Limited Classical Reprint Library

THE
DEATH OF CHRIST

BY

JAMES DENNEY, D.D.

REVISED AND ENLARGED EDITION
INCLUDING *THE ATONEMENT AND
THE MODERN MIND*

Foreword by
Dr. Cyril J. Barber

Klock & Klock Christian Publishers, Inc.
2527 GIRARD AVE. N.
MINNEAPOLIS, MINNESOTA 55411

Originally published by
Hodder & Stoughton
London, 1911

ISBN: 0-86524-090-6

Printed by Klock & Klock in the U.S.A.
1982 Reprint

FOREWORD

In the chapel of Trinity College, Glasgow, there is a stained glass window honoring the life and labors of Dr. James Denney. Beside the window on a plaque is inscribed, in part, the following:

James Denney, D.D.
(1856-1917)
. . . .
Supreme alike as scholar,
teacher, administrator,
and man of God,
to whom many owed their souls.

In paying tribute to Dr. Denney, Professor A.M. Hunter of Christ's College, Aberdeen, said:

> To scholarship of the first rank [Denney] brought a burning conviction of the truth and adequacy of the Gospel, and he would have no truck with those who, desiring to be in tune with the *Zeitgeist*, would have watered it down. In all his writing about the Christian faith he sought. . . to be Biblical, real, whole and clear, and he often declared that he had not the faintest interest in a theology which he could not preach.

Dr. Hunter goes on to point out that James Denney could write on all the chief doctrines of the Christian religion (though he evidenced a weakness when it came to eschatology) "but it was the Atonement which was the centre of his thinking." The cross, Dr. Denney believed was "the hiding place of God's power and the inspiration of all Christian praise."

Dr. Denney, however, died in 1917 and there are few today who know anything about him. A brief resume of his life, therefore, is in order.

Born in Paisley, Scotland, James Denney was reared a "Cameronian" or strict Reformed Presbyterian. His father was a deacon in the church, and all the fervor of Presbyterianism's long fight for freedom flowed through his veins. It is not surprising that, when further disruptions rocked the denomination, John Denney and his family withdrew and, with a large group of loyal independents, joined the Free Church of Scotland. Such zeal and committment to what was believed to be the truth were passed on to his son James.

Following his graduation from the local academy, James Denney enrolled in the University of Glasgow (1874) where he distinguished himself in both classical literature and philosophy. He graduated with honors and a Master of Arts degree in 1879 and immediately entered the Free Church College, Glasgow, where he had the good fortune to study under Robert S. Candlish, A. B. Bruce, and T. M. Lindsay. In 1883 he graduated with a Bachelor of Divinity degree.

Denney's only pastorate was at Broughty Ferry (1886-1897), where he took his young bride, the former Mary Brown. Their life together was one of happy companionship, and when she died in 1907 without bearing any children, James Denney found nothing to replace his keen sense of loss.

Mary Denney contributed much to her husband's ministry. He was inclined to be authoritarian, and under her kindly encouragement he became more compassionate. In addition, James Denney was disposed by his training to be theologically "liberal," and through her tender influence he became more evangelical. In fact, it was due to her recommendations that he began reading the writings of Charles Haddon Spurgeon, and the evangelical fervor of this British Baptist preacher radically changed the young Scot's ministry. One biographer records Denney saying, "Though it is my business to teach, the one thing I covet is to be able to do the work of an evangelist, and that at all events is the work that needs to be done."

With stress upon expository preaching characterizing his ministry at Broughty Ferry, Denney was invited to contribute two commentaries to *The Expositor's Bible*: "The Epistle to the Thessalonians" (1892) and "The Second Epistle to the Corinthians" (1894).

In 1894, James Denney was invited to deliver a series of lectures in theology at the Chicago Theological Seminary. Two things are significant about this invitation. First, Denney was a pastor with a pastor's heart, yet his abilities had brought him to the attention of those in need of a lecturer in theology; and second, the invitation extended to James Denney gives evidence of his influence beyond the borders of his native Scotland.

Before leaving for the United States, the University of Glasgow honored Denney with a Doctor of Divinity degree.

Of Dr. Denney's lectures at Chicago (later published under the title *Studies in Theology*) Dr. Hunter, writing in 1962, had this to say:

> Though forty years have passed since he died, Denney's work has not lost its relevance or its force. His writing has dated very little. . . . In [him] you will find what you do not always find in our modern theologians--what is in fact one of the first virtues of great theological writing--perfect lucidity of thought and expression.

In honor of his lectureship, the Chicago Theological Seminary conferred on James Denney a further Doctor of Divinity degree.

On his return to Scotland, Denney was soon called upon to succeed Dr. Robert S. Candlish as Professor of Systematic and Practical Theology in the Free Chruch College. Two years later, on the passing of Dr. A. B. Bruce, he was appointed to the chair of New Testament Language Literature, and Theology. Later, in 1915, he was invited to become principal of the college, succeeding Dr. T. M. Lindsay. His premature death brought his illustrious career to an untimely end.

While Professor Denney was at home expounding the text of a given book of the Bible, and was also a capable exegete (in 1900 he contributed a work on "The Epistle to the Romans" to *The Expositor's Greek Testament*), his greatest contribution was made as a theologian. In this respect, his *Death of Christ* (1902) may be regarded as his *magnum opus*.

Dr. Denney laid great stress upon Christ's physical sufferings. He emphasized the substitutionary nature of His sacrifice and expounded its effects to the believer with evangelical zeal. Such was his aversion to the teachings of certain mystics on the subject of the Atonement that he avoided all identification with mystical belief. In spite of this, his work on the death of Christ remains one of the most definitive discussions produced to date.

When James Denney died, Dr. H. R. McIntosh of Edinburgh was invited to pen a tribute to him. Here is part of what he wrote for *The Expository Times* (1917). His article is entitled "Principal James Denney as a Theologian."

At the time of his death [he] was at the summit of his power [and] in his passing evangelical religion throughout English-speaking lands has suffered a loss greater, we may say with sober truth, than would have been inflicted by the withdrawal of any other mind.

James Denney deserves to be remembered. His books are his finest memorial. It is hoped that pastors as well as seminarians will purchase and read this excellent treatise, here produced in its unabridged format. Those who do so will find their lives and ministries stimulated and enriched by what this great man of God has to impart.

Cyril J. Barber, D.Lit.
Author, *The Minister's Library*

PREFACE

THE first edition of *The Death of Christ* appeared in 1902. It contained the first six of the nine chapters in this book, and its purpose was to explain, in the light of modern historical study, the place held by the death of Christ in the New Testament, and the interpretation put upon it by the apostolic writers.

In its motive, the work was as much evangelical as theological. Assuming that the New Testament presents us with what must be in some sense the norm of Christianity, the writer was convinced that the death of Christ has not in the common Christian mind the place to which its centrality in the New Testament entitles it. It gets less than its due both in ordinary preaching and in ordinary theology. It is not too much to say that there are many indications of aversion to the New Testament presentation of it, and that there are large numbers of people, and even of preachers, whose chief embarrassment in handling the New Testament is that they cannot adjust their minds to its pronouncements on this subject. They are under a constant temptation to evade or to distort what was evidently of critical importance to the first witnesses to the gospel. It was with this in mind that the writer conducted his study of the subject, and while claiming to be impartial and scientific in his treatment of New Testament documents and ideas, he nowhere affected an insensibility he did not feel. He was and remains convinced that the New Testament presents us with a view of Christ's death which is consistent with itself, true to the whole being and relations of God and man as these have been affected by sin, and vital to Christian religion; and that on the discovery and appreciation of this—or if we prefer it so, on the rediscovery and fresh appreciation of it—the future and the power of Christianity depend. Without it we can have no renewal of Christian life and no large or deep restoration of Christian thought. It is quite true that there is a difference between religion and theology, and it may be argued (as the writer himself has argued elsewhere) that it is possible to have the same religion as the apostles without having the same theology; but the distinction is not absolute. In a religion which has at its heart a historical fact, it is impossible that the meaning of the fact should be a matter of indifference, and the whole question at issue here is the meaning of the fact that Christ died. The chapters in which the New Testament interpretation is examined have been carefully revised, but not essentially modified. A few sentences and paragraphs have been cancelled and a few inserted, but in substance the work is what it was before.

The Death of Christ, when published, was reviewed from various standpoints, and in particular it led to a considerable correspondence both with acquaintances and strangers which made still clearer to the writer the mental attitude

CONTENTS

INTRODUCTION

CHAPTER I

THE SYNOPTIC GOSPELS

and atmosphere to which the New Testament message has to be addressed. It was with this in view that the last three chapters were written. Originally delivered as lectures to a Summer School of Theology in Aberdeen, they appeared in *The Expositor* in the course of 1903, and were subsequently published under the title of *The Atonement and the Modern Mind*. No one could be more sensible than the writer of the disproportion between this title and what it covered; it could only be justified because, such as it was, the book was a real attempt, guided mainly by the correspondence referred to, to help the mind in which we all live and move to reach a sympathetic comprehension of the central truth in the Christian religion. As a rule, names are not mentioned in these chapters, but where opinions are stated or objections given within inverted commas, they are opinions and objections which have really been expressed, and they are given in the words of their authors, whether in print or manuscript. There are no men of straw among them, constructed by the writer merely to be demolished.

The close connection of *The Atonement and the Modern Mind* with *The Death of Christ* makes them virtually one work, and it seemed desirable, for various reasons, that they should appear together. The present volume contains both. The title of the earlier has been retained for the two in combination, and the publishers have made it possible, by resetting the whole in a slightly different form, to issue the two at the original price of the first.

The character and purpose of the book have not been affected by revision. It is not a complete dogmatic study

of the subject, but it contributes something to the preliminaries of such a study. It is governed as much by
interest in preaching as by interest in theology, and the
writer still hopes that it may do something to make evangelists theologians and theologians evangelists.

The full table of contents will enable the reader to
dispense with an index.

CHAPTER II

THE EARLIEST CHRISTIAN PREACHING

CONTENTS

CHAPTER III

THE EPISTLES OF ST. PAUL

CONTENTS xiii

CHAPTER IV

THE EPISTLE TO THE HEBREWS

CONTENTS

CHAPTER V

THE JOHANNINE WRITINGS

CHAPTER VI

b

CHAPTER VII

THE ATONEMENT AND THE MODERN MIND

CHAPTER VIII

SIN AND THE DIVINE REACTION AGAINST IT

CHAPTER IX

CHRIST AND MAN IN THE ATONEMENT

INTRODUCTION

Two assumptions must be made by any one who writes on
the death of Christ in the New Testament. The first is,
that there is such a thing as a New Testament; and the
second, that the death of Christ is a subject which has a
real place and importance in it. The first may be said to
be the more important of the two, for the denial of it
carries with it the denial of the other.

At the present moment there is a strong tendency in
certain quarters to depreciate the idea of a New Testament in the sense in which it has rightly or wrongly been
established in the Church. It is pointed out that the books
which compose our New Testament are in no real sense a
unity. They were not written with a view to forming the
volume in which we now find them, nor with any view of
being related to each other at all. At first, indeed, they
had no such relation. They are merely the chief fragments
that have survived from a primitive Christian literature
which must have been indefinitely larger, not to say richer.
The unity which they now possess, and in virtue of which
they constitute the New Testament, does not belong to them
inherently; it is factitious; it is the artificial, and to a considerable extent the illusive result of the action of the
Church in bestowing upon them canonical authority. The
age to which they historically belong is an age at which
the Church had no 'New Testament,' and hence what is
called New Testament theology is an exhibition of the
manner in which Christians thought before a New Testament

existed.   As a self-contradictory thing, therefore, it ought
to be abolished.   The 'dogma' of the New Testament, and
the factitious unity which it has created, ought to be superseded, and instead of New Testament theology we should
aim at a history of primitive Christian thought and life.
It would not be necessary for the purposes of such a history
to make any assumptions as to the unity of the 'New Testament' books; but though they would not form a holy
island in the sea of history, they would gain in life and
reality in proportion as the dogmatic tie which binds them
to each other was broken, and their living relations to the
general phenomena of history revealed.[1]

There is not only some plausibility in this but some
truth : all I am concerned to point out here is that it is not
the whole truth, and possibly not the main truth.   The
unity which belongs to the books of the New Testament,
whatever be its value, is certainly not fortuitous.   The
books did not come together by chance.   They are not held
together simply by the art of the bookbinder.   It would be
truer to say that they gravitated toward each other in the
course of the first century of the Church's life, and imposed
their unity on the Christian mind, than that the Church
imposed on them by statute—for when 'dogma' is used in
the abstract sense which contrasts it with fact or history,
this is what it means—a unity to which they were inwardly
strange.   That they are at one in some essential respects is
obvious.   They have at least unity of subject : they are all
concerned with Jesus Christ, and with the manifestation of
God's redeeming love to men in Him.   There is even a sense
in which we may say there is unity of authorship ; for all
the books of the New Testament are works of faith.

---

[1] As typical instances of this mode of thought, reference may be made to
Wrede's *Ueber Aufgabe und Methode der sogenannten neutestamentlichen
Theologie*, and G. Krüger's *Das Dogma vom Neuen Testament*.

Whether the unity goes further, and if so how far, are questions not to be settled beforehand. It may extend to modes of thought, to fundamental beliefs or convictions, in regard to Christ and the meaning of His presence and work in the world. It is not assumed here that it does, but neither is it assumed that it does not. It is not assumed, with regard to the particular subject before us, that in the different New Testament writings we shall find independent, divergent, or inconsistent interpretations of Christ's death. The result of an unprejudiced investigation may be to show that on this subject the various writings which go to make up our New Testament are profoundly at one, and even that their oneness on this subject, a oneness not imposed nor artificial, but essential and inherent, justifies against the criticism referred to above the common Christian estimate of the New Testament as a whole.

Without entering on abstract or general grounds into a discussion in which no abstract or general conclusion can be reached, it may be permitted to say, in starting, that in the region with which the New Testament deals we should be on our guard against pressing too strongly some current distinctions which, within their limits, are real enough, but which, if carried beyond their limits, make everything in the New Testament unintelligible. The most important of these is the distinction of historical and dogmatic, or of historico-religious and dogmatico-religious. If the distinction between historical and dogmatic is pressed, it runs back into the distinction between thing and meaning, or between fact and theory ; and this, as we shall have occasion to see, is a distinction which it is impossible to press. There is a point at which the two sides in such contrast pass into each other. He who does not see the meaning does not see the thing ; or to use the more imposing words, he who refuses to take a 'dogmatic' view proves by doing so

that he falls short of a completely ' historical ' one.   The
same kind of consideration has sometimes to be applied to
the distinction of ' Biblical ' or ' New Testament ' and ' systematic ' theology.   Biblical or New Testament theology deals
with the thoughts, or the mode of thinking, of the various
New Testament writers; systematic theology is the independent construction of Christianity as a whole in the mind
of a later thinker.   Here again there is a broad and valid
distinction, but not an absolute one.   It is the Christian
thinking of the first century in the one case, and of the
twentieth, let us say, in the other; but in both cases there
is Christianity and there is thinking, and if there is truth in
either there is bound to be a place at which the distinction
disappears.   It does not follow from the distinction, with
the inevitable limitations, that nothing in the New Testament can be accepted by a modern mind simply as it stands.
It does not follow that nothing in St. Paul or St. John—
nothing in their interpretation of the death of Jesus, for
example—has attained the character of finality.   There may
be something which has.   The thing to be dealt with is one,
and the mind, through the centuries, is one, and even in
the first century it may have struck to a final truth which
the twentieth will not transcend.   Certainly we cannot deny
this beforehand on the ground that Biblical theology is one
thing and Systematic or Philosophical theology another.
They may be taught in separate rooms in a theological
school, but, except to the pedant or the dilettante, the distinction between them is a vanishing one.   And the same
may be said, finally, about the distinction of matter and
form.   There is such a distinction: it is possible to put
the same matter in different forms.   But it does not follow
that the form in which a truth or an experience is put by a
New Testament writer is always unequal to the matter, or
that the matter must always be fused again and cast into a

new mould before it can be appropriated by us. The higher
the reality with which we deal, the less the distinction of
matter and form holds. If Christianity brings us into contact with the ultimate truth and reality, we may find that
the ' form ' into which it was cast at first is more essential
to the matter than we had supposed. Just as it would be a
rash act to venture to extract the matter of *Lycidas*, and to
exhibit it in a more adequate form, it may be a rash act to
venture to tell us what St. Paul or St. John meant in a form
more equal to the meaning than the apostles themselves
could supply. It is not necessary to say that it would be,
but only that it may be. The mind seems to gain freedom
and lucidity by working with such distinctions, but if we
forget that they are our own distinctions, and that in the
real world, in the very nature of things, a point is reached
sooner or later at which they disappear, we are certain to be
led astray. I do not argue against drawing them or using
them, but against making them so absolute that in the long-
run one of them must cease to be true, and forfeit all its
rights in favour of the other. The chief use, for instance, to
which many writers put them is to appeal to the historical
against the dogmatic; the historical is employed to drive
the dogmatic from the field. To do the reverse would of
course be as bad, and my object in these introductory
remarks is to deprecate both mistakes. It does not matter,
outside the class-room, whether an interpretation is called
historical or dogmatic, historico-religious or dogmatico-
religious; it does not matter whether we put it under the
head of Biblical or of philosophical theology; what we
want to know is whether it is true. In the truth such distinctions are apt to disappear.

Without assuming, therefore, the dogmatic unity of the
New Testament, either in its representation of Christianity
as a whole, or of the death of Christ in particular, we need

not feel precluded from approaching it with a presumption that it will exhibit some kind of coherence. Granting that the Church canonised the books, consciously or unconsciously, it did not canonise them for nothing. It must have felt that they really represented and therefore safeguarded the Christian faith, and as the Church of the early days was acutely conscious of the distinction between what did and what did not belong to Christianity, it must have had some sense at least of a consistency in its Christian Scriptures.[1] They did not represent for it two gospels or ten, but one. The view Christians took of the books they valued was instinctively dogmatic without ceasing to be historical; or perhaps we may say, with a lively sense of their historical relations the Church had an instinctive feeling of the dogmatic import of the books in its New Testament. It is in this attitude, which is not blind to either side of the distinction, yet does not let either annul the other, that we ought to approach the study of New Testament problems.

It is hardly necessary to prove that in the New Testament the death of Christ is a real subject. It is distinctly present to the mind of New Testament writers, and they have much to say upon it. It is treated by them as a subject of central and permanent importance to the Christian faith, and it is incredible that it should have filled the place it does fill in the New Testament had it ever been regarded as of trifling consequence for the understanding, the acceptance, or the preaching of the Gospel. As little is it necessary to say that in using the expression 'the death of Christ,' we are not speaking of a thing, but of an experience. Whether we view it as action or as passion, whatever enters into person-

---

[1] This, of course, does not exclude the idea that the native vigour of Christianity was shown in its power to assimilate as well as to reject extraneous matter.

ality has the significance and the worth of personality. The
death of Christ in the New Testament is the death of one
who is alive for evermore. To every New Testament writer
Christ is the Lord, the living and exalted Lord, and it is
impossible for them to think of His death except as an experience the result or virtue of which is perpetuated in His
risen life. Nevertheless, Christ died. His death is in some
sense the centre and consummation of His work. It is
because of it that His risen life is the hope which it is to
sinful men; and it needs no apology, therefore, if one who
thinks that it has less than its proper place in preaching
and in theology endeavours to bring out as simply as
possible its place and meaning in the New Testament. If
our religion is to be Christian in any sense of the term which
history will justify, it can never afford to ignore what, to say
the least of it, is the primary confession of Christian faith.

The starting-point in our investigation must be the life
and teaching of Jesus Himself. For this we shall depend in
the first instance on the synoptic gospels. Next will come
an examination of primitive Christian teaching as it bears
on our subject. For this we can only make use of the early
chapters in Acts, and with a reserve, which will be explained
at the proper place, of the First Epistle of Peter. It will
then be necessary to go into greater detail, in proportion
as we have more material at command, in regard to the
teaching of St. Paul. Of all New Testament writers he is
the one who has most deliberately and continually reflected
on Christ's death; if there is a conscious theology of it
anywhere it is with him. A study of the epistle to the
Hebrews and of the Johannine writings—Apocalypse, Gospel,
and Epistle—will bring the subject proper to a close; but I
shall venture to add, in a concluding chapter, some reflec-
tions on the importance of the New Testament conception of
Christ's death alike to the evangelist and the theologian.

CHAPTER I

THE SYNOPTIC GOSPELS

ALL the gospels describe the sufferings and death of Christ with a minuteness which has no parallel in their narratives of other events of His life, and they all, to a certain extent, by references to the fulfilment of Old Testament prophecy or otherwise, indicate their sense of its meaning and importance. This, however, reveals the mind of the evangelists rather than that of the Lord. It is in His life, rather than in the record of His death itself, that we must look for indications of His mind. But here we are at once confronted with certain preliminary difficulties. Quite apart from the question whether it is possible at all to know what Jesus thought or spoke about His death—a question which it is taken for granted is to be answered in the affirmative[1]—it has been asserted, largely upon general grounds, that Jesus cannot have entered on His ministry with the thought of His death present to Him; that He must, on the contrary, have begun His work with brilliant hopes of success; that only as these hopes gradually but irrevocably faded away did first the possibility and then the certainty of a tragic issue dawn upon Him; that it thus became necessary for Him to reconcile Himself to the idea of a violent death, and that in various ways, which can more or less securely be traced in the gospels, He did so; although, as the prayer in Gethsemane shows, there seemed a possibility to Him, even to the

---

[1] See the writer's *Jesus and the Gospel*, pp. 320-346.

last, that a change might come, and the will of the Father be done in some less tragic fashion. This is what is meant by an historical as opposed to a dogmatic reading of the life of Jesus, a dogmatic reading being one which holds that Jesus came into the world in order to die; and it is insisted on as necessary to secure for that life the reality of a genuine human experience. To question or impeach or displace this interpretation is alleged to be docetism; it gives us a phantom as a Saviour instead of the man Christ Jesus.

In spite of its plausibility, I venture to urge that this reading of the gospels requires serious qualification. It is almost as much an *a priori* interpretation of the history of Jesus as if it were deduced from the Nicene creed. It is derived from the word 'historical,' in the sense which that word would bear if it were applied to an ordinary human life, just as abstractly as another reading of the facts might be derived from the words 'ὁμοούσιος τῷ πατρί.' If any one wrote a life of Jesus, in which everything was subordinated to the idea that Jesus was 'of one substance with the Father,' it would no doubt be described as dogmatic, but it is quite as possible to be 'dogmatic' in history as in theology. It is a dogma, and an unreasoned dogma besides, that because the life of Jesus is historical, it neither admits nor requires for its interpretation any idea or formula that cannot be used in the interpretation of the common life of man. The Christian religion rests on the fact that there is not only an identity but a difference between His life and ours; and we cannot allow the difference (*and with it the Christian religion*) to be abolished *a priori* by a 'dogmatic' use of the term 'historical.' We must turn to our historical documents—the gospels—and when we do, there is much to give us pause.

All the gospels, we remark in the first place, begin with an account of the baptism of Jesus. Whatever may be doubtful about this it cannot be doubtful that it was the occasion of a great spiritual experience to Jesus. Ideas, as Dr. Johnson says, must be given through something; and Jesus, we must believe, gave His disciples an idea of what His experience at baptism was in the narratives which we now read in the gospels. The sum of that experience is often put by saying that He came then to the consciousness of His Sonship. But the manner in which Jesus Himself puts it is much more revealing. 'A voice came from heaven, Thou art My Son, the Beloved, in Thee I am well pleased.' A voice from heaven does not mean a voice from the clouds, but a voice from God; and it is important to notice that the voice from God speaks in familiar Old Testament words. It does not come unmediated, but mediated through psalm and prophecy. It is through the absorption of Old Testament Scripture that Jesus comes to the consciousness of what He is; and the Scriptures which He uses to convey His experience to the disciples are the 2nd Psalm, and the forty-second chapter of Isaiah. The first words of the heavenly voice are from the Psalm, the next from the prophet. Nothing could be more suggestive than this. The Messianic consciousness in Jesus from the very beginning was one with the consciousness of the Servant of the Lord. The King, to whom Jehovah says, Thou art My Son, this day have I begotten Thee (Psalm ii. 7),[1] is at the same time (in the mind of Jesus) that mysterious Servant

---

[1] In Luke iii. 22, *Codex Bezæ* gives the heavenly voice in this form. Probably Jesus told the stories of His baptism and temptation often, giving more or less fully, with brief allusions to Old Testament words or fuller citation of them, such hints of His experience as His hearers could appreciate. Certainly there could be no truer *index* to His life than a combination of Ps. ii. 7 with Isaiah xlii. 1 ff.—the Son of God as King, and the Servant of the Lord; and this combination, if we go upon the evidence and not upon any dogmatic conception of what is or is not historical, dates from the high hour in which Jesus entered on His public work, and is not an afterbirth of disappointing experiences.

of Jehovah—'My beloved, in whom I am well pleased'—
whose tragic yet glorious destiny is adumbrated in the
second Isaiah (xlii. 1 ff.). It is not necessary to inquire how
Jesus could combine beforehand two lines of anticipation
which at the first glance seem so inconsistent with each
other; the point is, that on the evidence before us, which
seems to the writer as indisputable as anything in the
gospels, He did combine them, and therefore cannot have
started on His ministry with the cloudless hopes which are
sometimes ascribed to Him. However 'unhistorical' it
might seem on general grounds, on the ground of the evidence which is here available we must hold that from the
very beginning of His public work the sense of something
tragic in His destiny—something which in form might only
become definite with time, but in substance was sure—was
present to the mind of Jesus. When it did emerge in
definite form it brought necessities and appeals along with
it which were not there from the beginning; it brought
demands for definite action, for assuming a definite attitude,
for giving more or less explicit instruction; but it did not
bring a monstrous and unanticipated disappointment to
which Jesus had to reconcile Himself as best He could. It
was not a brutal *démenti* to all His hopes. It had a
necessary relation to His consciousness from the beginning,
just as surely as His consciousness from the beginning had
a necessary relation to the prophetic conception of the
Servant of the Lord.

This is confirmed if we look from the baptism to that
which in all the gospels is closely connected with it, and is
of equal importance as illustrating our Lord's conception of
Himself and His work—the temptation. Nothing can be
more gratuitous than to ascribe this wonderful narrative to
the 'productive activity' of the Church, and to allege that
the temptations which it records are those which Jesus

encountered during His career, and that they are antedated
for effect, or for catechetical convenience. Psychologically,
the connection of the temptations with the baptism is
strikingly true, and two of the three are connected even
formally with the divine voice, Thou art My Son (Matt. iii.
17; iv. 3, 6). The natural supposition is that Jesus spoke
often to His disciples of a terrible spiritual experience which
followed the sublime experience of the baptism—sometimes
without detail, as in Mark, who mentions only a prolonged
conflict with Satan, during which Jesus was sustained by
the ministry of angels; sometimes, as in Matthew and
Luke, with details which gave insight into the nature of
the conflict.   It does not matter that the temptations
which are here described actually assailed Jesus at later
stages in His life. Of course they did. They are the
temptations of the Christ, and they not only assailed Him
at particular moments, some of which we can still identify
(Matt. xvi. 22 f.; John vi. 15), they must in some way
have haunted Him incessantly.[1]   But they were present to
His mind *from the outset of His career*; that is the very
meaning of the temptation story, standing where it stands.
The Christ sees the two paths that lie before Him, and He
chooses at the outset, in spiritual conflict, that which He

[1] Wellhausen asserts that the temptation in Mark i. 12 f. is not Messianic ;
the Messianic temptation in Mark does not follow the baptism, but the
Messianic confession of Peter at ch. viii. 29 ; and it is Peter, not 'der leib-
haftige Satan,' to whom the severe rebuke of Jesus is historically addressed.
This is one of his main arguments for regarding Mark as older than Q,
the source to which the temptation narratives of Matthew and Luke are
traced.   But it surely needs no proof that however summarily he may refer
to it, the temptation associated by Mark with the baptism must have had its
character determined by the baptism ; and on Wellhausen's own showing
the whole significance of the baptism *for Mark* is that it indicates the birth
of the Messianic consciousness in Jesus.   He entered the water an ordinary
Israelite, and emerged the Messiah.   A temptation in this context can have
been nothing but a Messianic temptation.—*Einleitung in die drei ersten
Evangelien* (2nd edition), 65 f.

knows will set Him in irreconcilable antagonism to the hopes and expectations of those to whom He is to appeal. A soul which sees its vocation shadowed out in the Servant of the Lord, which is driven of the Spirit into the wilderness to face the dreadful alternatives raised by that vocation, and which takes the side which Jesus took in conflict with the enemy, does not enter on its life-work with any superficial illusions: it has looked Satan and all he can do in the face; it is prepared for conflict; it may shrink from death, when death confronts it in the path of its vocation, as hideous and unnatural, but it cannot be startled by it as by an unthought of, unfamiliar thing. The possibility, at least, of a tragic issue to His work—when we remember the Servant of the Lord, far more than the possibility—belongs to the consciousness of Jesus from the first. Not that His ultimate triumph is compromised, but He knows before He begins that it will not be attained by any primrose path. If there was a period in His life during which He had other thoughts, it is antecedent to that at which we have any knowledge of Him.

These considerations justify us in emphasising, in relation to our subject, not merely the fact of Jesus' baptism, but its meaning. It was a baptism of repentance with a view to remission of sins, and there is undoubtedly something paradoxical, at a first glance, in the idea of Jesus submitting to such a baptism. Neither here nor elsewhere in the gospel does He betray any consciousness of sin. The opinion of a recent writer on the life of Jesus,[1] who ascribes to the fragments of the gospel according to the Hebrews an authority equal, and at this point superior, to that of the canonical gospels, is not likely to find many supporters. Jerome tells us that in this gospel, which in his day was still used by the Nazarenes, and could be seen in the library

---

[1] O. Holtzmann.

at Caesarea, the narrative ran : 'Behold the mother of the
Lord and His brethren said to Him : John Baptist is
baptizing with a view to remission of sins : let us go and
be baptized by him.   But He said to them : 'What sin
have I done that I should go and be baptized by him?
unless, indeed, this very word I have spoken is *ignorantia*,'
i.e. a sin of ignorance or inadvertence (cf. ἀγνόημα, Heb. ix.
7, and שְׁגָגָה in Old Testament).[1] We should have to suppose
in this case that Jesus went up to Jordan half reluctantly,
His first thought being that a baptism like John's could
mean nothing to Him, His next that possibly this proud
thought, or the utterance of it, indicated that He might
have something to repent of after all, and more perhaps
than He knew.   This mingling of what might not unfairly
be called petulance with a sudden access of misgiving, as of
one who was too sure of himself and yet not quite sure, is
as unlike as anything could be to the simplicity and truth of
Jesus ;[2] and surely it needs no proof that it is another mood
than this to which the heavens are opened, and on which divine
assurance and divine strength are bestowed.   We must abide
by the canonical narratives as consistent in themselves, and
consistent with the New Testament as a whole.   What we see
there is Jesus, who, according to all apostolic testimony, and
according to the suggestion of the Baptist himself in Matt. iii.
14, knew no sin, submitting to a baptism which is defined as
a baptism of repentance.   It would not have been astonishing
if Jesus had come from Galilee to baptize along with John,

[1] Hier. *Contra Pelag.*, 3, 2.   Nestle, *Novi Testamenti Graeci Supplementum* (77, 81), quotes in the same sense from Cyprian *De Rebaptismate* :
'Confictus liber qui inscribitur *Pauli predicatio* in quo libro contra omnes
scripturas et de peccato proprio confitentem invenies Christum, qui solus
omnino nihil deliquit et ad accipiendum Joannis baptisma paene invitum a
matre sua esse compulsum.'
[2] Soltau, *Unsere Evangelien*, p. 58 : 'Der Zusatz ist nicht mehr naiv,
sondern ganz kasuistisch.'

if He had taken His stand by John's side confronting the people; the astonishing thing is that being what He was He came to be baptized, and took His stand side by side with the people. He identified Himself with them. As far as the baptism could express it, He made all that was theirs His. It is as though He had looked on them under the oppression of their sin, and said: On Me let all that burden, all that responsibility descend. The key to the act is to be found in the great passage in Isaiah liii. in which the vocation of the Servant of the Lord, which, as we have seen, was present to our Lord's mind at the moment, is most amply unfolded. The deepest word in that chapter, He was numbered with the transgressors, is expressly applied to our Lord by Himself at a later period (Luke xxii. 37); and however mysterious that word may be when we try to define it by relation to the providence and redemption of God—however appalling it may seem to render it as St. Paul does, Him who knew no sin, God made to be sin for us—here in the baptism we see not the word but the thing: *Jesus numbering Himself with the transgressors*, submitting to be baptized with their baptism, identifying Himself with them in their relation to God as sinners, making all their responsibilities His own. It was 'a great act of loving communion with our misery,' and in that hour, in the will and act of Jesus, the work of atonement was begun. It was no accident that now, and not at some other hour, the Father's voice declared Him the beloved Son, the chosen One in whom His soul delighted. For in so identifying Himself with sinful men, in so making their last and most dreadful responsibilities His own, Jesus approved Himself the true Son of the Father, the true Servant and Representative of Him whose name from of old is Redeemer.[1] It

[1] See Garvie's *Studies in the Inner Life of Jesus*, ch. iv. 'The Vocation Accepted,' pp. 117 ff. 'It is in His vicarious consciousness and the sacrifice

is impossible to have this in mind, and to remember the career which the fifty-third chapter of Isaiah sets before the Servant of the Lord, without feeling that from the moment He entered on His ministry our Lord's thoughts of the future must have been more in keeping with the reality than those which are sometimes ascribed to Him as alone consistent with a truly human career. His career was truly His own as well as truly human, and the shadow of the world's sin lay on it from the first.[1]

Starting from this point, we may now go on to examine the facts as they are put before us in the gospels.

It is only, indeed, after the great day of Caesarea Philippi, on which Jesus accepts from the lips of His disciples the confession of Messiahship, that He begins expressly to teach the necessity of His death. But there are indications earlier than this that it was not alien to His thoughts, as indeed there was much to prompt the thought of it. There was the experience of ancient prophets, to which He refers from the sermon on the mount, at the opening of His ministry (Matt. v. 10-12), to the great denunciation of the Pharisees at its close (Matt. xxiii. 37). There was the fate of John the Baptist, which, though the precise date of it is uncertain, was felt by Jesus to be parallel to His own (Mark ix. 12, 13). There was the sense underlying all His early success, to speak of it in such language, of an irreconcilable antipathy in His adversaries, of a temper which would incur the guilt of eternal sin

---

which this would ultimately involve that Jesus fulfilled all righteousness. There is a higher righteousness than being justified by one's own works, a higher even than depending on God's forgiveness ; and that belongs to Him who undertakes by His own loving sacrifice for sinners to bring God's forgiveness to them.'

[1] Compare Kähler, *Zur Lehre von der Versöhnung,* 179 : 'Die Taufe im Jordan nimmt jene Taufe voraus, der er mit Bangen entgegenblickt, die letzte, schwerste Versuchung.'

rather than acknowledge His claims (Mark iii. 20-30);
there was the consciousness, going back, if we can trust the
evangelic narrative at all, to very early days, that the most
opposite parties were combining to destroy Him (Mark iii. 6).
And there is one pathetic word in which the sense of the
contrast between the present and the future comes out with
moving power. 'Can the children of the bride-chamber
fast while the bridegroom is with them? As long as they
have the bridegroom with them they cannot fast. But
days will come when the bridegroom shall be taken away
from them, and then shall they fast in that day' (Mark ii.
19 f.). The force of this exquisite word has been evaded in
two ways. (1) Hollmann [1] has argued that v. 20, in which
the taking away of the bridegroom is spoken of, is not
really a word of Jesus, but due to the productive activity
of the Church. It is irrelevant in the circumstances, and
it is only made possible by the parable of Jesus being
treated as an allegory. All that is apposite to the occasion
is the first clause: Can the children of the bride-chamber
fast while the bridegroom is with them? But the allegory,
which is thus used to discredit v. 20, must, as Wellhausen
has fairly pointed out, be assumed if we are to get any
pertinent meaning even for v. 19; and few will follow
him in expunging both verses alike.[2] (2) It has been
argued that the words do not necessarily refer to a
violent or premature or unnatural death, but merely to
the parting which is inevitable in the case of all human
relations, however joyful they may be, and which perhaps
suggests itself the more readily the more joyful they
are.[3] But there is nothing elsewhere in the words of

---

[1] *Die Bedeutung des Todes Jesu*, p. 16 ff.
[2] See *Jesus and the Gospel*, 314 ff.
[3] Cf. Haupt, *Die eschatol. Aussagen Jesu*, p. 108; Holtzmann, *Neut. Theologie*, i. p. 287.

Jesus so sentimental and otiose as this. He does not aim at cheap pathetic effects, like the modern romance writers, who studiously paint the brightness and gaiety of life against the omnipresent black background of death. The taking away of the bridegroom from the bridal party is *not* the universal experience of man, applied to an individual case ; it is something startling, tragic, like sudden storm in a summer sky ; and it is as such that it is present to the mind of Jesus as a figure of His own death. Even in the Galilean springtime, when His fortune seems to rise like the rising tide, there is this sad presentiment at His heart, and once at least He suffers it to break through.

It is not possible, for critical reasons, to insist in the same way on the saying about being three days and three nights in the heart of the earth, as Jonah was three days and three nights in the whale's belly (Matthew xii. 40) ; in the parallel passage in Luke xi. 29 f. the sign of Jonah must be interpreted without any such reference to the fortunes of Jesus. But even if Jesus did make an allusion of this sort to the issue of His life—an allusion which none of His hearers could understand—it does not carry us any way into the understanding of His death. It only suggests that it is not a final defeat, but has the true victory of His cause beyond it. What He came to do will be effectively done, not before He dies, but after He has come again through death. And this is the only sign which His enemies can have.[1]

But leaving these allusive references to His death, let us

---

[1] Cf. Rev. C. F. Burney in *Contentio Veritatis*, p. 202. ' If, as is probable, Jonah represents the nation of Israel emerging as though by a miracle from the Exile in order to carry out its mission to the world at large, it may be noticed that the idea of the restoration from the exile as a resurrection is elsewhere current in the prophetic writings (Hos. vi., Ezek xxxvii.) and that it is thus highly fitting that the allegory of the death and resurrection of the nation should be also the allegory of the death and resurrection of the nation's true Representative.'

proceed to those in which it is the express subject of our Lord's teaching.

All the synoptics introduce it, in this sense, at the same point (Mark viii. 31, Matthew xvi. 21, Luke ix. 22). Matthew lays a peculiar emphasis on the date, using it to mark the division of his gospel into two great parts. 'From that time Jesus began,' he says in iv. 17, 'to preach and to say : Repent, for the Kingdom of Heaven is at hand.' 'From that time,' he says in xvi. 21, 'Jesus began to show to His disciples that He must go up to Jerusalem and be killed.' A comparison of the evangelists justifies us in saying broadly that a new epoch in our Lord's ministry had now begun. His audience is not so much the multitudes as the twelve; His method is not so much preaching as teaching; His subject is not so much the Kingdom as Himself, and in particular His death. All the evangelists mention three occasions on which He made deliberate and earnest efforts to initiate the disciples into His thoughts (Mark viii. 31, ix. 31, x. 32, with parallels in Matthew and Luke). Mark, especially, whose narrative is fundamental, lays stress on the continued and repeated attempts He made to familiarise them with what was drawing near (notice the imperfects ἐδίδασκεν, ἔλεγεν in ix. 31). There is no reason whatever to doubt this general representation. It is mere wantonness to eliminate from the narrative one or two of the three passages on the ground that they are but duplicates or triplicates of the same thing. In Mark, especially, they are distinctly characterised by the varying attitude of the disciples. Further, in the first we have the presumptuous protest of Peter, which guarantees the historicity of the whole, if anything could. In the second the disciples are silent. They could not make him out (ἠγνόουν τὸ ῥῆμα), and with the remembrance of the overwhelming rebuke which Peter had drawn down on himself, they were afraid to put any question to Him (ix. 32). The third is attached to that never-to-be-forgotten incident in which, as they were on the way to Jerusalem, Jesus took the lead in some startling manner, so that they followed in amazement and fear. If anything in the gospels has the stamp of real and live recollection upon it, it is this. It is necessary to insist on this repeated instruction of the disciples by Jesus as a fact, quite apart from what He was able to teach or they to learn. It is often said that the death of Christ has a place in the epistles out of all proportion to that which it has in the gospels. This is hardly the fact, even if the space were to be estimated merely by the number of words devoted to it in the gospels and epistles respectively ; but it is still less the fact when we remember that that which, according to the gospels themselves, characterised the last months of our Lord's life was a deliberate and thrice-repeated attempt to teach His disciples something about His death.

The critical questions which have been raised as to the contents of these passages need not here detain us. It has been suggested that they must have become more detailed in the telling—that unconsciously and involuntarily the Church put into the lips of the Lord words which were only supplied to its own mind by its knowledge of what actually took place—that the references to mocking, scourging, spitting, in particular, could not have been so explicit—above all, that the resurrection on the third day must, if spoken of at all, have been veiled in some figurative form which baffled the disciples at the moment. It has been suggested, on the other hand, that it may have been the idea of a resurrection on the third day, and not on the familiar great day at the end of all things, which put them out. It may not be possible, and it is certainly not necessary, to say beforehand that there is nothing in any of these suggestions.[1]   But one

---

[1] It is undoubtedly disappointing that in spite of the reiterated assertion that Jesus did teach His disciples about His death, Mark does not tell us

may hold sincerely, and with good grounds, that there is very little in them, and that even that little is persuasive rather for dogmatic than for historical reasons. Surely we cannot imagine Jesus iterating and reiterating (as we know He did), with the most earnest desire to impress and instruct His followers, such vague, elusive, impalpable hints of what lay before Him as some critics would put in the place of what they regard, for extra-historical reasons, as impossibly definite predictions. Jesus must have had something entirely definite and sayable to say, when He tried so persistently to get it apprehended. He did not live in cloudland; what He spoke of was the sternest of realities; and for whatever reason His disciples failed to understand Him, it cannot have been that He talked to them incessantly and importunately in shadowy riddles: the thing could not be done. As far, however, as our present purpose is concerned, it is not affected by any reasonable opinion we may come to on the critical questions here in view. The one point in which all the narratives agree is that Jesus taught that He *must* go up to Jerusalem and die; and the one question it is of importance to answer is, What is meant by this *must* (δεῖ)?

There are obviously two meanings which it might have. It might signify that His death was inevitable; the *must* being one of outward constraint. No doubt, in this sense it was true that He must die. The hostile forces which were arrayed against Him were irreconcilable, and were only waiting their time. Sooner or later it would come, and they would crush Him without remorse. But it might also signify that His death was indispensable, the *must* being one of inward constraint. It might signify that death was something He was bound to accept and contemplate if the work He came to do was to be done, if the vocation with which he

even remotely what He taught. There is no memorable word of Jesus preserved from His teaching.

was called was to be fulfilled. These two senses, of course, are not incompatible; but there may be a question as to their relation to each other. Most frequently the second is made to depend upon the first. Jesus, we are told, came to see that His death was inevitable, such were the forces arrayed against Him; but being unable, as the well-beloved Son of the Father, merely to submit to the inevitable, merely to encounter death as a blind fate, He reconciled Himself to it by interpreting it as indispensable, as something which properly entered into His work and contributed to its success. It became not a thing to endure, but a thing to do. The passion was converted into the sublimest of actions. We do not need to say that this reasoning has nothing in it; but it is too abstract, and the relation in which the two necessities are put to one another does not answer to the presentation of the facts in the gospels. The inward necessity which Jesus recognised for His death was not simply the moral solution which He had discovered for the fatal situation in which He found Himself. An inward necessity is identical with the will of God, and the will of God for Jesus is expressed, not primarily in outward conditions, but in that Scripture which is for Him the word of God. We have seen already that from the very beginning our Lord's sense of His own vocation and destiny was essentially related to that of the Servant of the Lord in the Book of Isaiah, and it is there that the ultimate source of the δεῖ is to be found. The divine necessity for a career of suffering and death is primary; it belongs, in however vague and undefined a form, to our Lord's consciousness of what He is and what He is called to do; it is not deduced from the malignant necessities by which He is encompassed; it rises up within Him, in divine power, to encounter these outward necessities and subdue them.

This connection of ideas is confirmed when we notice that

what Jesus began to teach His disciples is the doctrine of a
suffering *Messiah*. As soon as they have confessed Him to
be the Christ, He begins to give them this lesson. The
necessity of His death, in other words, is not a dreary, incomprehensible somewhat that He is compelled to reckon with
by untoward circumstances; for Him it is given, so to speak,
with the very conception of His person and His work. When
He unfolds Messiahship it contains death. This was the
first and last thing He taught about it, the first and last
thing He wished His disciples to learn. In Matthew xvi. 21,
Westcott and Hort read, 'From that time began Jesus
Christ to show to His disciples that He must go to Jerusalem
and suffer many things,' while Mark and Luke, in the corresponding passage, speak of *the Son of Man*. The official
expressions, or, to use a less objectionable term, the names
which denote the vocation of Jesus, 'the Christ' and 'the
Son of Man,' show that in this lesson He is speaking out of
the sense of his vocation, and not merely out of a view of
His historical circumstances. The necessity to suffer and
die, which was involved in His vocation, and the dim sense
of which belonged to His very being, so that without it He
would not have been what He was, was now beginning to
take definite shape in His mind. As events made plain the
forces with which He had to deal, He could see more clearly
how the necessity would work itself out. He could go
beyond that early word about the taking away of the bridegroom, and speak of Jerusalem, and of rejection by the
elders and chief priests and scribes. And this consideration
justifies us in believing that these details in the evangelic
narrative are historical. But the manner in which the
necessity did work itself out, and the greater or less detail
with which, from a greater or less distance, Jesus could
anticipate its course, do not affect in the least the character
of that necessity itself. It is the necessity involved in the

divine vocation of one in whom the Old Testament prophecy of the Servant of the Lord is to be fulfilled.

It must be admitted that in none of the three summary references which the evangelists make to our Lord's teaching on His death do they say anything of explicitly theological import. They tell us (1) that it was necessary—in the sense, we now assume, which has just been explained; (2) that it should be attended by such and such circumstances of pain and ignominy ; and (3) that it should be speedily followed by His resurrection. The repeated assurances that His disciples could not understand Him must surely refer to the meaning and necessity which He wished them to see in His death. They cannot but have understood His words about dying and rising, unless, as has been suggested already, the date of the rising puzzled them. All that remains is to suppose that the incomprehensible element in the new teaching of Jesus was the truths He wished to convey to them about the necessity, the meaning, the purpose, the power, of His death. But if we observe the unanimity with which every part of the early Church taught that Christ died for our sins according to the Scriptures—if, as will be shown below, we see how in Acts, in Peter, in Hebrews, in John, in Paul, passages referring to the Servant of the Lord, and especially to His bearing sin, and being numbered with the transgressors, are applied to Christ—it becomes very difficult to believe that this consent, in what might seem by no means obvious, can have any other source than the teaching of Jesus Himself. Hollmann, indeed, makes a remarkable attempt to prove that Jesus never applied the fifty-third chapter of Isaiah to Himself except in Luke xxii. 37, and that there, when He says (with singular emphasis), 'that which is written must be fulfilled in Me,—the word : and He was numbered with transgressors,' He is not thinking of His death at all as having expiatory value in relation to sin : He is only thinking of the dreary fact that His countrymen are going to treat Him as a criminal instead of as the Holy One of God.[1]   But there is surely no reason why the most superficial sense of profound words, a sense, too, which evacuates them of all their original associations, should be the only one allowed to Jesus.   If there is any truth at all in the connection we have asserted between His own consciousness of what He was and the Old Testament conception of the Servant of the Lord, it is surely improbable that He applied to Himself the most wonderful expression in Isaiah liii. in a shallow verbal fashion, and put from Him the great meanings of which the chapter is full, and which the New Testament writers embrace with one accord.   On the strength of that quotation, and of the consent of the New Testament as a whole, which has no basis but in Jesus, we are entitled to argue from the δεῖ of the evangelists—in other words, from the divine necessity Jesus saw in His death—that what He sought in those repeated lessons to induce His disciples to do was to recognise in the Messiah the person who should fulfil the prophecy of Isaiah liii.   The ideal in their minds was something far other than this, and there is no dead lift so heavy as that which is required to change an ideal.   We do not wonder that at the moment it was too much for Him and for them. We do not wonder that at the moment they could not turn, one is tempted to say bodily round, so as to see and understand what He was talking about.   And just as little do we

---

[1] *Die Bedeutung des Todes Jesu*, 69 ff.

Ritschl (*Rechtf. u. Versöhnung*, ii. 67) had already described as 'an unproved conjecture' the idea that Isaiah liii. had any decisive influence upon the mind of Jesus.   He argues that the two express words of our Lord about His death (Matt. xx. 28, xxvi. 28) have no connection with that chapter, and he discredits Luke xxii. 37 (which Hollmann accepts) as part of a passage (Luke xxii. 24-38) which he regards as 'eine Anschwemmung von unsicheren Erinnerungen.'

wonder that when the meaning of His words broke on them
later, it was with that overwhelming power which made the
thing that had once baffled them the sum and substance of
their gospel.   The centre of gravity in their world changed,
and their whole being swung round into equilibrium in
a new position.   Their inspiration came from what had
once alarmed, grieved, discomfited them.   The word they
preached was the very thing which had once made them
afraid to speak.

But we are not limited, in investigating our Lord's teaching
on His death, to inferences more or less secure.   There are
at least two great words in the gospels which expressly refer
to it—the one contained in His answer to James and John
when they asked the places at His right hand and His left
in His kingdom, the other spoken at the Supper.   We now
proceed to consider these.

Part of the difficulty we always have in interpreting
Scripture is the want of context; we do not know what
were the ideas in the minds of the original speakers or
hearers to which the words that have been preserved for us
were immediately related.   This difficulty has perhaps been
needlessly aggravated, especially in the first of the passages
with which we are concerned.   Yet the context here, even
as we have it, is particularly suggestive.   Jesus and His
disciples are on the way to Jerusalem, when Jesus takes the
start of them, apparently under some overpowering impulse,
and they follow in amazement and fear (Mark x. 32).   He
takes them aside once more, and makes the third of those
deliberate attempts to which reference has already been
made, to familiarise them with His death.   'Behold, we go
up to Jerusalem; and the Son of Man shall be delivered to
the chief priests and the scribes; and they shall condemn
Him to death, and shall deliver Him unto the Gentiles:
and they shall mock Him, and shall spit upon Him and

scourge Him, and shall kill Him ; and after three days He shall rise again ' (Mark x. 33 f.). It was while Jesus was in the grip of such thoughts—setting His face steadfastly, with a rapt and solemn passion, to go to Jerusalem—that James and John came to Him with their ambitious request. How was He to speak to them so that they might understand Him ? As Bengel finely says, He was dwelling in His passion ; He was to have others on His right hand and on His left before that ; and their minds were in another world. How was He to bridge the gulf between their thoughts and his own ? ' Are ye able,' He asks, ' to drink the cup which I drink, or to be baptized with the baptism with which I am baptized ? ' The cup and the baptism are poetic terms in which the destiny which awaits Him is veiled and transfigured. They are religious terms, in which that destiny is represented, in all its awfulness, as something involved in the will of God, and involving in itself a consecration. The cup is put into His hand by the Father, and if the baptism is a flood of suffering in which He is overwhelmed, it has through the very name which He uses to describe it the character of a religious act assigned to it ; He goes to be baptized with it, as He takes the cup which the Father gives Him to drink. That the reference in both figures is to His death, and to His death in that tragic aspect which has just been described in the immediately preceding verses, is not open to doubt. And just as little is it open to doubt that in the next scene in the gospel—that in which Jesus speaks to the disciples who were indignant with James and John for trying to steal a march upon them—a reference to His death is so natural as to be inevitable. True greatness, He tells them, does not mean dominance, but service. That is the law for all, even for the highest. It is by supremacy in service that the King in the Kingdom of God wins his place. ' Even the

Son of Man came not to be ministered unto but to minister, and to give His life a ransom for many.'

It is not inept to insist on the sequence and connection of ideas throughout this passage, because when it is really understood it puts the last words—' to give His life a ransom for many '—beyond assault. It is often asserted that these words are an indication of Pauline influence in the second evangelist. Let us hope that one may be forgiven if he says frankly that this is an assertion which he cannot understand. The words are perfectly in place. They are in line with everything that precedes. They are words in the only key, of the only fulness, which answers to our Lord's absorption at the time in the thought of His death. A theological aversion to them may be conceived, but otherwise there is no reason whatever to call them in question. There is no critical evidence against them, and their psychological truth is indubitable. So far from saying that Jesus could not have uttered anything so definitely theological, we should rather deny that the words are theological, in the technical question-begging sense of the term, yet maintain that in an hour of intense preoccupation with His death no other words would have been adequate to express the whole heart and mind of our Lord.

From this point of view, we must notice a common evasion of their import even by some who do not question that Jesus spoke them. It is pointed out, for instance, that the death is here set in line with the life of our Lord. He came not to be ministered unto but to minister, and (in particular, and at last, as His crowning service) to give His life a ransom for many. His death is the consummation of His life, and the consummation of His ministry ; but it has no other end than His life, and we must not seek another interpretation for it. An extreme example of this is seen in Hollmann,[1]

---

[1] *Die Bedeutung des Todes Jesu*, 99 ff.

whose exegesis of the passage brings out the following result. Jesus came into the world to serve men, and especially to serve them by awakening them to that repentance which is the condition of entering the Kingdom of God and inheriting its blessings. So far, His ministry has not been without success; some have already repented, and entered into the Kingdom. But even where He has not proved successful, it is not yet necessary to despair : many will be won to repentance by His death who resisted all the appeal of His life. It is scarcely necessary to point out that the connection of ideas here is not in the least that which belongs to the words of Jesus. Hollmann actually speaks of a *Glaubensurtheil*, a conviction which Jesus held by faith, that even His death (tragic and disconcerting as we must suppose it to be) will, by the grace of the Father, nevertheless contribute to the success of His work, and win many whom He has yet failed to reach. But this completely leaves out the one thing to which the words of Jesus gives prominence—the fact, namely, that the Son of Man came expressly to do a service which involved the giving of His life a ransom for many. Hollmann's interpretation means that Jesus could by faith in the Father reconcile Himself to His death as something which would, though it is not clear how, contribute to the carrying out of His vocation—something which, in spite of appearances, would not prove inconsistent with it ; but what the words in the gospel mean is that the death of Jesus, or the giving of His life a ransom for many, is itself the very soul of His vocation. He does not say that He can bear to die, because His death will win many to repentance who are yet impenitent, but that *the object of His coming* was to give His life a ransom for many.

The same consideration discredits an interpretation like Wendt's,[1] which finds the key to the passage in Matthew xi.

[1] *Lehre Jesu*, ii. 509 ff.

29 f. Wendt lays all the stress on the effect to be produced on human character by realising what the death of Jesus is. If men would only put on the yoke of Jesus and learn of Him—if they would drink of His cup and be baptized with His baptism—if, as St. Paul says, they would be conformed to His death, their souls would be liberated from the restless passions of pride and ambition by which James and John, and the other ten not less than they, were tormented, and death itself would cease to be a terror to them. However true this may be, one cannot look at the text without being impressed by its irrelevance as an interpretation. There is nothing in it to explain the introduction of Christ's death at all as the very end contemplated in His coming. There is nothing in it to explain either λύτρον, or ἀντί, or πολλῶν, or λύτρον ἀντὶ πολλῶν. In spite of the attention it has attracted, it is an ingenious vagary which has surely merited oblivion.

In what direction, then, are we to seek the meaning? The only clue is that which is furnished by the passages in which our Lord Himself speaks of the soul and of the possibility of losing or ransoming it. Thus in Mark viii. 34 f., immediately after the first announcement of His death, He calls the multitude to Him with His disciples, and says: 'If any man will come after Me, let him deny himself, and take up his cross and follow Me. For whoso *will* save his life (ψυχήν) shall lose it: but whoso shall lose his life (ψυχήν) for My sake and the gospel's, shall find it. For what does it profit a man to gain the whole world and forfeit his life (ψυχήν)? For what can a man give in exchange for his life (ἀντάλλαγμα τῆς ψυχῆς αὐτοῦ)?' It is clear from a passage like this that Jesus was familiar with the idea that the ψυχή or life of man, in the higher or lower sense of the term, might be lost, and that when it was lost there could be no compensation for it, as there was no

means of buying it back. It is in the circle of such ideas
that the words about giving His life a ransom for many
must find their point of attachment, and it is not only far
the simplest and most obvious interpretation, but far the
most profound and the most consonant with the New Testament as a whole, that Jesus in this passage conceives the
lives of the many as being somehow under forfeit, and
teaches that the very object with which He came into the
world was to lay down His own life as a ransom price that
those to whom these forfeited lives belonged might obtain
them again. This was the supreme service the Son of Man
was to render to mankind; it demanded the supreme
sacrifice, and was the path to supreme greatness. Anything
short of this is in the circumstances an anti-climax ; it falls
far beneath the passion with which our Lord condenses
into a single phrase the last meaning of His life and death.

Nothing has been gained for the understanding of this
passage by the elaborate investigation of the Hebrew or
Aramaic equivalents of λύτρον. In truth it does not matter
whether כֹּפֶר or פִּדְיוֹן, whether גְּאֻלָּה or מְחִיר or *purkana* is
most akin to it in the language which Jesus spoke ; if δοῦναι
τὴν ψυχὴν αὐτοῦ λύτρον ἀντὶ πολλῶν does not convey His
idea, it will certainly not be conveyed by any of the precarious equivalents for this Greek expression which are
offered for our acceptance. The best fruit of these
attempts to get behind the Greek has been Ritschl's
reference to Psalm xlix. 7 f., Job xxxiii. 23 f., as
passages furnishing a real clue to the mind of Christ. In
both of these the Hebrew word כֹּפֶר occurs, which Ritschl
regards as the equivalent of λύτρον, and in both also the
verb פָּדָה is used, with which, rather than with כֹּפֶר, Hollmann would connect the word of Jesus. But the ideas
which the words express are inseparable : the כֹּפֶר is in both
passages that by means of which, or at the cost of which,

the action of the verb פָּדָה (to deliver) is accomplished.[1]
The Psalm makes it particularly plain. What no man can
do for his brother—namely, give to God a ransom for him
(כָּפְרוֹ) so that he may still live always and not see corruption ;
what no man can do for his brother, because the redemption
(פִּדְיוֹן) of their soul is precious, and must be let alone for
ever, this the Son of Man claims to do for many, and to do
by giving His life a ransom for them. It seems hardly open
to doubt that the world in which our Lord's mind moved as
He spoke was that of the writer of the Psalm, and if this be so,
it is possible to find in it confirmation for the meaning just
assigned to His words. Dr. Driver [2] defines כֹּפֶר as ' properly *a covering* (viz. of an offence), hence *a propitiatory gift*,
but restricted by usage to a gift offered to propitiate or
satisfy the avenger-of-blood, and so *the satisfaction offered
for a life*, i.e. *a ransom*.' Without going into meaningless
questions as to how the ransom was fixed, or to whom it
was paid, it is important to recognise the fact that our Lord
speaks of the surrender of His life in this way. A ransom
is not wanted at all except where life has been forfeited, and
the meaning of the sentence unambiguously is that the forfeited lives of many are liberated by the surrender of Christ's
life, and that to surrender His life to do them this incalculable service was the very soul of His calling. If we find the
same thought in St. Paul, we shall not say that the evangelist has Paulinised, but that St. Paul has sat at the feet
of Jesus. And if we feel that such a thought carries us
suddenly out of our depth—that as the words fall on our
minds we seem to hear the plunge of the lead into fathom-
less waters—we shall not for that imagine that we have lost
our way. By these things men live, and wholly therein is

---

[1] Ritschl, *Rechtf. u. Versöhnung*, ii. 69 ff. Hollmann, *Die Bedeutung
des Todes Jesu*, 99 ff.

[2] In Hastings' *Bible Dictionary*, s.v. *Propitiation* (vol. iv. 128).

the life of our spirit. We cast ourselves on them, because they outgo us ; in their very immensity, we are assured that God is in them.[1]

One almost despairs of saying anything about the Lord's Supper which will not seem invalid to some upon critical or more general grounds. Our main interest is in the words which Jesus spoke, and in the light which these words throw on His own conception of His death. Here we are confronted at once by the paradoxical view of Spitta that in

---

[1] Compare Kähler, *Zur Lehre von der Versöhnung*, 166 : ' We put our whole faith in reconciliation into this word, and have a right to do so.' I do not think anything whatever is gained by trying all possible permutations and combinations of the words in the text, and deciding whether ἀντὶ πολλῶν is to be construed with λύτρον or with δοῦναι, or with the two in combination, or in some other ingenious or perverse way. It is a *sentence* which leaves meaning on the mind, not the bits into which it can be broken. Ritschl sums up his interpretation thus : ' Der Sinn des Ausdrucks Jesu ist also : Ich bin gekommen anstatt derer, welche eine Werthgabe als Schutzmittel gegen das Sterben für sich oder für Andere an Gott zu leisten vergeblich erstreben würden, dasselbe durch die Hingebung meines Lebens im Tode an Gott zu verwirklichen, aber eben nur anstatt derer, welche durch Glauben und selbstverleugnende Nachfolge meiner Person die Bedingung erfüllen, unter der allein meine Leistung den erwarteten Schutz für sie vermitteln kann.'— *R. u. V.* ii. 86. For a criticism of Ritschl's views on כֹּפֶר and כִּפֶּר see the last paragraph of Driver's article on *Propitiation* referred to above. Feine, in his *Theologie des Neuen Testaments*, 127 f., mentions four points of attachment for this ransom saying in Isaiah liii., which show in combination that we are justified in using the ideas of that prophecy as a key to it. (1) The words δοῦναι τὴν ψυχὴν αὐτοῦ recall the παρεδόθη εἰς θάνατον ἡ ψυχὴ αὐτοῦ of Isa. liii. 12. (2) The general idea of *service* pervades both. The subject of Isa. liii. is the humiliation and exaltation of the Servant of the Lord—His humiliation (as here that of Jesus) as the way to exaltation. (3) The peculiar use of ' many' in both : My righteous Servant shall justify ' many,' He bare the sin of ' many ' ; to give His life a ransom for ' many.' (4) The correspondence in meaning between the λύτρον as that by which a forfeited life is redeemed, and the giving of the life or soul as an אָשָׁם or guilt-offering by which legal satisfaction was rendered for an injury or wrong (Isa. liii. 10). There is a worth or goodness in Jesus' surrender of His life which outweighs the whole wrong which the world's sin inflicts upon God ; and He came that at this cost the sin of the world might be outweighed.

what actually took place on the occasion there was no reference to the death of Christ at all. What Jesus did in the upper room (so we are to suppose) was to anticipate with His disciples the Messianic Supper of the world to come. In that supper, according to Rabbinical and Apocalyptic writers, the good to be enjoyed is the Messiah Himself, and it is to this that Jesus refers when He speaks of the bread and wine as His own body and blood. He is preoccupied with the completion of His work, with the blessed prospect of the time when God shall have brought His kingdom to victory, and when from Him, the Messiah sent of God, the powers of knowledge and of eternal life shall flow unimpeded into the disciples as the gift of the meal which God prepares for those who are faithful to Him. The representation of the Supper in the evangelists is quite different, Spitta admits ; but the form it there assumes is due to the intervening death of Jesus, which compelled the disciples to give His words another turn. I do not feel it necessary to contest this construction of what took place. A conception of the Supper which sets aside the whole testimony of the New Testament to what it meant, which ignores its association with the Passover, the explicit references in every account of it to the shedding of Jesus' blood, and above all, the character expressly stamped upon it in the evangelists as a meal in which Jesus knew that He was sitting with the Twelve for the last time and was preoccupied with the idea of His parting from them, does not demand refutation. Nor is it entitled to forbid our asking —on the basis of the narratives in our hands—what Jesus said and did, and what is the bearing of this on the interpretation of His death.[1]

---

[1] Spitta's views are given in his treatise on *Die urchristlichen Traditionen über Ursprung und Sinn des Abendmahls* (*zur Geschichte u. Litteratur des Urchristenthums*).

There is at least a general consent in this, that Jesus took bread, and when He had broken it, or as He broke it, said, *This is My body*; that He took a cup with wine in it, or a cup into which He poured wine, saying as He did so, *This is My blood, which is poured out for many*. This is all that is admitted, *e.g.* by Hollmann, and it enables him to give the same interpretation to the supper as he gives to the word about the λύτρον.[1] Christ's death is in question, certainly, but it has no reference to those who are sitting at the table, and who are members of the Kingdom of God. The many in whose interest it takes place—the many who are to have benefit by it—are the same as the many for whom the ransom is to be given; they are the numbers, as yet impenitent, who will be won to penitence by the death of Jesus. According to this interpretation, the idea of a supper is a complete mistake. The persons at the table had really no interest in the death of Christ; they had already all that God could give. Hollmann, therefore, expunges from Mark as a liturgical insertion, intended to adapt the narrative to ecclesiastical custom, the very first word spoken by Jesus: *Take* (λάβετε). In propriety, the disciples should not have taken, as His death meant nothing to them. He quotes, with approval, a remark of Schmiedel: 'The most significant thing is, at least in the first instance, the breaking of the bread and the pouring out of the wine. The distribution of these foods to be partaken of attaches itself to this as a second thing. So far as the main matter is concerned, it might have been treated as superfluous; but as they were sitting at table any how, it was natural.' It is difficult to believe that this sort of thing is written seriously: if courtesy compels us to acknowledge that it is, we can only draw the melancholy conclusion that it is possible for the human mind to be serious even when it has completely lost

[1] *Die Bedeutung des Todes Jesu*, 133 ff.

contact with reality. The primary narrative of Mark begins by saying plainly, ' He took bread, and when He had given thanks He brake it and gave it to them and said, Take, this is My body. Then He took a cup, and when He had given thanks He gave it to them, and they drank of it every one (πάντες last and emphatic). And He said to them, This is My blood of the covenant shed for many.' This is not qualified by any other of the New Testament authorities, nor by the practice of the Church as the New Testament reveals it ; and I submit that it is not open to any one to go behind it, and to tell us blankly out of his own head (for that is the only authority left) that the bearing of what took place was really quite independent of this giving and taking, eating and drinking; and that while the death of Jesus was the subject of the symbolical actions of breaking the bread and pouring out the wine, and was no doubt meant to benefit some persons, it was a thing in which those who were present, and who at Jesus' word ate and drank the symbols of it, had no interest at all. Jesus made the bread and wine symbols of His death : this is not denied. He handed them to His disciples, pronouncing as He did so the very words in which He conferred on them this symbolical character : this also is not denied. But when He did so, it was not that the disciples might take them in this character. On the contrary, it was only because they were at their supper anyhow, and because bread and wine are naturally eaten and drunk. That is how bread and wine are disposed of in this world, but it has nothing to do with the story. If there is anybody in the world who finds this convincing, presumably it cannot be helped.

But it is not only necessary to insist on the eating and drinking of the bread and wine, which as broken and outpoured symbolised Christ's death, and as eaten and drunk symbolised the interest of the disciples in that death, and their making

it somehow their own; it is necessary to insist on what was
further said by Jesus. All the evangelists in their narratives
introduce the word ' covenant ' (διαθήκη) in some construction
or other. Mark has, This is My blood of the covenant
(xiv. 24). Matthew, according to some authorities (including
that combination of Latin and Syriac versions to which
critics seem inclined to ascribe a higher value than once
seemed probable) has, This is My blood of the new covenant
(xxvi. 28). Luke has what is apparently a Pauline form,
This cup is the new covenant in My blood (xxii. 20). For
long it was an admitted point among critics that this was an
indubitable word of Jesus. Brandt, whose criticism is
sceptical enough, holds that the only historically certain
words in the whole story are, This is My covenant blood,
drink ye all of it. But even these words have lately been
assailed in the determined effort to get behind the gospels.
Three grounds have been assigned for questioning them.[1]
The first is that the expression τὸ αἶμά μου τῆς διαθήκης is
awkward in Greek; the second, that it is impossible to
translate it into Hebrew or Aramaic; and the third, that
the conception of the covenant owes its place in Christianity
to St. Paul. Of these reasons the last obviously begs the
question. It does not follow that because St. Paul makes
use of an idea he originated it. There are very great ideas,
indeed, of which St. Paul says, I delivered unto you that
which also I received (1 Corinthians xv. 3 f.): why should
not this be one of them? Does he not himself declare that it
is one, when he prefaces his account of the supper—including
in it the idea of the new covenant in the blood of Jesus—
with the words, I received of the Lord that which also I
delivered unto you? (1 Corinthians xi. 23). The idea of a
new covenant, and that of covenant blood, are Old Testament

---

[1] See Preuschen's *Zeitschrift*, i. 69 ff., and on the other side O. Holtzmann,
War Jesus Ekstatiker? 110 ff.

ideas; and if Jesus was conscious, nay, if it was the very essence of His consciousness, that, in relation both to law and prophecy, He came not to destroy but to fulfil, why should not He Himself have spoken the creative word? As for the other two reasons, that 'My blood of the covenant' is awkward in Greek, and that there are persons who cannot translate it into Hebrew, however true or interesting they may be, they are obviously irrelevant. It may be awkward in Greek or in any language to combine in one proposition the two ideas this is My blood, and this is covenant blood; but however awkward it may be, since they really are ideas which the mind can grasp, it must be possible to do it, in Greek or in any language. It does not, therefore, seem open to question, on any serious ground whatever, that Jesus at the last supper spoke of His blood as covenant blood. Now, what does this imply? To what set of ideas in the minds of His hearers, to what Old Testament associations does it attach itself, so as to be not merely a word, but an element in a living mind? We get the clue to the answer when we notice the form in which the words appear in Matthew, This is My blood of the *new* covenant, shed for many *unto remission of sins*. The added words here may be no more than an interpretative expansion of what Jesus said, but if they are no more than this they are also no less. They are an interpretative expansion by a mind in a position naturally to know and understand what Jesus meant.

The Old Testament twice speaks of 'covenant,' in the sense in which God makes a covenant with his people. There is the covenant made with sacrifice at Sinai, in the account of which we have the phrase, Behold the blood of the covenant which the Lord hath made with you upon all these conditions (Exodus xxiv. 8). Here, it is sometimes said, is the original of the words found in our evangelists; and as nothing is said in Exodus about the forgiveness of sins, and

as the sacrifices mentioned there are not sin or guilt offerings,
but burnt offerings and peace offerings, it is argued that the
insertion in Matthew of the clause 'for forgiveness of sins'
is a mistake.[1]   The inference is hasty.   Covenant blood is
sacrificial blood, and we have every reason to believe that
sacrificial blood universally, and not only in special cases,
was associated with propitiatory power.   'The atoning
function of sacrifice,' as Robertson Smith put it, speaking of
primitive times, 'is not confined to a particular class of
oblation, but belongs to all sacrifices.'[2]   Dr. Driver has
expressed the same opinion with regard to the Levitical
legislation in which the key to the language of our passage
must be found.   Criticising Ritschl's explanation of sacrifice
and its effect, he says : ' It seems better to suppose that
though the burnt-, peace-, and meat-offerings were not offered
expressly, like the sin- and guilt-offerings, for the forgiveness
of sin, they nevertheless (in so far as *Kipper* is predicated of
them) were regarded as " covering," or neutralising, the
offerer's unworthiness to appear before God, and so, though
in a much less degree than the sin- or guilt-offering, as
effecting *Kappārā* in the sense ordinarily attached to the
word, viz. " propitiation." '[3]   Instead of saying 'in a much
less degree,' I should prefer to say 'with a less specific
reference or application,' but the point is not material.
What it concerns us to note is that the New Testament,
while it abstains from interpreting Christ's death by any
special prescriptions of the Levitical law, constantly uses
sacrificial language to describe that death, and in doing so
unequivocally recognises in it a propitiatory character—in

[1] Holtzmann, *Neut. Theologie*, i. 302, says : ' The figure of covenant blood,
which alone retains its validity, points, indeed, to a covenant sacrifice, but
not necessarily also to an expiatory sacrifice, with which last alone have been
combined the later ideas of exchange and substitution.'

[2] *Religion of the Semites*, 219.

[3] Hastings' *Dictionary of the Bible*, s.v. *Propitiation*, p. 132.

other words, a reference to sin and its forgiveness. But
there is something further to be said. The passage in Exodus
is not the only one in the Old Testament to which reference is here made. In the thirty-first chapter of Jeremiah
we have the sublime prophecy of a new covenant—a new
covenant which is indeed but the efficacious renewal of the
old, for there is but one God, and His grace is one—a new
covenant, the very condition and foundation of which is the
forgiveness of sins. 'They shall all know Me from the least
to the greatest, *for* I will forgive their iniquities, and I will
remember their sins no more' (Jeremiah xxxi. 34). It is
this which is present to the mind of our Lord as He says of
the outpoured wine, This is My blood of the covenant. He
is establishing, at the cost of His life, the new covenant, the
new religious relation between God and man, which has the
forgiveness of sins as its fundamental blessing. He speaks
as knowing that that blessing can only become ours through
His death, and as the condition upon which it depends His
death can be presented as a propitiatory sacrifice. It is as
though He had pointed to the prophecy in Jeremiah, and
said, This day is this Scripture fulfilled before your eyes.
He had already, we might think, attached to Himself all that
is greatest in the ideals and hopes of the Old Testament—
the Messianic sovereignty of the 2nd and of the 110th Psalm,
and the tragic and glorious calling of the Servant of the
Lord; but there is something which transcends both, and
which gives the sublimest expression to our Lord's consciousness of Himself and His work, when He says, This is My
blood of the covenant. It is a word which gathers up into
it the whole promise of prophecy and the whole testimony
of the apostles; it is the focus of revelation, in which the
Old Testament and the New are one. The power that is in
it is the power of the passion in which the Lamb of God
bears the sin of the world. It is no misapprehension, there-

fore, but a true rendering of the mind of Christ, when
Matthew calls the covenant *new*, and defines the shedding
of blood by reference to the remission of sins.

There is really only one objection which can be made, and
it is made unceasingly, to this interpretation of the words
of Jesus. It is that it is inconsistent with what is elsewhere
His unmistakable teaching. The very burden of His message,
we are told, is that God forgives unconditionally, out of His
pure fatherly love. This love reaches of itself deeper far
than sin, and bestows pardon freely and joyfully on the
penitent. It is nothing less than a direct contradiction of
this gospel of the free love of God when we make forgiveness
dependent upon a sacrificial, that is a propitiatory, virtue in
the death of Christ. It misrepresents God's character, and
in so doing destroys the gospel. We cannot, it is argued,
on the strength of one word, and that a dubious word, run
counter to the sense and spirit of our Lord's teaching as a
whole. So, in substance, a large school of critics and
theologians. How can we answer such a contention?

As for the alleged dubiety of the word, we have said
enough already; it only remains to deal with its alleged
inconsistency with the rest of our Lord's teaching. This is
usually asserted in the most unqualified fashion, but if we look
back on what we have already seen to be our Lord's conception of Himself and His calling from the beginning we may
well question it. The love of God, according to Jesus, is
no doubt unconditionally free, but it is not an abstraction.
It does not exist *in vacuo*: so far as the forgiveness of sins
is concerned—and it is with the love of God in this relation
that we have to do—it exists in and is represented by Jesus'
own presence in the world: His presence in a definite
character, and with a definite work to do, which can only be
done at a definite cost. The freeness of God's love is not
contradicted by these facts; on the contrary, it is these facts

which enable us to have any adequate idea of what that love really is. To say that it is inconsistent with God's free love to make the forgiveness of sins dependent on the death of Jesus, is exactly the same (in one particular relation) as to say (in general) that it is inconsistent with God's free love that entrance into His kingdom and participation in its blessings should only be possible through the presence of Jesus in the world, His work in it, and the attitude which men assume towards Him. Those who accept the latter should not deny the former. If we give any place at all to the idea of mediation, there is no reason why we should reject the idea of propitiation : for propitiation is merely a mode of mediation, a mode of it no doubt which brings home to us acutely what we owe to the Mediator, and makes us feel that though forgiveness is free to us it does not cost nothing to Him. Of course, if we choose to say that the Son has no place in the gospel at all, but only the Father, we may reject the great word about covenant-blood, or rather we must reject it ; if He has no place in the gospel at all, we have no obligations to Him ; we do not owe Him anything, least of all are we indebted to His death for the forgiveness of sins. But there is something in such language which when confronted with the gospels can only strike one as utterly abstract, unconvincing, and unreal. It does not answer to the relation of sinful souls to Jesus, to their devotion, their gratitude, their sense of undying obligation. It was not for a forgiveness with which He had in the last resort nothing to do that they poured their precious oint-ment on His head and wet His feet with tears. No ; but in the depths of their being they had the dim sense of His passion in their pardon, and were conscious of an obligation for it to Him which they could never repay. The love of God, I repeat, free as it is to sinful men, unconditionally free, is never conceived in the New Testament, either by our

Lord Himself or by any of His followers, as an abstraction. Where the forgiveness of sin is concerned, it is not conceived as having reality or as taking effect apart from Christ. It is a real thing to us as it is mediated through Him, through His presence in the world, and ultimately through His death. The love of God by which we are redeemed from sin is a love which we do not know except as it comes in this way and at this cost; consequently, whatever we owe as sinners to the love of God, we owe to the death of Jesus. It is no more a contradiction of God's free love to the sinful, when we say that Christ's death is the ground of forgiveness, than it is a contradiction of God's fatherly goodwill to men in general, when we admit the word of Jesus, No man cometh unto the Father but by Me. In both cases equally, Christ stands between God and man; in both cases equally it is at cost to Him that God becomes our God. Why should we be loth to become His debtors? The Christian faith is a specific form of dependence on God, and to cavil at the atonement is to begin the process of giving it away in bits. It is to refuse to allow it to be conditioned by Christ at the central and vital point, the point at which the sinner is reconciled to God; and if we can do without Christ there, we can do without Him altogether. The process which begins with denying that we owe to Him and to His death the forgiveness of sins, ends by denying that He has any proper place in the gospel at all. It is not either from His own lips, or from the lips of any of the apostles, that we so learn Christ.

CHAPTER II

THE EARLIEST CHRISTIAN PREACHING

I. Thus far we have confined ourselves to the words of Jesus. The divine necessity of His death, indicated in the Old Testament and forming the basis of all His teaching regarding it, is the primary truth; the nature of that necessity begins to be revealed as the death is set in relation to the ransoming of many, and to the institution of a new covenant —that is, a new religion, having as its fundamental blessing the forgiveness of sins. I do not think this view of our Lord's mind as to His own death can be shaken by appealing to His experience in the garden, as though that proved that to the last day of His life the inevitableness of death remained for Him an open question.

The divine necessity to lay down His life for men, which we have been led to regard as a fixed point in His mind, did not preclude such conflicts as are described in the last pages of the gospel; rather was it the condition of our Lord's victory in them. At a distance, it was possible to think of death in its heroic and ideal aspects only, as the fulfilment of a divine calling, an infinite service rendered in love to man; but as the fatal hour approached, its realistic and repellent aspects predominated over everything; it stood out before the mind and imagination of Jesus—we might almost say it obtruded itself upon His senses—as a scene and an experience of treachery, desertion, hate, mockery, injustice, anguish, shame. It is not hard to conceive that in these circumstances Jesus should have prayed as He did in the garden : O My Father, if it be possible, let this cup pass from Me, even though the unmoved conviction of His soul was that He had come to give His life a ransom for many. It is one thing to have the consciousness of so high a calling, another to maintain and give effect to it under conditions from which all that is ideal and divine seems to have withdrawn. It is one thing not to count one's life dear, or to make much of it, in comparison with great ends which are to be attained by laying it down ; it is another to lay it down, encompassed not by the gratitude and adoration of those for whom the sacrifice is made, but by mocking and spitting and scorn. This was what Jesus did, and He attained to it through the agony in the garden. The agony does not represent a doubt as to His calling, but the victorious assertion of His calling against the dreadful temptation to renounce it which came in the hour and with the power of darkness. Not that I should venture to say, as is sometimes said, that the realisation, as they approached, of the sensible and moral horrors of the death He was to die was all that wrung from Jesus that last appeal to the Father, all that made His soul exceeding sorrowful even unto death, and put Him in *agonia* —that is, in deadly fear : [1] this does not answer to what we know of the courage of martyrs. Though one shrinks from analysing the cry of the heart to God in its anguish, it is difficult to avoid the impression that both here and in the experience of forsaking on the cross, we are in contact with something out of proportion to all that men could do to Jesus, something that seems to call for connection, if we would

[1] See Field, *Notes on the New Testament*, p. 77, where decisive proof of this is given ; and Armitage Robinson, *Gospel according to Peter*, pp. 84, 87 (ἀγωνιάω).

understand it, with realities more mysterious and profound.
Language like Calvin's,[1] who says plainly that Jesus endured
in His soul the dreadful torments of a condemned and lost
man, may well be repellent to us; there is something unrealisable and even impious in such words. But it does not
follow that there was nothing true, nothing in contact with
reality, in the state of mind which inspired them.[2] Not
with any logical hardness, not as carrying out aggressively
to its issue any theological theory, but sensible of the thick
darkness in which, nevertheless (we are sure), God is, may
we not urge that these experiences of deadly fear and of
desertion are of one piece with the fact that in His death
and in the agony in the garden through which He accepted
that death as the cup which the Father gave Him to drink,
Jesus was taking upon Him the burden of the world's sin,
consenting to be, and actually being, numbered with the
transgressors? They cannot but have some meaning, and
it must be part of the great meaning which makes the Cross
of Christ the gospel for sinful men. No doubt there are
those who reject this meaning altogether; it is dogmatico-
religious, not historico-religious, and no more is needed to
condemn it. But a dogmatico-religious interpretation of
Christ's death—that is, an interpretation which finds in it
an eternal and divine meaning, laden with gospel—is so far
from being self-evidently wrong, that it is imperatively
required by the influence which that death has had in the
history of the Christian religion. Such an interpretation
carries out, through the experiences of His death, thoughts

---

[1] *Institutio,* II. xvi. 10.

[2] Calvin has, in point of fact, many more adequate utterances on this subject: 'Invisibile illud et incomprehensibile judicium quod coram Deo sustinuit';
'neque tamen innuimus Deum fuisse unquam illi vel adversarium vel iratum';
'illic personam nostram gerebat'; and especially the following: 'Atqui
haec nostra sapientia est probe sentire quanti constiterit Dei filio nostra
salus.'

as to its significance which we owe to Jesus Himself, and connects these thoughts and experiences with the subsequent testimony of the apostles. In other words, to read the accounts of Gethsemane and Calvary in this sense is to read them in line at once with the words of Jesus and with the words of those who were first taught by His spirit; it is to secure at once the unity of the gospels with themselves, and their unity, in the main truth which it teaches, with the rest of the New Testament. To call such an interpretation dogmatico-religious as opposed to historico-religious either has no meaning, or has a meaning which would deny to the Person and Work of Jesus any essential place in the Christian religion. But if the death of Jesus has *eternal* significance—if it has a meaning which has salvation in it for all men and for all times; a meaning which we discover in Scripture as we look back from it and look forward; a meaning which is the key to all that goes before and to all that comes after (and such a meaning I take it to have, indisputably)—then Gethsemane and Calvary cannot be invoked to refute, but only to illustrate, the 'dogmatic' interpretation. They are too great to be satisfied by anything else.[1]

It does not follow, of course, that they were understood at once, even in the light of our Lord's words, by those whom He left as His witnesses. The mind can easily retain words the meaning of which it only imperfectly apprehends. It can retain words by which it is in the first instance moved and impressed, rather than enlightened. It can retain words which are sure, when reflection awakens, to raise many questions, to ask for definition in a great variety of relations; and it can retain them without at first having

[1] Compare Kähler, *Zur Lehre von der Versöhnung*, pp. 181, 401. On the other side Fairbairn, *Philosophy of the Christian Religion*, p. 425 ff.

any consciousness of these questions whatever. It is in the highest degree probable that it was so with the disciples of Jesus. We can easily believe that they had right impressions from our Lord's words, before they had clear ideas about them. We can understand even that it might be natural enough for them to ascribe to Jesus directly what was only indirectly due to Him, because in the absence of philosophical reflection they were not conscious of the difference. Not that one would include under this head the creative words of Jesus already referred to about the ransom and the covenant blood; these bear the stamp of originality, not of reflection, upon them; it is their greatness to explain all things and to be explained by none. But before proceeding to examine the ideas of the primitive Christian Church on this subject, it is necessary to give an explicit utterance on the Resurrection, and the gospel presentation of it.

The Resurrection of Jesus from the dead is here assumed to have taken place, and, moreover, to have had the character which is ascribed to it in the New Testament. It is not sufficient to say that there were appearances of the Jesus who had died to certain persons—appearances the significance of which is exhausted when we say that they left on the minds of those who were favoured with them the conviction that Jesus had somehow broken the bands of death. It is quite true that St. Paul, in setting before the Corinthians the historical evidence for the Resurrection, enumerates various occasions on which the Risen Lord was seen, and says nothing about Him except that on these occasions He appeared to Peter, to James, to the Twelve, to more than five hundred at once, and so on: this was quite sufficient for his purpose. But there is no such thing in the New Testament as an appearance of the Risen Saviour in which He merely appears. He is always repre-

sented as entering into relation to those who see Him in
other ways than by a flash upon the inner or the outer
eye: He establishes other communications between Himself and His own besides those which can be characterised
in this way. It may be that a tendency to materialise the
supernatural has affected the evangelical narrative here or
there—that Luke, for instance, who makes the Holy Spirit
descend upon Jesus in bodily form as a dove went involuntarily beyond the apostolic tradition in making the
Risen One speak of His flesh and bones, and eat a bit of
roast fish before the disciples, to convince them that He
was no mere ghost; it may be so, though the mode of
Christ's being, in the days before His final withdrawal, is
so entirely beyond our comprehension, that it is rash to be
too peremptory about it; but even if it were so, it would
not affect the representation as a whole which the gospels
give of the Resurrection, and of the relation of the Risen
One to His disciples. It would not affect the fact that
He not only appeared to them, but spoke to them. It
would not affect the fact that He not only appeared to
them, but taught them, and in particular gave them a
commission in which the meaning of His own life and
work, and their calling as connected with it, are finally
declared.

Without going in detail into the critical questions here
involved, yet claiming to speak with adequate knowledge
of them, I feel it quite impossible to believe that this
representation of the gospels has nothing in it. How
much the form of it may owe to the conditions of trans-
mission, repetition, condensation, and even interpretation,
we may not be able precisely to say, since these conditions
must have varied indefinitely and in ways we cannot
calculate; but the *fact* of a great charge, the general
import of which was thoroughly understood, seems indis-

putable. All the gospels give it in one form or another; and even if we concede that the language in which it is expressed owes something to the Church's consciousness of what it had come to possess through its risen Lord, this does not affect in the least the fact that every known form of the evangelic tradition puts such a charge, or instruction, or commission, into the lips of Jesus after His Resurrection.[1]

What, then, is the content of this teaching or commission of the Risen Saviour, which all the evangelists give in one form or another? Luke has some peculiar matter in which he tells how Jesus opened the minds of His disciples to understand the Scriptures, recalling the words He had spoken while He was yet with them, how that all things must be fulfilled which were written in the law of Moses and in the Prophets and in the Psalms concerning Him. If Jesus spoke to His disciples at all about what had befallen Him, all that we have already seen as to His teaching prepares us to believe that it was on this line. Alike for Him and for the disciples the divine necessity for His death could only be made out by connecting it with intimations in the Word of God. But apart from this instruction, which is referred to by Luke alone, there is the common testimony with which we are mainly concerned. In Matthew it runs thus: 'Jesus came and spoke to them saying, All power has been given to Me in heaven and on earth. Go and make disciples of all the nations, baptizing them into the name of the Father and of the Son and of the Holy Spirit, teaching them to observe all things that I have commanded you. And lo, I am with you all the days until the end of the world' (Matt. xxviii. 18 ff.). Here we notice as the essential things in our Lord's words (1) the universal mission; (2) baptism; (3) the promise of a

[1] For a fuller statement on this point see *Jesus and the Gospel*, 153 ff.

spiritual presence. In Mark, as is well known, the original ending has been lost. The last chapter, however, was in all probability the model on which the last in Matthew was shaped, and what we have at present instead of it reproduces the same ideas. 'Go into all the world and preach the gospel to every creature. He that believeth and is baptized shall be saved; but he that disbelieveth shall be condemned' (Mark xvi. 15 f.). What follows, as to the signs which should attend on those who believe —'in My name they shall cast out demons, they shall speak with new tongues, they shall take up serpents, and if they drink any deadly thing it shall not hurt them, they shall lay hands on the sick, and they shall recover'— shows how easy it was to expand the words of Jesus on the basis of experience, just as a modern preacher sometimes introduces Jesus speaking in His own person, and promising what the preacher knows by experience He can and will do; but it does not follow from this that the commission to preach and its connection with baptism are unhistorical. In Luke the commission is connected with the teaching above referred to. 'He said to them, Thus it is written that the Christ should suffer, and should rise from the dead on the third day, and that repentance for remission of sins should be preached in His name to all the nations, beginning from Jerusalem' (Luke xxiv. 46 f.). Here again we have (1) the universal commission; (2) repentance and remission of sins. In John what corresponds to this runs as follows: 'Jesus therefore said to them again, Peace be unto you. As the Father hath sent Me, even so send I you. And when He had said this, He breathed on them and saith to them, Receive ye the Holy Spirit: whose soever sins ye forgive they are forgiven unto them: whose soever sins ye retain they are retained' (John xx. 21 f.). Here once more we have (1) a mission, though its range is not defined; (2) a message, the sum and substance of which has to do with forgiveness of sins; and (3) a gift of the Holy Ghost. 'But what,' it may be asked, 'has all this to do with the death of Jesus? The death of Jesus is not expressly referred to here, except in what Luke tells about His opening the minds of the disciples to understand the Scriptures, and that simply repeats what we have already had before us.'

The answer is apparent if we consider the context in which the ideas found in this commission are elsewhere found in the New Testament. In all its forms the commission has to do either with baptism (so in Matthew and Mark) or with the remission of sins (so in Luke and John). These are but two forms of the same thing, for in the world of New Testament ideas baptism and the remission of sins are inseparably associated. But the remission of sins has already been connected with the death of Jesus by the words spoken at the supper, or if not by the very words spoken, at least by the significance ascribed to His blood as covenant-blood; and if the Risen Saviour, in giving His disciples their final commission, makes the forgiveness of sins the burden of the gospel they are to preach, which seems to me indubitable, He at the same time puts at the very heart of the gospel His own covenant-founding, sin-annulling death. This inference from the evangelic passages which record the intercourse of the Risen Lord with His disciples may strike some, at the first glance, as artificial; but the air of artificiality will pass away, provided we admit the reality of that intercourse, and its relation both to the past teaching of Jesus and to the future work of the apostles. There is a link wanted to unite what we have seen in the gospels with what we find when we pass from them to the other books of the New Testament, and that link is exactly supplied by a charge of Jesus to His disciples to make the forgiveness of sins the centre of their gospel, and to attach it to the rite by which men were admitted to the Christian society. In an age when baptism and remission of sins were inseparable ideas—when, so to speak, they interpenetrated each other—it is no wonder that the sense of our Lord's charge is given in some of the gospels in one form, in some in the other : that here He bids them baptize, and there preach the forgiveness of sins. It is not the form on which we can lay stress, but only the import. The import, however, is secure. Its historicity can only be questioned by those who reduce the resurrection to mere appearances of Jesus to the disciples—appearances which, as containing nothing but themselves, and as unchecked by any other relation to reality, are essentially visionary. And its significance is this : it is the very thing which is wanted to evince the unity of the New Testament, and the unity and consistency of the Christian religion, as they have been presented to us in the historical tradition of the Church. Here, where the final revelation is made by our Lord of all that His presence in the world means and involves, we find Him dealing with ideas—baptism and forgiveness—which alike in His own earlier teaching, and in the subsequent teaching of the apostles, can only be defined by relation to His death.

When we pass from the gospels to the earliest period of the Church's life we are again immersed in critical difficulties. It is not easy to use the book of Acts in a way which will command universal agreement. Renan's remark that the closing chapters are the most purely historical of anything in the New Testament, while the opening ones are the least historical, is at least plausible enough to make one cautious. But while this is so, there is a general consent that in the early chapters there is a very primitive type of doctrine. The Christian imagination may have transfigured the day of Pentecost, and turned the ecstatic praise of the first disciples into a speaking in foreign languages,[1] but some source or sources of the highest value underlie the speeches of Peter. They do not represent the nascent catholicism of the beginning of the second century, but the very earliest type of preaching Jesus by men who had kept company with Him. It would be out of place here to dwell on the primitive character of the Christology, but it is necessary to refer to it as a guarantee for the historical character of the speeches in which it occurs. Consider, then, passages like these : 'Jesus of Nazareth, a man approved of God unto you by mighty works and wonders and signs which God did by Him in the midst of you, even as ye yourselves know' (ii. 22); 'God hath made Him both Lord and Christ, this Jesus whom ye crucified' (ii. 36); 'Jesus of Nazareth, how that God anointed Him with the Holy Ghost and with power; who went about doing good, and healing all that were oppressed of the devil, for God was with Him' (x. 38). It is impossible to deny that in words like these we have a true echo of the earliest Christian preaching. And it is equally impossible to deny that the soteriology which accompanies this Christology is as truly primitive. What then is it, and what, in particular, is the place taken in it by the death of Jesus ?

It is sometimes asserted broadly that the real subject of these early speeches in Acts is not the death of Jesus but the resurrection ; the death, it is said, has no significance assigned to it ; it is only a difficulty to be got over. But there is a great deal of confusion in this. No doubt the apostles were witnesses of the resurrection, and the discourses in these chapters are specimens of their testimony. The resurrection is emphasised in them with various motives. Sometimes the motive may be called apologetic : the idea

---

[1] For the best examination of this see Chase's *Hulsean Lectures* and Vernon Bartlet's *Acts* (Century Bible).

is that in spite of the death it is still possible to believe in Jesus as the Messiah ; God by raising Him from the dead has exalted Him to this dignity. Sometimes it may be called evangelistic. You killed Him, the preacher says again and again (ii. 23 f., iii. 14 f., v. 30 f.), and God exalted Him to His right hand. In these two appreciations of Jesus lies the motive for a great spiritual change in sinful men. Sometimes, again, the resurrection is referred to in connection with the gift of the Spirit ; the new life in the Church, with its wonderful manifestations, attests the exaltation of Jesus (ii. 33). Sometimes, once more, it is connected with His return, either to bring times of refreshing from the presence of the Lord (iii. 20 f.), or as Judge of the quick and the dead (x. 42). But this preoccupation with the resurrection in various aspects and relations does not mean that for the first preachers of the gospel the death of Jesus had no significance, or no fundamental significance. Still less does it mean that the death of Jesus was nothing to them but a difficulty in the way of retaining their faith in His Messiahship, a difficulty which the resurrection enabled them to surmount—its sinister significance being discounted, so to speak, by the splendour of this supreme miracle. This last idea, that the cross *in itself* is nothing but a scandal, and that all the New Testament interpretations of it are but ways of getting over the scandal, cannot be too emphatically rejected. It ignores, in the first place, all that has been already established as to our Lord's own teaching about the necessity and the meaning of His death—which has nothing to do with its being a σκάνδαλον. And it ignores, in the second place, the spiritual power of Christ's death in those who believe in Him, alike as the New Testament exhibits it, and as it is seen in all subsequent ages of the Church. The gospel would never have been known as ' the word of the cross' if the interpretation of the cross had merely been an apologetic device for surmounting the theoretical difficulties involved in the conception of a crucified Messiah. Yet nothing is commoner than to represent the matter thus. The apostles, it is argued, had to find some way of getting over the difficulty of the crucified Messiah theoretically, as well as practically; the resurrection enabled them to get over it practically, for it annulled the death; and the various theories of a saving significance ascribed to the death enabled them to get over it theoretically—that is all. Nothing, I venture to say, could be more hopelessly out of touch alike with New Testament teaching and with all Christian experience than such a reading of the facts. A doctrine of the death of Jesus, which was merely the solution of an abstract difficulty—the answer to a conundrum— could never have become what the doctrine of the death of Jesus is in the New Testament—the centre of gravity in the Christian world. It could never have had stored up in it the redeeming virtue of the gospel. It could never have been the hiding-place of God's power, the inspiration of all Christian praise. Whatever the doctrine of Jesus' death may be, it is the feeblest of all misconceptions to trace it to the necessity of saying something about the death which should as far as possible remove the scandal of it. 'I delivered unto you first of all,' says St. Paul to the Corinthians, 'that which I also received, that Christ died for our sins, according to the Scriptures' (1 Cor. xv. 3). St. Paul must have received this doctrine from members of the primitive Church. He must have received it in the place which he gave it in his own preaching—that is, as the first and fundamental thing in the gospel. He must have received it within seven years—if we follow some recent chronologies, within a very much shorter period—of the death of Jesus. Even if the book of Acts were so preoccupied with the resurrection that it paid no attention to the independent significance of the death, it would be perfectly fair, on the ground of this explicit reference of St. Paul, to supplement its outline of primitive Christian doctrine with some definite teaching on atonement; but when we look closely at the speeches in Acts, we find that our situation is much more favourable. They contain a great deal which enables us to see how the primitive Church was taught to think and feel on this important subject.

Here we have to consider such points as these. (1) The death of Christ is repeatedly presented, as in our Lord's own teaching, in the light of a divine necessity. It took place 'by the determined counsel and foreknowledge of God' (ii. 23). That His Christ should suffer, was what God foretold by the mouth of all His prophets (iii. 18). In His death, Jesus was the stone which the builders rejected, but which God made the head of the corner (iv. 1). All the enemies of Jesus, both Jew and Gentile, could only do to Him what God's hand and counsel had determined before should be done (iv. 28). A divine necessity, we must remember, is not a blind but a seeing one. To find the necessity for the death of Jesus in the word of God means to find that His death is not only inevitable but indispensable, an essential part of the work He had to do. Not blank but intelligible and moral necessity is meant here.

Hence (2) we notice further the frequent identification, in these early discourses, of the suffering Messiah with the Servant of the Lord in the Book of Isaiah. 'The God of our Fathers hath glorified His Servant Jesus' (iii. 13). 'Of a truth, in this city, both Herod and Pontius Pilate were gathered together against Thy Holy Servant Jesus' (iv. 27). The same identification is involved in the account of Philip and the Ethiopian eunuch.   The place of the Scripture which the eunuch read was the fifty-third chapter of Isaiah, and beginning from that Scripture Philip preached to him Jesus (viii. 35).   We cannot forget that the impulse to this connection was given by our Lord Himself, and that it runs through His whole ministry, from His baptism, in which the heavenly voice spoke to Him words applied to the Servant of the Lord in Isaiah xlii. 1, to the last night of His life when He applied to Himself the mysterious saying, He was numbered with transgressors (Luke xxii. 37).   The divine necessity to suffer is here elevated into a specific divine necessity, namely, to fulfil through suffering the vocation of one who bore the sins of many, and made intercession for the transgressors.

This connection of ideas in the primitive Church is made clearer still, when we notice (3) that the great blessing of the gospel, offered in the name of Jesus, is the forgiveness of sins.   This is the refrain of every apostolic sermon.   Thus in ii. 38 : 'Repent and be baptized every one of you in the name of Jesus Christ unto remission of your sins.'   In iii. 19, immediately after the words, 'the things that God declared before through the mouth of all the prophets, that His Christ should suffer, He thus fulfilled,' we read : 'Repent therefore and turn, that your sins may be blotted out.'   In v. 31 Jesus is exalted a Prince and a Saviour to give repentance to Israel and forgiveness of sins.   In x. 43, after rehearsing in outline the life, death, and resurrection of Jesus, Peter concludes his sermon in the house of Cornelius : 'To Him bear all the prophets witness, that every one who believes in Him shall receive forgiveness of sins through His name.'   This prominence given to the remission of sins is not accidental, and must not be separated from the context essential to it in Christianity.   It is part of a whole or system of ideas, and other parts which belong to the same whole

with it in the New Testament are baptism and the death of
Christ. The book of Acts, like all other books in the New
Testament, was written inside of the Christian society, and
for those who were at home inside; it was not written for
those who had no more power of interpreting what stood on
the page than the letter itself supplied. It does not seem to
me in the least illegitimate, but on the contrary both natural
and necessary, to take all these references to the forgiveness
of sins and to baptism as references at the same time to the
saving significance (in relation to sin) of the death of Jesus.
This is what is suggested when Jesus is identified with the
Servant of the Lord. This is what we are prepared for by
the teaching of Jesus, and by the great commission ; and we
are confirmed in it by what we find in the rest of the New
Testament.   It is not a sufficient answer to this to say that
the connection of ideas asserted here between the forgiveness
of sins or baptism, on the one hand, and the death of Jesus
on the other, is not explicit; it is self-evident to any one
who believes that there is such a thing as Christianity as a
whole, and that it is coherent and consistent with itself, and
who reads with a Christian mind. The assumption of such
a connection at once articulates all the ideas of the book
into a system, and shows it to be at one with the gospels
and epistles ; and such an assumption, for that very reason,
vindicates itself.

Besides the references to baptism and the forgiveness of
sins, we ought to notice also (4) the reference in ii. 42 to
the Lord's Supper. ' They continued stedfastly . . . in the
breaking of the bread.' It may seem to some excessively
venturous to base anything on the Sacraments when everything connected with them is being brought into dispute,
and their very connection with Jesus is denied. But
without going into the infinite and mostly irrelevant discussions which have been raised on the subject, I venture to say

that the New Testament nowhere gives us the idea of an unbaptized Christian—by one Spirit we were all baptized into one body (1 Cor. xii. 13)—and that Paul, in regulating the observance of the Supper at Corinth, regulates it as part of the Christian tradition which goes back for its authority, through the primitive Church, to Christ Himself. ‘I received of the Lord that which also I delivered unto you’ (1 Cor. xi. 23). In other words, there was no such thing known to Paul as a Christian society without baptism as its rite of initiation, and the Supper as its rite of communion. And if there was no such thing known to Paul, there was no such thing in the world. There is nothing in Christianity more primitive than the Sacraments, and the Sacraments, wherever they exist, are witnesses to the connection between the death of Christ and the forgiveness of sins. It is explicitly so in the case of the Supper, and the expression of St. Paul about being baptized into Christ's death (Rom. vi. 3) shows that it is so in the case of the other Sacrament too. The apostle was not saying anything of startling originality, when he wrote the beginning of Rom. vi. : ‘ Know ye not that all we who were baptized into Christ Jesus were baptized into His death ? ’ Every Christian knew that in baptism what his mind was directed to, in connection with the blessing of forgiveness, was the death of Christ. Both Sacraments, therefore, are memorials of the death, and it is not due to any sacramentarian tendency in Luke, but only brings out the place which the death of Christ had at the basis of the Christian religion, as the condition of the forgiveness of sins, when he gives the sacramental side of Christianity the prominence it has in the early chapters of Acts. From the New Testament point of view, the Sacraments contain the gospel in brief; they contain it in inseparable connection with the death of Jesus; and as long as they hold their place in the Church the saving significance of that death has a witness which it will not be easy to dispute.

It is customary to connect with the Petrine discourses in Acts an examination of the First Epistle of Peter. It is not, indeed, open to dispute that the First Epistle of Peter shows traces of dependence upon one or perhaps more than one epistle of Paul. There are different ways in which this may be explained. Peter and Paul were not at variance about the essentials of Christianity, as even the second chapter of the Epistle to the Galatians proves; if they had any intimate relations at all, it is *a priori* probable that the creative mind of Paul would leave its mark on the more receptive intelligence of Peter; something also may be due to an amanuensis, Silvanus (1 Pet. v. 12) or another, who had seen (as was possible enough in Peter's lifetime) letters of Paul like those to the Romans or Ephesians. But we must take care not to exaggerate either the originality of Paul, or the secondary character of Peter. Paul's originality is sometimes an affair rather of dialectic than invention; he is original rather in his demonstration of Christianity than in his statement of it. The thing about which he thinks and speaks with such independent and creative power is not his own discovery; it is the common tradition of the Christian faith; that which he delivers to others, and on which he expends the resources of his original and irrepressible mind, he has himself in the first instance received (1 Cor. xv. 3). And Peter may often be explained, where explanation is necessary, not by reference to Paul, but by reference to the memory of Jesus in the first instance, and to the suggestions of the Old Testament in the next. His antecedents, properly speaking, are not Pauline, but prophetic and evangelic. And if there are formal characteristics of his epistle which have to be explained by reference to his great colleague, the substance of it, so far as our subject is concerned, points not

so much to Paul as to Jesus and the ancient Scriptures.
What ideas, then, we may ask, does the First Epistle of
Peter connect with the death of Jesus?

To begin with, the death of Jesus has the central place in
the writer's mind which it everywhere has in the New
Testament. He describes himself as a 'witness of the sufferings of the Christ' (v. 1). Μάρτυς is to be taken here in
its full compass; it means not only a spectator of, but one
who bears testimony to. The writer's testimony to the
sufferings of the Christ is one in which their significance is
brought out in various aspects; but though this sense of
'witness' is emphasised, it by no means excludes the other;
rather does it presuppose it. Peter seems to prefer 'sufferings' to 'death' in speaking of the Christ, perhaps because
he had been an eye-witness, and because 'sufferings' served
better than 'death' to recall all that his Lord had endured.
Death might be regarded merely as the end of life, not so
much a moral reality, as a limit or termination to reality;
but sufferings are a part of life, with moral content and
meaning, which may make an inspiring or pathetic appeal
to men. In point of fact it is the moral quality of the
sufferings of the Christ, and their exemplary character, which
first appeal to the apostle. As he recalls what he had seen
as he stood by the great sufferer, what impresses him most
is His innocence and patience. He had done no sin, neither
was guile found in His mouth. When He was reviled, He
reviled not again; when He suffered He did not threaten,
but committed himself to Him who judges righteously
(ii. 22 f.). In this character of the patient and innocent
sufferer Peter commends Jesus to Christians, especially to
slaves, who were having their first experience of persecution,
and finding how hard it was not only to suffer without cause,
but actually to suffer for doing well, for loving fidelity to God
and righteousness. It is not necessary to press the parallel

unduly, or to argue (as Seeberg has done[1]) that the suffering of Christians in imitation of the Christ will have in all
respects the same kind of result, or the same kind of influence,
as His. Yet Peter identifies the two to some extent when
he says, in iv. 13, Ye are partakers in the sufferings of the
Christ. This is a genuinely evangelical point of view. Jesus
calls on all His followers to take up their cross, and walk in
His steps. The whole mass of suffering for righteousness'
sake, which has been since the world began and will be to
its close, is 'the sufferings of the Christ'; all who have any
part in it are partners with Him in the pain, and will be
partners also in the glory which is to be revealed. So far, it
may be said, there is no theological reflection in the epistle;
it occupies the standpoint of our Lord's first lesson on the
Cross: I must suffer for righteousness' sake, and so must all
who follow Me (Matt. xvi. 21-24)—with the admonition
annexed, Let it be in the same spirit and temper, not with
amazement, irritation, or bitterness.

But the epistle has other suggestions which it is necessary
to examine. The first is found in the salutation. This is
addressed to the elect who are sojourners of the Dispersion
in Pontus, Galatia, Cappadocia, Asia, and Bithynia, according to the foreknowledge of God the Father, in sanctification
of the Spirit, unto obedience and sprinkling of the blood of
Jesus Christ (i. 1 f.). In this comprehensive address, a whole
world of theological ideas is involved. Christians are what
they are as elect according to the foreknowledge of God.
Their position does not rest on assumptions of their own, or on
any movable basis, but on the eternal goodwill of God which
has taken hold of them. This goodwill, which they know to
be eternal—that is, to be the last reality in the world—has
come out in their consecration by the Spirit. The Spirit,
standing as it does here between God the Father and Christ,

---

[1] Seeberg, *Der Tod Christi*, p. 292.

must be the Holy Spirit, not the spirit of the Christian ; the consecration is wrought not upon it but by it. The readers of the epistle would no doubt connect the words, and be intended by the writer to connect them, with their baptism ; it was in baptism that the Spirit was received, and that the eternal goodwill of God became a thing which the individual (of course through faith) grasped in time. But what is in view in this eternal goodwill and its manifestation in time ? It has in view 'obedience and the sprinkling of the blood of Jesus Christ.' We cannot miss the reference here to the institution of the covenant in Exodus xxiv. There we find the same ideas in the same relation to each other. 'Moses took the book of the covenant, and read in the audience of the people ; and they said, All that the Lord hath spoken will we do, and be obedient. And Moses took the blood, and sprinkled it on the people and said, Behold the blood of the covenant which the Lord hath made with you upon all these conditions.' Such a sprinkling with covenant blood, after a vow of obedience, is evidently in Peter's mind here. We have already seen, in connection with the institution of the Lord's Supper, what covenant blood means. As sacrificial, it is sin-covering ; it is that which annuls sin as the obstacle to union with God. Within the covenant, God and man have, so to speak, a common life. God is not excluded from human life ; He enters into it and achieves His ends in the world through it. Man is not excluded from the divine life ; God admits him to His friendship and shows him what He is doing ; he becomes a partaker in the divine nature, and a fellow-worker with God. But the covenant is made by sacrifice ; its basis and being are in the blood. In this passage, therefore, election and consecration have in view a life of obedience, in union and communion with God ; and such a life, it is assumed, is only possible for those who are sprinkled with the blood of Jesus

Christ. In other words, it is this only which has abiding power in it to annul sin as that which comes between God and man. It is sometimes said that the position of the blood in this passage—after obedience—points to its sanctifying virtue, its power to cleanse the Christian progressively, or ever afresh, from all sin ; but if we use technical language at all, we should rather say that its character as covenant-blood obviously suggests that on its virtue the Christian is perpetually dependent for his justification before God. With this blood on us we have peace with Him, and the calling to live in that peace.

The second express reference to the saving significance of our Lord's death occurs in ch. i. 18 ff. Peter is exhorting those to whom he writes to a life of holiness, and he uses various arguments in support of his plea for sanctification.[1] First, it answers to the essential relations between man and God. ' As He who called you is holy show yourselves also holy in all your behaviour' (i. 15). Second, it is required in view of the account they must render. ' If ye invoke as Father Him who without respect of persons judges according to every man's work, pass the time of your sojourning here in fear' (i. 17). And, third, they have been put in a position to live a holy life by the death of Christ. ' Knowing that you were ransomed, not with corruptible things, silver and gold, from your vain manner of life, handed down from your fathers ; but with precious blood, as of a lamb without blemish and without spot, even the blood of Christ' (i. 18 f.). A lamb without blemish and without spot is a sacrificial lamb, and the virtue here ascribed to the blood of Christ is some sort of sacrificial virtue. The preciousness of the blood cannot be otherwise explained than by saying that it was Christ's blood. But what is the virtue here ascribed

---

[1] Compare Kähler, *Zur Lehre von der Versöhnung*, p. 239.

to it ? By it Christians were ransomed from a vain manner
of life handed down from their fathers. The ἐλυτρώθητε of
this passage is no doubt an echo of the λύτρον ἀντὶ πολλῶν
in Mark x. 45. The effect of Christ's death was that for
Christians a peculiar kind of servitude ended ; when it told
on them their life was no longer in bondage to vanity and
to custom. The expression ἐκ τῆς ματαίας ὑμῶν ἀναστροφῆς
πατροπαραδότου is a very striking one. Life before the
death of Christ has touched it is ματαία : i.e. it is futile,
it is a groping or fumbling after something it can never find ;
it gets into no effective contact with reality ; it has no abiding fruit. From this subjection to vanity it is redeemed by
the blood of Christ. When the power of Christ's Passion
enters into any life it is not futile any more : there is no more
the need or the inclination to cry ματαιότης ματαιοτήτων,
all is vanity. Nothing can be more real or satisfying than
the life to which we are introduced by the death of Christ ;
it is a life in which we can have fruit, much fruit, and fruit
that abides ; hence the introduction to it, as ἐλυτρώθητε
suggests, is a kind of emancipation. Similarly, life before
the death of Christ has touched it is πατροπαράδοτος ; it is
a kind of tradition or custom, destitute of moral originality
or initiative. A man may think he is himself, and that he
is acting freely and spontaneously, when he is only indulging
self-will, or yielding to impulses of nature in him through
which a genuine moral personality has never been able to
emerge ; but it is the power of Christ's passion descending
into the heart which really begets the new creature, to whom
moral responsibility—his own—is an original thing, a kind
of genius, in virtue of which he does what nobody in the
world ever did before, and feels both free and bound to do
so. The moral originality of the New Testament life is a
miracle that never grows old ; and whatever in the form of
this epistle may be due to a mind more creative than that

of the writer, at this point, at any rate, we catch the note of an independent experience. Now this new life of the Christian, with its satisfying reality, and its wonderful freedom, was bought with the blood of Christ.

It is possible to argue that the new life is called forth *immediately* by the death of Christ—that is, that the impression produced by the spectacle of the cross, if we may so speak, quite apart from its interpretation, emancipates the soul. But there is something unreal in all such arguments. The death of Christ was never presented to the world merely as a spectacle. It was never presented by any apostle or evangelist apart from an interpretation. It was the death of Christ so interpreted as to appeal irresistibly to the heart, the conscience, the imagination, perhaps we should sometimes include the very senses of men, which exercised the emancipating power. And the only hint which is here given of the line of interpretation is that which is involved in the reference to the sacrificial lamb. It was the death of Christ not uninterpreted (which is really equivalent to non-significant) but interpreted in some way as a death for our sins which exercised this beneficent power to liberate and to recreate the soul.

A clearer light is cast on the nature of the connection between Christ's death and the moral emancipation of believers by the third passage in which the apostle makes a detailed reference to the subject. It is that in which the example of Christ in His sufferings is set before Christian slaves who are called to suffer unjustly. Peter pleads with them to be patient. 'What glory is it if when you do wrong and are beaten you take it patiently? But if when you do good and suffer for it you take it patiently this is acceptable with God. For this is what you were called for: for Christ also suffered for you (ὑπὲρ ὑμῶν ἔπαθεν), leaving you an example that ye should follow in His steps.' So ii.

20 f. It is the exemplary character of the sufferings of Christ
that is in view when the writer goes on : ' Who did no sin,
neither was guile found in His mouth : who when He was
reviled reviled not again, under suffering did not threaten,
but committed His cause to Him who judges righteously.'
In all this (ii. 22 f.) the appeal of the example is clear. It
is equally clear that in what follows the exemplary character
of Christ's sufferings is left behind, or transcended, and that
they are put in another aspect. It is as though the apostle
could not turn his eyes to the Cross for a moment without
being fascinated and held by it ; he saw far more in it
habitually, and he saw far more in it now, than was needed
to point his exhortation to the wronged slaves ; it is not
their interest in it, as the supreme example of suffering
innocence and patience, but the interest of all sinners in it
as the only source of redemption, by which he is ultimately
inspired : ' Who His own self bare our sins in His body upon
the tree, that we having died unto (the) sins might live unto
righteousness : by whose stripes ye were healed.' The enlargement of view is shown by the change to the first person
(He bore *our* sins, that *we* might live, etc.), the writer including himself and all Christians with those whom he
addresses in the benefits of Christ's death ; it is only in the
last clause—' by whose wound you were healed '—that he
returns to his immediate subject, the slaves who were
buffeted for doing well. What, then, precisely is it which
is here affirmed of Christ in His death ?

Literally, it is that He Himself bore our sins in His
body on to the tree. The use of ἀναφέρειν with ἁμαρτίαν
is not common : it occurs only in Is. liii. 12 and Num.
xiv. 33, the more usual expression being λαμβάνειν. But
it seems absurd for this reason, and for the reason
that ἀναφέρειν τι ἐπὶ τὸ θυσιαστήριον is a common
expression, to argue that here the tree or cross is regarded

as an altar, to which sin was literally carried up to be slain.[1] That which is slain at the altar is always regarded as a gift acceptable to God: the slaying is only the method in which it is irrevocably made His; and nothing is more perverse than the attempt to present sin in this light. The words of the apostle must be interpreted as the simple sense of Christians always has interpreted them: that Christ bore our sins in His body as He ascended the Cross, or ascended to it. There is something in the words ἐν τῷ σώματι and ἐπὶ τὸ ξύλον which leaves a singular and even poignant impression of reality on the mind. To us the Passion is idealised and transfigured; 'the tree' is a poetic name for the Cross, under which the hard truth is hidden. But σῶμα means flesh and blood, and ξύλον means timber. We may have wondered that an apostle and eye-witness should describe the sinlessness and the suffering of Jesus, as the writer of this epistle does, almost entirely in words quoted from the Old Testament; but even as we wonder, and are perhaps visited with misgivings, we are startled by these words in which the Passion is set before us as a spectacle of human pain which the writer had watched with his own eyes as it moved to its goal at the Cross. But this reminiscent pictorial turn which he has given to his expression does not alter the meaning of the principal words—'Who His own self bore our sins.'[2] This is the interpretation of the Passion: it was a bearing of sin. Now, to bear sin is not an expression for which we have to invent or excogitate a meaning: it is a

---

[1] See, for instance, Alford's note on the passage, and the qualified support given to it in Bigg's *Commentary*.

[2] In his *Bible Studies* (E. Tr. p. 88 ff.) Deissmann argues that there is no suggestion here of the special ideas of substitution or sacrifice: all that is meant is that when Christ *bears up to the cross* the sins of men, then men have their sins no more: the *bearing up to* is a *taking away*. In view of the other references in the epistle and of the Old Testament parallels, this is rather a refusal to think out the apostle's thoughts than a stricter interpretation of his words.

familiar expression, of which the meaning is fixed.   Thus,
to take the instance referred to above (Num. xiv. 34) : ' After
the number of the days in which ye spied out the land,
even forty days, for every day a year, shall ye bear your
iniquities': the meaning clearly is, bear the consequences of
them, take to yourselves the punishment which they involve.
Or again, in Lev. v. 17 : ' If any one sin, and do any of the
things which the Lord hath commanded not to be done,
though he knew it not, yet is he guilty, and shall bear his
iniquity': the meaning is as clearly, he shall underlie the consequences attached by the law to his act.   Or again, in Ex.
xxviii. 43, where the sons of Aaron are to observe punctually
the laws about their official dress, ' that they bear not iniquity
and die': to die and to bear iniquity are the same thing,
death being the penalty here denounced against impiety.
Expressions like these indicate the line on which we are to fill
out the meaning of the words, ' Who His own self bare our
sins.'   They are meant to suggest that Christ took on
Him the consequences of our sins—that He made our responsibilities, as sin had fixed them, His own.   He did so
when He went to the Cross—*i.e.* in His death.   His death,
and His bearing of our sins, are not two things, but one.   It
may be true enough that He bore them on His spirit,
that He saw and felt their exceeding sinfulness, that
He mourned over them before God ; but however true and
moving such considerations may be, they are not what the
apostle means in the passage before us.   He means that all the
responsibilities in which sin has involved us—responsibilities
which are summed up in that death which is the wages of
sin—have been taken by Christ upon Himself.   His interpretation of the Passion is that it is a bearing of sin—more
precisely, that it is the bearing of others' sin by one who is
Himself sinless.   (Num. xxx. 15, Heb. 16.)   The apostle does
not raise the question whether it is possible for one to assume

the responsibilities of others in this way; he assumes (and the assumption, as we shall see, is common to all the New Testament writers) that the responsibilities of sinful men have been taken on Himself by the sinless Lamb of God. This is not a theorem he is prepared to defend; it is the gospel he has to preach. It is not a precarious or a felicitous solution of an embarrassing difficulty—the death of the Messiah; it is the foundation of the Christian religion, the one hope of sinful men. It may involve a conception of what Christ is, which would show the irrelevance of the objection just referred to, that one man cannot take on him the responsibilities of others; but leaving that apart for the moment, the idea of such an assumption is unquestionably that of this passage. It is emphasised by the very order of the words—ὃς τὰς ἁμαρτίας ἡμῶν αὐτὸς ἀνήνεγκεν; it was *not His own* but *our* sins that were borne at Calvary.

To that which was so done Peter annexes the aim of it. *He* bore *our* sins, that having died to the sins, we might live to righteousness. It is not possible to argue from ἀπο-γενόμενοι that our death was involved in His—that we actually or ideally died when He did, and so have no more relation to sins. It is quite fair to render, 'that we might die to our sins and live to righteousness.' A new life involves death to old relations, and such a new life, involving such death, is the aim of Christ's bearing of our sins. How this effect is mediated the apostle does not say. Once we understand what Christ's death means—once we receive the apostolic testimony that in that death He was taking all our responsibilities upon Him—no explanation may be needed. The love which is the motive of it acts immediately upon the sinful; gratitude exerts an irresistible constraint; His responsibility means our emancipation; His death our life; His bleeding wound our healing. Whoever says 'He bore our sins' says substitution; and to say substitution is to say something which involves an immeasurable obligation to Christ, and has therefore in it an incalculable motive power. This is the answer to some of the objections which are commonly made to the idea of substitution on moral grounds. They fail to take account of the sinner's sense of debt to Christ for what He has done, a sense of debt which it is not too much to designate as the most intimate, intense, and uniform characteristic of New Testament life. It is this which bars out all ideas of being saved from the consequences of sin, while living on in sin itself. It is so profound that the whole being of the Christian is changed by it; it is so strong as to extinguish and to create at once; under the impression of it, to use the apostle's words here, the aim of Christ's bearing of our sins is fulfilled in us—we die to the sins and live to righteousness.

This interpretation of the passage in the second chapter is confirmed when we proceed to the one in the third. The subject is still the same, the suffering of Christians for righteousness' sake. 'It is better,' says the apostle in iii. 17, 'if the will of God should have it so, to suffer doing well than doing ill. For Christ also died once for sins, the righteous for the unrighteous, that He might conduct us to God.' Here, as in the previous passage, an exemplary significance in Christ's sufferings is assumed, and to it apparently the writer reverts in iv. 1 ('as Christ therefore suffered in the flesh, arm yourselves likewise with the same mind'), but it is not this exemplary significance on which he enlarges. On the contrary, it is a connection which the death of Christ, or His Passion, has with sins. Christ, he says, died in connection with sins once for all ($ἅπαξ$); His death has a unique significance in this relation. What the special connection was is indicated in the words $δίκαιος\ ὑπὲρ\ ἀδίκων$. It is the obvious implication of these words that the death on which such stress is laid was something to which the unrighteous were liable because of their sins, and that in their

interest the Righteous One took it on Himself.   When He
died for them, it was *their* death which He died.   His death
has to be defined by relation to sin, but it is the sin of others,
not His own.   The writer no more asks here than he asked
in the previous case, How can such things be?   He does not
limit the *will* of love—he does not, in a world made and ruled
by God, limit beforehand the *power* of love—to take on it
to any extent the responsibility of others.   This is his gospel,
that a Righteous One has once for all faced and taken up
and in death exhausted the responsibilities of the unrighteous,
so that they no more stand between them and God; his
business is not to prove this, but to preach it.   The only
difference is that whereas in the second chapter, if we can
draw such a distinction in the New Testament, the aim is a
moral one (that we may die to sin and live to righteousness),
in the present case it is *religious* (that He might conduct us to
God).   The word προσάγειν has always a touch of formality
in it; it is a great occasion when the Son who has assumed
our responsibilities for us takes us by the hand to bring us
to the Father.   We find the same idea of the προσαγωγή
as the great Christian privilege in Rom. v. 2, Eph. ii. 18.
Sin, it is implied, keeps man at a distance from God; but
Christ has so dealt with sin on man's behalf that its separa-
tive force is annulled; for those who commit themselves to
Christ, and to the work which He has done for them in His
Passion, it is possible to draw near to God and to live in His
peace.   This is the end contemplated in His dying for sins
once, the righteous for the unrighteous.   We can only repeat here what has just been said in connection with the
previous passage.   If Christ died the death in which sin had
involved us—if in His death He took the responsibility of
our sins upon Himself—no word is equal to this which falls
short of what is meant by calling Him our substitute.   Here
also, as in the second chapter, the substitution of Christ in

His death is not an end in itself: it has an ulterior end in view.　And this end is not attained except for those who, trusting in what Christ has done, find access to God through Him.　Such access, we must understand, is not a thing which can be taken for granted.　It is not for the sinful to presume on acceptance with God whenever they want it.　Access to God is to the Apostle the most sublime of privileges, purchased with an unspeakable price; for such as we are it is only possible because for our sins Christ died.　And just as in the ancient tabernacle every object used in worship had to be sprinkled with atoning blood, so all the parts of Christian worship, all our approaches to God, should consciously rest on the atonement.　They should be felt to be a privilege beyond price; they should be penetrated with the sense of Christ's Passion, and of the love with which He loved us when He suffered for sins once for all, the just for the unjust, *that He might conduct us to God.*

There is no other passage in the First Epistle of Peter which speaks with equal explicitness of the saving significance of Christ's death.　But the passages which have just been reviewed are all the more impressive from the apparently incidental manner in which they present themselves to us.　The apostle is not avowedly discussing the theology of the Passion.　There is nothing in his epistle like that deliberate grappling with the problem of the justification of the ungodly which we find, for example, in the third and fourth chapters of the Epistle to the Romans.　His general purpose, indeed, is quite different.　It is to exhort to patience and constancy Christians who are suffering for the first time severe persecution, and who are disposed to count it a strange thing that has befallen them; the suffering Christ is held up to them as an example.　He is the first of martyrs, and all who suffer for righteousness' sake, as they share the suffering which He endured, should

confront it in the same spirit which He displayed. But
the imitation of Jesus is not an independent thing for the
apostle; at least he never speaks of it by itself. It is the
sense of obligation to Christ which enables us to lift our
eyes to so high an example; and Peter glides insensibly, on
every occasion, from Christ the pattern of innocence and
patience in suffering to Christ the sacrificial lamb, Christ
the bearer of sin, Christ who died, righteous for unrighteous
men. It is here the inspiration is found for every genuine
imitatio Christi, and the unforced, inevitable way in which
the apostle falls regularly back on the profounder interpretation of the death of Christ, shows how central and
essential it was in his mind. He does not dwell anywhere
of set purpose on the attitude of the soul to this death, so
as to make clear the conditions on which it becomes effective
for the Christian's emancipation from a vain and custom-
ridden life, for his death to sin, or for his introduction to
God. As has been already remarked, the sense of obligation to Christ, the sense of the love involved in what he has
done for men, may produce all these effects immediately.
But there are two particulars in which the First Epistle
of Peter makes a near approach to other New Testament
books, especially to Pauline ones, in their conception of the
conditions on which the blessings of the gospel are enjoyed,
and it may not be out of place to refer to them here. The
first is the emphasis it lays on faith. The testing of the
Christian life is spoken of as 'the trying of your faith'
(i. 7); the salvation of the soul is 'the end of your faith'
(i. 9); Christians are those 'who through Him'—that is,
through Christ—'have faith in God' (i. 21). The other is
the formula 'in Christ,' which has sometimes been treated
almost as if it were the signature of St. Paul. It occurs in
the last verse of the epistle: 'Peace be to you all that
are in Christ.' Probably it is not too bold to suggest that

in these two ideas—that of 'faith' and that of being 'in Christ'—we have here, as elsewhere in the New Testament, a clue to the terms on which all the Christian facts, and most signally the death of Christ, as the apostle interprets it, have their place and efficacy in the life of men.

It is not possible to base anything on the Second Epistle ascribed to Peter. The one expression to be found in it, bearing on our subject, is the description of certain false teachers in ch. ii. 1, as 'denying the Master who bought them' (τὸν ἀγοράσαντα αὐτοὺς δεσπότην ἀρνούμενοι). The idea of ἀγοράζειν is akin to that of λυτροῦσθαι, and the New Testament in other places emphasises the fact that we are bought with a price (1. Cor. vi. 20, vii. 23), and that the price is the blood of Christ (Rev. v. 9.); but though these ideas no doubt underlie the words just quoted, there is no expansion or application of them in the context. The passage takes for granted the common faith of Christians in this connection, but does not directly contribute to its elucidation.

CHAPTER III

THE EPISTLES OF ST. PAUL

WHEN we pass from primitive Christian preaching to the epistles of St. Paul, we are embarrassed not by the scantiness but by the abundance of our materials. It is not possible to argue that the death of Christ has less than a central, or rather than the central and fundamental place, in the apostle's gospel. But before proceeding to investigate more closely the significance he assigns to it, there are some preliminary considerations to which it is necessary to attend. Attempts have often been made, while admitting that St. Paul teaches what he does teach, to evade it—either because it is a purely individual interpretation of the death of Jesus, which has no authority for others; or because it is a theologoumenon, and not a part of the apostolic testimony; or because it is not a fixed thing, but a stage in the development of apostolic thought, which St. Paul was on the way to transcend, and would eventually have transcended, and which we (by his help) can quite well leave behind us; or because it is really inconsistent with itself, a bit of patchwork, pieced out here and there with incongruous elements, to meet the exigencies of controversy; or because it unites, in a way inevitable for one born a Pharisee, but simply false for those who have been born Christian, conceptions belonging to the imperfect as well as to the perfect religion—conceptions which it is our duty to allow to lapse. I do not propose to consider such criticisms of St. Paul's teaching on the death of Christ directly. For one thing, abstract discussion of such statements, apart from their application to given cases, never leads to any conclusive results; for another, when we do come to the actual matters in question, it often happens that the distinctions just suggested disappear; the apostolic words have a virtue in them which enables them to combine in a kind of higher unity what might otherwise be distinguished as testimony and theology. But while this is so it is relevant, and one may think important, to point out certain characteristics of St. Paul's presentation of his teaching which constitute a formidable difficulty in the way of those who would evade it.

The first is, the assurance with which he expresses himself. The doctrine of the death of Christ and its significance was not St. Paul's theology, it was his gospel. It was all he had to preach. It is with it in his mind—immediately after the mention of our Lord Jesus Christ, *who gave Himself for our sins, that He might deliver us from this present world with all its evils*—that he says to the Galatians: 'Though we or an angel from heaven preach a gospel to you contravening the gospel which we preached, let him be anathema. As we have said before, so say I now again, if any man is preaching a gospel to you contravening what you received, let him be anathema' (Gal. i. 4, 8 f.). I cannot agree with those who disparage this, or affect to forgive it, as the unhappy beginning of religious intolerance. Neither the Old Testament nor the New Testament has any conception of a religion without this intolerance. The first commandment is, 'Thou shalt have none other gods beside Me,' and that is the foundation of the true religion. As there is only one God, so there can be only one gospel. If God has really done something in Christ on which the

ASSURANCE OF ST. PAUL

salvation of the world depends, and if He has made it known, then it is a Christian duty to be intolerant of everything which ignores, denies, or explains it away. The man who perverts it is the worst enemy of God and men; and it is not bad temper or narrowmindedness in St. Paul which explains this vehement language, it is the jealousy of God which has kindled in a soul redeemed by the death of Christ a corresponding jealousy for the Saviour. It is intolerant only as Peter is intolerant when he says, ' Neither is there salvation in any other' (Acts iv. 12), or John, when he says, ' He that hath the Son hath the life; he that hath not the Son of God hath not the life' (1 John v. 12); or Jesus Himself when He says, ' No man knoweth the Father save the Son, and he to whomsoever the Son willeth to reveal him' (Matt. xi. 27). Intolerance like this is an essential element in the true religion; it is the instinct of self-preservation in it; the unforced and uncompromising defence of that on which the glory of God and the salvation of the world depends. If the evangelist has not something to preach of which he can say, If any man makes it his business to subvert this, let him be anathema, he has no gospel at all. Intolerance in this sense has its counterpart in comprehension; it is when we have the only gospel, and not till then, that we have the gospel for all. It is a great argument, therefore, for the essential as opposed to the casual or accidental character of St. Paul's teaching on Christ's death—for it is with this that the Epistle to the Galatians is concerned—that he displays his intolerance in connection with it. To touch his teaching here is not to do something which leaves his gospel unaffected; as he understands it, it is to wound his gospel mortally.

Another consideration of importance in this connection is St. Paul's relation to the common Christian tradition. No doubt the apostle was an original thinker, and in the Epistle to the Galatians he is concerned to vindicate his originality, or at least his independence; but his originality is sometimes exaggerated. He did not invent Christianity; there were apostles and preachers and men in Christ before him. And he tells us expressly that in the fundamentals of Christianity he not only agreed with them, but was indebted to them. 'I delivered unto you first of all that which I also *received*, that Christ died for our sins according to the Scriptures, and that He was buried, and that He hath been raised the third day, according to the Scriptures' (1 Cor. xv. 3). It is impossible to leave out of the tradition which St. Paul had himself received, and which he transmitted to the Corinthians, the reference to the meaning of Christ's death —' He died *for our sins* according to the Scriptures '—and to limit it to the fact : the fact needed no such authentication. It is the fact in its meaning for sinners which constitutes a gospel, and this, he wishes to assert, is the only gospel known. ' Whether it be I or they—whether it be I or the twelve apostles at Jerusalem—this is the way we preach, and it was thus that you became believers' (1 Cor. xv. 11). And the doctrinal tradition of Christianity, if we may call it so, was supplemented and guaranteed by the ritual one. In the same Epistle to the Corinthians St. Paul says again, speaking of the Supper, ' I received of the Lord that which also I delivered unto you' (1 Cor. xi. 23). An immediate supernatural revelation of what took place on the last night of our Lord's life has no affinity to anything we know of revelations : we must understand St. Paul to say that what he had handed on to the Corinthians had before been handed on to him, and went back originally to the Lord Himself. The Lord was the point from which it started. But Paul could not receive this ritual tradition, and we know he did not, without receiving at the same time the great interpretative words about the new covenant in

Christ's blood, which put the death of Christ, once for all, at the foundation of the Gospel.[1] It is not Paulinism which does this, it is the Christianity of Christ. The point at issue between the apostle and his Jewish Christian adversaries was not whether Christ had died for sins; every Christian believed that. It was rather how far this death of Christ reached in the way of producing or explaining the Christian life. To St. Paul it reached the whole way; it explained everything; it supplanted everything he could call a righteousness of his own; it inspired everything he could call righteousness at all. To his opponents, it did not so much supplant as supplement: but for the atoning death, indeed, the sinner is hopeless; but even when he has believed in it, he has much to do on his own account, much which is not generated in him by the sense of obligation to Christ, but must be explained on other principles—*e.g.* that of the authority of the Jewish law. It is not necessary to enter into this controversy here, but what may fairly be insisted upon is the fact, which is evident in all the epistles, that underneath the controversy St. Paul and his opponents agreed in the common Christian interpretation of Christ's death as a death in which sin had been so dealt with that it no longer barred fellowship between God and those who believed in Jesus. This, again, should make us slow to reject anything on this subject in St. Paul as being merely Pauline—an idiosyncrasy of the individual. We must remember that his great argument against Judaising

---

[1] Cf. Soltau, *Unsere Evangelien*, S. 85 : 'The apostles and evangelists who went about two by two from church to church preaching everywhere the Word of God, must have had a fixed basis for the instruction they gave. And when Paul (1 Cor. xi. 23) declares of his account of the Supper, 'I have received it from the Lord,' he points in doing so to a formulation of Christian teaching once for all fixed and definite.' In a note he adds that St. Paul's words, ' the Lord Jesus on the night on which He was betrayed,' even show an affinity to the synoptic narrative.

F

Christians is that they are acting inconsistently : they are unwittingly doing something which contravenes, not Paulinism, but the gospel they have already received of redemption through the death of Christ.

Again, the perception of St. Paul's place in Christian tradition, and of his debt to it, should make us slow to lay stress on the development which has been discovered in his writings. Leaving out the Pastorals, Paul wrote his other epistles within the space of ten years. But he had been preaching the gospel, in which the death of Christ had from the beginning the place and significance which we have just seen, at least fifteen years before any of the extant epistles were written. Is it credible that he had no intellectual life at all for those fifteen years, and that then, all of a sudden, his brain began to work at high pressure, and continued to work so till the end of his life ? It is true that in the epistles of the imprisonment, as they may be conveniently called— Colossians, Ephesians, Philippians—we see the whole gospel in other relations than those in which it is exhibited in the epistles of the great missionary period—Thessalonians, Corinthians, Galatians, Romans. But this is something quite different from a development in the gospel itself ; and in point of fact we cannot discover in St. Paul's interpretation of Christ's death anything which essentially distinguishes his earliest epistles from his latest. To suppose that a great expansion of his thoughts took place between the letters to the Thessalonians and those to the Corinthians is to ignore at once the chronology, the nature of letters, and the nature of the human mind. St. Paul tells us himself that he came to Corinth determined to know nothing among the Corinthians but Jesus Christ and Him crucified. But he came in that mood straight from Thessalonica, and in that mood he wrote from Corinth the letters to Thessalonica, in which, nevertheless, there is, as we shall see, only a passing allusion to Christ's death. Nothing could demonstrate more clearly how entirely a matter of accident it is—that is, how entirely it depends upon conditions which we may or may not have the means of discovering—whether any particular part of the apostle's whole conception of Christianity shall appear in any given epistle. If development might be asserted anywhere, on general grounds, it would be in this case and on this subject; there is far more about Christ's death, and far more that is explicit, in the First Epistle to the Corinthians than in the First to the Thessalonians. Yet precisely at this point our knowledge of St. Paul's mind when he reached Corinth (1 Cor. ii. 1 f.), and of the brief interval which lay between this and his visit to Thessalonica, puts the idea of development utterly out of the question. As far as the evidence goes—the evidence including St. Paul's epistles on the one hand, and St. Paul's admitted relation to the doctrinal and ritual tradition of Christianity on the other—the apostle had one message on Christ's death from first to last of his Christian career. His gospel, and it was the only gospel he knew, was always ' the Word of the Cross ' (1 Cor. i. 18), or ' the Word of reconciliation ' (2 Cor. v. 19). The applications might be infinitely varied, for, as has been already pointed out, everything was involved in it, and the whole of Christianity was deduced from it; but this is not to say that it was in process of evolution itself.

There are two other sets of questions which might be raised here, either independently or in relation to each other —the questions involved in the experimental, and in the controversial or apologetic, aspects of St. Paul's theology. How much of what he tells us of the death of Christ is the interpretation of experience, and has value as such? How much is mere fencing with opponents, or squaring of accounts with his own old ways of thinking about God and the soul, but has no value now, because the conditions to which it is relative no longer exist ?   These questions, as has been already remarked, are not to be discussed abstractly, because taken abstractly the antitheses they present are inevitably tainted with falsehood.   They assume an opposition which does not exist, and they ignore the capacity of the truth to serve a variety of intellectual and spiritual purposes.   St. Paul could use his gospel, no doubt, in controversy and in apology, but it was not devised for controversial or apologetic ends.   The truth always has it in itself to be its own vindication and defence.   It can define itself in all relations, against all adversaries ; but it is not constituted truth, it is only exhibited as truth, when it does so.   The fact that Christ died for our sins—that His death is an atoning death —is a magnificent apology for the Cross, turning its shame into glory ; but it is not philosophy or criticism, it is mere unintelligence, to maintain that it was invented or believed just in order to remove the offence of the Cross.   In St. Paul it is not an apologetic or a controversial truth, or a truth relative to the exigencies of Jewish prejudice ; it is an independent, eternal, divine truth, the profoundest truth of revelation, which for that very reason contains in it the answer to all religious questions whether of ancient or of modern times.   It is so far from being a truth which only a mind of peculiar antecedents or training could apprehend, that it is of all truths the most universal.   It was the sense of it, in its truth, that made St. Paul a missionary to all men.   When he thought of what it meant, it made him exclaim, Is God a God of Jews only ? (Rom. iii. 29).   Is the God who is revealed in the death of Christ for sin a God who speaks a language that only one race can understand ? Incredible.   The atoning death of Christ, as a revelation of God, is a thing in itself so intelligible, so correspondent to a universal need, so direct and universal in its appeal, that it must be the basis of a universal religion.   It is so far from being a truth (if we can speak of truth on such terms) relative only to one race, or one upbringing, or one age, or one set of prejudices, that it is the one truth which for all races and in all ages can never admit of any qualification. In itself true, it can be used as a weapon, but it was no necessity of conflict which fashioned it. It is the very heart of revelation itself.

The same attitude of mind to the Pauline teaching which would discount some of it as controversial or apologetic, as opposed to experimental or absolute, is seen in the disposition to distinguish in that teaching, as the expression is, fact from theory. In all probability this also is a distinction which it will not repay us to discuss *in vacuo* : everything depends on the kind of fact which we are supposed to be theorising. The higher we rise in the scale of reality the more evanescent becomes the distinction between the thing 'itself' and the theory of it. A fact like the one with which we are here concerned, a fact in which the character of God is revealed, and in which an appeal is to be made to the reason, the conscience, the heart, the whole moral being of man, is a fact which must be, and must be seen to be, full of rational, ethical, and emotional content. If instead of 'theory' we use an equivalent word, say 'meaning,' we discover that the absolute distinction disappears. The fact is not known to us at all unless it is known in its meaning, in that which constitutes it a revelation of God and an appeal to man; and to say that we know it in its meaning is to say that we know it theoretically, or in or through a theory of it. A fact of which there is no theory is a fact in which we can see no meaning ; and though we can apply this distinction so far when we are speaking of physical facts, and argue that it is fire which burns and not the theory of heat, we cannot apply it at all when we are speaking of a fact which has to tell on us in other than physical ways : through conscience, through the heart, through the intelligence, and therefore in a manner to which the mind can really respond. St. Paul's own words in Romans v. 11 enable us to illustrate this. We have received, he says, or taken, the reconciliation. If we could take it physically, as we take a doctor's prescription, which would tell on us all the same whatever our spiritual attitude to it might be, then we might distinguish clearly between the fact and the theory of it, and argue that as long as we accepted the fact, the theory was neither here nor there ; but if the fact with which we are dealing cannot be physically accepted at all—if it addresses itself to a nature which is higher than physical, a nature of which reason, imagination, emotion, conscience, are the elements, then the fact itself must be seen to be one in which there is that which appeals to all these elements; that is, to repeat the truth, it must be an interpreted fact, something in which fact and theory are indissolubly one. The Cross must be exhibited in ὁ λόγος τοῦ σταυροῦ, the Reconciliation in ὁ λόγος τῆς καταλλαγῆς ; and λόγος is always a rational, a theoretical word. It is much easier to say there is a distinction of fact and theory, a distinction between the testimony and the theology of St. Paul, than to prove it ; it is much easier to imagine that one can preach the gospel without any theory of the death of Christ than, knowing what these words mean, to do so. The simplest preacher, and the most effective, is always the most absolutely theoretical. It is a theory, a tremendous theory, that Christ's death is a death *for sin*. But unless a preacher can put some interpretation on the death—unless he can find a meaning in it which is full of appeal—why should he speak of it at all ? Is it the want of a theory that deprives it of its place in preaching ?

There is one other subject to which also it is necessary to refer before going into detail on St. Paul's teaching—the connection between Christ's death and His resurrection. The tradition of Protestant theology undoubtedly tends to isolate the death, and to think of it as a thing by itself, apart from the resurrection ; sometimes, one is tempted to say, apart even from any distinct conception of Him who died.   But we know that St. Paul himself puts an extraordinary emphasis on the resurrection.   Sometimes it is co-ordinated with the death.   'If we believe that Jesus died and rose again,' he writes to the Thessalonians, including in this the whole of the Christian faith (1 Thess. iv. 14).   'He was delivered for our offences, and raised again for our justification,' he says to the Romans, making the resurrection as essential as the death (Rom. iv. 25). It is the same with the summary of fundamental truths, which constituted the gospel as he preached it at Corinth, and which has been repeatedly referred to already : 'first of all that Christ died for our sins according to the Scriptures, and that He was buried, and that He rose again the third day according to the Scriptures' (1 Cor. xv. 3 f.). But there are passages in which he gives a more exclusive emphasis to the resurrection.   Thus in Rom. x. 9 he writes : 'If thou shalt confess with thy mouth that Jesus is Lord, and believe in thy heart that God raised Him from the dead, thou shalt be saved '; and in 1 Cor. xv. 17 : 'If Christ is not risen, your faith is vain ; ye are yet in your sins.'   It is possible, however, to do full justice to all such expressions without qualifying in the slightest the prominence given in St. Paul to Jesus Christ as crucified.   It was the appearance of the Risen One to St. Paul which made him a Christian.   What was revealed to him on the way to Damascus was that the Crucified One was Son of God, and the gospel that He preached afterwards was that of the Son of God crucified.   There can be no salvation from sin unless there is a living Saviour : this explains the emphasis laid by the apostle on the resurrection. But the Living One can only be a Saviour because He has died : this explains the emphasis laid on the Cross. The Christian believes in a living Lord, or he could not believe at all ; but he believes in a living Lord who died an atoning death, for no other can hold the faith of a soul under the doom of sin.

The importance of St. Paul's teaching, and the fact that dissent from any specifically New Testament interpretation of Christ's death usually begins with it, may justify these preliminary observations ; we now go on to notice more precisely what the apostle does teach. What then, let us ask, are the relations in which St. Paul defines the death of Christ ? What are the realities with which he connects it, so that in these connections it becomes an intelligible thing—not a brute fact, like the facts of physics, while their laws are as yet unknown, but a significant, rational, ethical, appealing fact, which has a meaning, and can act not as a cause but as a motive ? In other words, what is the doctrinal construction of this fact in virtue of which St. Paul can preach it to man as a gospel ?

(1) To begin with, he defines it by relation to *the love of God*. The death of Christ is an illustration or rather a demonstration of that love. It is a demonstration of it which can never be surpassed. There are great, though rare examples of love among men, but nothing which could give any suggestion of this. 'Scarcely for a righteous man will one die ; for the good man possibly one might dare even death : but God commends *His* love to us in that while we were yet sinners Christ died for us' (Rom. v. 7 f.). We shall return to this, and to St. Paul's inferences from it, when the passage in Romans comes before us ; but meanwhile we should notice that the interpretation of Christ's

death through the love of God is fundamental in St. Paul. In whatever other relations he may define it, we must assume, unless the contrary can be proved, that they are consistent with this. It is the commonest of all objections to the propitiatory doctrine of the death of Christ that it is inconsistent with the love of God ; and not only amateur, but professional theologians of all grades have rejected St. Paul's doctrine of propitiation as inconsistent with Jesus' teaching on the love of the Father ; but if a mind like St. Paul teaches both things—if he makes the death of Christ in its propitiatory character the supreme demonstration of the Father's love—is there not an immense probability that there is misunderstanding somewhere ? It may be a modern, it is certainly not a Pauline idea, that a death for sins, with a view to their forgiveness, is inconsistent with God's love. Whatever the process, St. Paul related that death to God's love as the supreme proof of it.

(2) Further, the apostle defines Christ's death by relation to *the love of Christ*. 'The Son of God loved me,' he says, 'and gave Himself for me' (Gal. ii. 20). 'The love of Christ constraineth us, because we thus judge, that one died for all' (2 Cor. v. 14). ' Walk in love, as Christ also loved us, and gave Himself for us an offering and a sacrifice to God for a sweet-smelling savour' (Eph. v. 2). 'Christ loved the church, and gave Himself for it, that He might sanctify it to Himself' (Eph. v. 25).   Christ is not an instrument, but the agent, of the Father in all that He does. The motive in which God acts is the motive in which He acts : the Father and the Son are at one in the work of man's salvation. It is this which is expressed when the work of Christ is described, as it is in Phil. ii. 8 and Rom. v. 19, as obedience—obedience unto death, and that the death of the Cross.   The obedience is conceived as obedience to the loving will of the Father to save men—that is, it is

obedience in the vocation of Redeemer, which involves death for sin. It is not obedience merely in the sense of doing the will of God as other men are called to do it, keeping God's commandments ; it is obedience in this unique and incommunicable yet moral calling, to be at the cost of life the Saviour of the world from sin. Hence it is in the obedience of Christ to the Father that the great demonstration of *His* love to men is given—'He loved me,' as the apostle says, 'and gave Himself for me.' In His obedience, in which He makes His great sacrifice, Christ is fulfilling the will of God ; and the response which He evokes by His death is a response toward God. It is at this point, in the last resort, that we become convinced of the deity of Christ. It is a work of God which He is working, and the soul that is won for it is won for God in Him.

(3) The relation of Christ's death to the love of God and of Christ is its fundamental relation on one side ; on the other side, St. Paul relates it essentially *to sin*. It is a death for sin, whatever else may be said of it. 'First of all, Christ died for our sins.' It was sin which made death, and not something else, necessary as a demonstration of God's love and Christ's. Why was this so ? The answer of the apostle is that it was so because sin had involved *us* in death, and there was no possibility of Christ's dealing with sin effectually except by taking *our* responsibility in it on Himself—that is, except by dying for it. Of course it is assumed in this that there is an ethical connection of some kind between death and sin, and that such a con- nection of words as, 'The wages of sin is death,' (Rom vi. 23) really has meaning. No doubt this has been denied. Death, it is argued, is the debt of nature, not the wages of sin ; it has no moral character at all. The idea of moral liability to death, when you look at the universality of death quite apart from moral considerations, is a piece of

pure mythology. In spite of the assurance with which this argument is put forward it is not difficult to dissent from it. What it really does is to treat man abstractly, as if he were no more than a physical being; whereas, if we are to have either religion or morality preserved in the world, it is essential to maintain that he is more. The argument is one of the numberless class which proves nothing, because it proves too much. It is part of a vaster argument which would deny at the same time the spiritual nature and the immortality of man. But while it is right to say that death comes physically, that through disease, or accident, or violence, or mere physical exhaustion, it subdues to itself everything that lives, this does not touch the profounder truth with which St. Paul is dealing, that death comes from God, and that it comes in man to a being who is under law to Him. Man is not like a plant or an animal, nor is death to him what it is at the lower levels of life. Man has a moral nature in which there is a reflection of the holy law of God, and everything that befalls him, in-cluding death itself, must be interpreted in relation to that nature. *Conscience*, quickened by the law of God, has to look at death, and to become alive, not to its physical antecedents, but to its divine meaning. *What is God's voice in death to a spiritual being?* It is what the apostle represents it—death is the wages of sin.[1] It is that in which the divine judgment on sin comes home to the conscience. The con-nection between the two things is real, though it is not physical; and because it is what it is—because death by God's ordinance has in the conscience of sinful men the tremendous significance which it does have—because it is a power by which they are all their lifetime held in bondage

---

[1] Compare Kähler, p. 399. In Empfindung, Mythus, Bild, Religion und Betrachtung ist der Tod, wie wir Sünder ihn sterben, der Prediger der Verantwortlichkeit geblieben.

—because it is the expression of God's implacable and final opposition to evil—He who came to bear our sin must also die our death. Death is the word which sums up the whole liability of man in relation to sin, and therefore when Christ came to give Himself for our sins He did it by dying. It does not occur to St. Paul to ask how Christ could die the death which is the wages of sin, any more than it occurred to St. Peter (see p. 70 f.) to ask how He could bear the sins of others. If any one had argued that the death which Jesus died, since it had not the shadow of a bad conscience cast upon it, was not the death which is the wages of sin, can we not conceive him asking, ' What death, then, was it ? Is there any other ? The death He died was the only death we know ; it was death in all that tragic reality that we see at Calvary ; and the sinlessness of Jesus—when we take His love along with it—may have been so far from making it impossible for Him to know and feel it as all that it was, that it actually enabled him to realise its awful character as no sinful soul had ever done or could do. Instead of saying, *He* could not die the death which is the wages of sin, it may be far truer to say, None *but* He could.' [1]

It may not be amiss here to point out that analysis of the term ' death ' as it is used by St. Paul almost invariably misleads. According to M. Ménégoz, [2] the apostle's doctrine of the expiation of sin by death is fatally vitiated by the ambiguity of the term. Paul confounds in it two distinct things : (1) death as *l'anéantissement complet et définitif ;* (2) death as *la peine de mort, le décès.* If we take the word in the first sense, Christ did not die, for He was raised again, and therefore there is no expiation. If we take it in the second sense, there was no need that He should die, for we can all expiate our own sins by dying ourselves. This kind

[1] Compare Kähler, *Zur Lehre von der Versöhnung,* 397 ff.
[2] *Le Péché et la Rédemption,* p. 258 f.

of penetration is hardly to be taken seriously. When Paul spoke of Christ's death as a death for sin, he had not a definition in his mind, whether *l'anéantissement complet et définitif*, or *la peine de mort*; but neither had he a vague or blurred idea which confused both; he had the awful fact of the crucifixion, with everything, physical and spiritual, which made it real; *that* was the bearing of sin and expiation of it, whether it answered to any one's abstract definition or not. The apostle would not have abandoned his gospel because some one demonstrated *à priori*, by means of definitions, that expiation of sin by death was either (1) impossible, or (2) unnecessary. He lived in another region. With these general remarks on the different relations in which St. Paul defines the death of Christ, we may now proceed to consider the teaching of the epistles in detail, keeping as far as possible to chronological order.

(I.) The Epistles to the Thessalonians do not yield us much. The only indisputable passage is in the first epistle, ch. v. 10 : 'God did not appoint us to wrath, but to the obtaining of salvation through our Lord Jesus Christ, who died for us, that whether we wake or sleep we should live together with Him.' If the question is raised, What did Christ do for us with a view to our salvation, St. Paul has only one answer : He died for us. There is nothing in the epistles like the language of the hymn :—

> ' For us despised, for us He bore
>   His holy fast, and hungered sore;
>   For us temptations sharp He knew,
>   For us the Tempter overthrew.'

The only thing He is said to have done for us is to die, and this He did, because it was determined for Him by sin. The relation of sin and death in the nature of things made it binding on Him to die if He was to annul sin. The purpose here assigned to Christ's death, that whether we

wake or sleep we should live together with Him, suggests
that His power to redeem is dependent on His making all
our experiences His own.   If we are to be His in death
and life, then He must take our death and life to Himself.
If what is His is to become ours, it is only on the condition
that what is ours He first makes His.   There is the same
suggestion in Romans xiv. 9 : 'To this end Christ died and
lived, that He might be Lord both of dead and living.'
Not as though death made Him Lord of the dead, and
rising again, of the living ; but as One to whom no human
experience is alien, He is qualified to be Lord of men
through all.   The particular character elsewhere assigned to
death as the doom of sin is not here mentioned, but it does
not follow that it was not felt.   On the contrary, we should
rather hold that St. Paul could never allude to the death
of Christ without becoming conscious of its propitiatory
character and of what gave it that character.   The word
would fill of its own accord with the meaning which it
bears when he says, First of all, Christ died for our sins.

(II.) When we pass to the First Epistle to the Corinthians, we have much fuller references to the subject.   For
one thing, its supreme importance is insisted on when we
find the gospel described as ' the word of *the cross* ' (i. 18),
and the apostle's endeavours directed to this, ' that *the cross*
of Christ may not be made void ' (i. 17).   It is in the same
spirit that he contrasts the true gospel with the miracles
claimed by the Jews, and the wisdom sought by the Greeks :
' We preach *Christ crucified*, the power of God and the
wisdom of God.'   So again in the second chapter he reminds
the Corinthians how he came to Achaia determined to know
nothing among them but Jesus Christ and Him crucified :
his whole gospel, the testimony of God, as he calls it, was
in this (ii. 1 f.).   In other passages he refers to the death
of Christ in general terms which suggest the cost at which

man's redemption was achieved. Twice over, in chapters vi. 20, and vii. 23, he writes, Ye were bought *with a price;* making it in the first instance the basis of an exhortation to glorify God in the nature He had made His own at so dear a rate ; and in the other, of an exhortation to assume all the responsibilities of that freedom for which they had been so dearly ransomed, and not to become servants of men, *i.e.* not to let the conventions, or judgments, or consciences of others invade a responsibility which had obligations to the Redeemer alone. It may not be possible to work out the figure of a price, which is found in these passages, in detail; we may not be able to say what it answered to, who got it, how it was fixed, and so on. But what we may legitimately insist upon is the idea that the work of man's salvation was a costly work, and that the cost, however we are to construe it, is represented by the death of Christ. Ye were bought with a price, means, Ye were not bought for nothing. Salvation is not a thing which can be assumed, or taken for granted; it is not an easy thing, about which no difficulty can possibly be raised by any one who has any idea of the goodness of God. The point of view of the New Testament is the very opposite. Salvation *is* a difficult thing, an incredible thing, an impossible thing ; it is the miracle of miracles that such a thing should be ; the wonder of it never ceases, and it nowhere finds a more thrilling expression than in St. Paul's words, Ye were bought with a price. St. Paul will show us in other ways why cost was necessary, and the cost of Christ's death in particular; but it is a great step in initiation into the gospel he preached to see that cost, as Bushnell puts it in his book on *Forgiveness and Law,* had to be made, and actually was made, that men might be redeemed for God.

There is another passage in the First Epistle to the

Corinthians on which I should lay greater stress than is usually done in connection with the apostle's teaching on Christ's death : it is that in the tenth and eleventh chapters in which St. Paul speaks of the Sacraments. He is concerned about the recrudescence of immorality among the saints, about the presumptuous carelessness with which they go into temptation, relying apparently on their sacramental privileges to ensure them against peril. He points out that God's ancient people had had similar privileges, indeed identical ones, yet had fallen in the wilderness owing to their sins. You are baptized into Christ? Yes, and all our fathers were baptized into Moses in the cloud and in the sea ; they formed one body with him, and were as sure of God's favour. You have supernatural meat and supernatural drink in the Holy Supper, meat and drink which have the assurance of a divine and immortal life in them ? So had they in the manna and the water from the rock. They all ate the same supernatural meat as you do, they all drank the same supernatural drink ; they drank of a supernatural rock which followed them, and the rock was Christ.[1] It is obvious from this passage (1 Corinthians x. 1-4) as well as from the references to baptism in i. 13 f., xii. 13, and from the full explanation of the Supper in xi. 23 ff., that the Sacraments had a large place in the church at Corinth, and

---

[1] I have rendered πνευματικὸν here 'supernatural' rather than 'spiritual,' because it suggests better the element of mystery, or rather of divineness, which all through this passage is connected with the Sacraments. Baptism is not a common washing, nor is the Supper common meat and drink ; it is a divine cleansing, a divine nourishment, with which we have to do in these rites ; there is a mysterious power of God in them, which the Corinthians were inclined to conceive as operating like a charm for their protection in situations of moral ambiguity or peril. This is so far suggested to the Greek reader by πνευματικὸν, for πνεῦμα and its derivatives always involve a reference to God ; but as it is not necessarily suggested to the English reader by 'spiritual,' I have ventured on the other rendering. The indefiniteness of 'supernatural' is rather an advantage in the context than a drawback.

not only a large place, but one of a significance which can hardly be exaggerated. And, as has been pointed out already, there is no interpretation of the Sacraments except by reference to the death of Christ. Baptism has always in view, as part at least of its significance, the forgiveness of sins; and as the rite which marks the believer's initiation into the new covenant, it is essentially related to the act on which the covenant is based, namely, that which Paul delivered first of all to this Church, that Christ died for our sins. When, in another epistle, Paul argues that baptism into Christ means baptism into His death, he is not striking out a new thought, of a somewhat venturesome originality, to ward off a shrewd blow suddenly aimed at his gospel; he is only bringing out what was all along to him the essential meaning of this ordinance. The Supper, again, of which he speaks at length in 1 Corinthians x. and xi., bears an unmistakable reference to Christ's death. The cup is specially defined as the new covenant in His blood, and the apostle sums up the meaning of the Sacrament in the words, As often as ye eat this bread and drink the cup, ye publish the Lord's death till He come (1 Cor. xi. 26). In all probability καταγγέλλετε (publish) implies that the Sacrament was accompanied by words in which its significance was expressed; it was not only a picture in which the death of Christ was represented and its worth to the Church declared; there was an articulate confession of what it was, and of what the Church owed to it. If we compare the sixth chapter of Romans with the tenth and eleventh of 1st Corinthians, it seems obvious that modern Christians try to draw a broader line of distinction between the Sacraments than really exists. Partly, no doubt, this is owing to the fact that in our times baptism is usually that of infants, while the Supper is partaken of only by adults, whereas, in New Testament times, the significance of both was defined in relation to conscious faith.   But it would not be easy to show, from St. Paul's epistles, that in contents and meaning, in the blessings which they represented and which were conveyed through them, there is any very great distinction. The truth seems rather to be that both the Sacraments are forms into which we may put as much of the gospel as they will carry ; and St. Paul, for his part, practically puts the whole of his gospel into each.   If Baptism is relative to the forgiveness of sins, so is the Supper.   If Baptism is relative to the unity of the Church, so is the Supper.   We are not only baptized into one body (1 Cor. xii. 13), but because there is one bread, we, many as we are who partake of it, are one body (1 Cor. x. 17).   If Baptism is relative to a new life in Christ (Rom. vi. 4 f.), in the Supper Christ Himself is the meat and drink by which the new life is sustained (1 Cor. x. 3 f.).   And in both the Sacraments, the Christ to whom we enter into relation is Christ who died ; we are baptized into His death in the one, we proclaim His death till the end of time in the other.   I repeat, it is hardly possible to exaggerate the significance of these facts, though it is possible enough to ignore them altogether.   The superstition that has gathered round the Sacraments, and that has tempted even good Christians to speak of abolishing them, probably showed itself at a very early date ; there are unmistakable traces of it in the First Epistle to the Corinthians itself, especially in the tenth chapter ; but instead of lessening, it increases our assurance of the place which these ordinances had in Christianity from the beginning.   And although the rationale of the connection between the death of Christ and the blessings of the gospel is not elucidated by them, it is presupposed in them.   In ordinances with which every Christian was familiar, and without which a place in the Christian community could neither be acquired nor retained, the death of Christ was perpetually kept before all as a death essentially related in some way to the forgiveness of sins.

Not much light falls on our subject from the one sacrificial allusion to Christ's death in 1 Corinthians v. 7: 'For our passover also has been sacrificed—Christ.' No doubt τὸ πάσχα here, as in Mark xiv. 12, means the paschal lamb, and the apostle is thinking of Christ as the Lamb of God, by whose sacrifice the Church is called and bound to a life of holiness. It is because of this sacrifice that he says, 'Let us therefore keep festival, not in old leaven, nor in leaven of malice and wickedness, but in the unleavened bread of sincerity and truth.' It is implied here certainly that there is an entire incongruity between a life of sin, and a life determined by a relation to the sacrificial death of Christ ; but we could not, from this passage alone, make out what, according to St. Paul, was the ground of this incongruity. It would be wrong, in a passage with this simply allusive reference to the passover, to urge the significance of the lamb in the twelfth and thirteenth chapters of Exodus, and to apply this to interpret the death of Christ. There is no indication that the apostle himself carried out his thought on these lines.

We now come to the Second Epistle to the Corinthians, which is here of supreme importance. In one point of view, it is a defence of St. Paul's apostleship, and of his work in the apostolic office. The defence rests mainly on two pillars ; first, his comprehension of the gospel ; and second, his success in preaching it. There are one or two references in the earlier chapters to the sufferings and even the death of Jesus in an aspect with which we are not here specially concerned. Thus in i. 5, Paul says : 'The sufferings of Christ abound toward us' ; meaning by this that in his apostolic work he suffered abundantly just as Christ had suffered ; the weariness and peril from which Jesus could not escape haunted him too ; the Lord's experience was continued in him. Similarly, in iv. 10, when he speaks of always bearing about in the body τὴν νέκρωσιν τοῦ Ἰησοῦ— the dying of Jesus—he means that his work and its attendant sufferings are killing him as they killed his Master; every day he feels his strength lessen, and the outer man perish. But it is not in these passages that the great revelation is made of what Christ's death is in relation to sin. It is in chapter v., in which he is defending his conduct in the apostolic office against the assaults of his enemies. Extravagant or controlled, the motive of his conduct was always the same. 'The love of Christ constrains us,' he writes, ' because we thus judge, that one died for all (so then all died), and died for all that they who live should no longer live for themselves, but for Him who died for them, and rose again.' The importance of this passage is that it connects the two relations in which St. Paul is in the habit of defining Christ's death—its relation to the love in which it originated, and to the sin with which it dealt; and it shows us how to construe these two things in relation to each other. Christ's death, we are enabled to see, was a loving death, so far as men are concerned, only because in that death He took the responsibilities of men upon Himself: deny that, and it will be impossible to show any ground on which the death can be construed as a loving death at all. It it necessary to examine the passage in detail.

The love of Christ, the apostle argues, constrains us, because we thus judge—*i.e.*, because we put a certain interpretation on His death. Apart from this interpretation, the death of Christ has no constraining power. Here we find in St. Paul himself a confirmation of what has been said above about the distinction of fact and theory. It is in virtue of a certain theory of Christ's death that the fact has its power to constrain the apostle. If it were not susceptible of such an interpretation, if this theory were inapplicable

to it, it would cease to constrain. What, then, is the
theory? It is that one died for all; ὑπὲρ πάντων means
that the interest of all was aimed at and involved in the
death of the one. How it was involved in it these words
alone do not enable us to say. They do not by themselves
show the connection between Christ's death and the world's
good. But St. Paul draws an immediate inference from
them : 'so then all died.' In one sense, it is irrelevant and
interrupts his argument. He puts it into a hurried paren-
thesis, and then eagerly resumes what it had suspended.
'One died for all (so then all died), and died for all that
they who live should no longer live to themselves, but to
Him who died for them and rose again.' Yet it is in this
immediate inference—that the death of Christ *for* all involved the death *of* all—that the missing link is found. It
is because Christ's death has this inclusive character—
because, as Athanasius puts it, 'the death of all was fulfilled
in the Lord's body '—that His death has in it a power
which puts constraint on men to live for Him.[1] I cannot
agree with Mr. Lidgett when he says that the words can
only be understood in connection with the apostle's declaration elsewhere, that he has been 'crucified with Christ.'[2]
That declaration is a declaration of Christian experience,
the fruit of faith ; but what the apostle is dealing with here
is something antecedent to Christian experience, something
by which all such experience is to be generated, and which,
therefore, is in no sense identical with it. The problem
before us is to discover what it is in the death of Christ
which gives it its power to generate such experience, to exercise on human hearts the constraining influence of which
the apostle speaks ; and this is precisely what we discover in
the inferential clause : ' so then all died.' This clause puts

[1] *De Incarnatione*, c. xx. §. 5.
[2] J. S. Lidgett, *The Spiritual Principle of the Atonement*, p. 39.

as plainly as it can be put the idea that His death was equivalent to the death of all; in other words, it was the death of all men which was died by Him. Were this not so, His death would be nothing to them. It is beside the mark to say, as Mr. Lidgett does, that His death is died by them rather than theirs by Him; the very point of the apostle's argument may be said to be that in order that they may die His death He must first die theirs. Our dying His death is not, in the New Testament, a thing which we achieve on our own initiative, or out of our own resources; it is the fruit of His dying ours. If it is our death that Christ died on the Cross, there is in the Cross the constraint of an infinite love; but if it is not our death at all—if it is not our burden and doom that He has taken to Himself there—then what is it to us? His death can put the constraint of love upon all men, only when it is thus judged— that the death of all was died by Him. When the apostle proceeds to state the purpose of Christ's death for all—'that they which live should not henceforth live to themselves, but to Him who died for them and rose again'—he does it at the psychological and moral level suggested by the words: The love of Christ constrains us. He who has done so tremendous a thing as to take our death to Himself has established a claim upon our life. We are not in the sphere of mystical union, of dying with Christ and living with Him; but in that of love transcendently shown, and of gratitude profoundly felt.[1] But it will not be easy for any one to be grateful for Christ's death, especially with a gratitude which will acknowledge that his very life is Christ's,

---

[1] The way in which theologians in love with the ' mystical union ' depreciate gratitude must be very astonishing to psychologists. See Juncker, *Die Ethik des Ap. Paulus*, 161, and Rothe, *Dogmatik* II. i. 223 (a remark on this passage in 2 Cor. v.) : ohne Ihn und seinen Tod hätten Alle sterben müssen ; das Leben das sie leben verdanken sie also gänzlich Ihm, und müssen es deshalb ganz und gar Ihm widmen.

un!ess he reads the Cross in the sense that Christ there made the death of all men His own.

It is in this same passage that St. Paul gives the fullest explanation of what he means by reconciliation (καταλλαγή), and an examination of this idea will also illustrate his teaching on the death of Christ. Where reconciliation is spoken of in St. Paul, the subject is always God, and the object is always man. The work of reconciling is one in which the initiative is taken by God, and the cost borne by Him ; men are reconciled in the passive, or allow themselves to be reconciled, or receive the reconciliation. We never read that God has been reconciled. God does the work of reconciliation in or through Christ, and especially through His death. He was engaged, in Christ, in reconciling the world—or rather, nothing less than a world—to Himself (2 Cor. v. 19). He reconciled us to Himself through Christ (v. 20). When we were enemies, we were reconciled to God by the death of His Son (Rom. v. 10). Men who once were alienated, and enemies in mind through wicked works, yet now He has reconciled in the body of His flesh through death (Col. i. 21 f.). It is very unfortunate that the English word reconcile (and also the German *versöhnen*, which is usually taken as its equivalent) diverge seriously, though in a way of which it is easy to be unconscious, from the Greek καταλλάσσειν. We cannot say in English, God reconciled us to Himself, without conceiving the persons referred to as being actually at peace with God, as having laid aside all fear, distrust, and love of evil, and entered, in point of fact, into relations of peace and friendship with God. But καταλλάσσειν, as describing the work of God, or καταλλαγή, as describing its immediate result, do not necessarily carry us so far. The work of reconciliation, in the sense of the New Testament, is a work which is *finished*, and which we must conceive to be finished, *before the gospel is preached*. It is the good tidings of the Gospel, with which the evangelists go forth, that God has wrought in Christ a work of reconciliation which avails for no less than the world, and of which the whole world may have the benefit. The summons of the evangelist is—'*Receive* the reconciliation; consent that it become effective in your case.' The work of reconciliation is not a work wrought upon the souls of men, though it is a work wrought in their interests, and bearing so directly upon them that we can say God has reconciled the world to Himself; it is a work—as Cromwell said of the covenant—*outside of us*, in which God so deals in Christ with the sin of the world, that it shall no longer be a barrier between Himself and men.

From this point of view we can understand how many modern theologians, in their use of the word reconciliation, come to argue as it were at cross purposes with the apostle. Writers like Kaftan,[1] for example, who do not think of the work of Christ as anything else than the work which Christ is perpetually doing in winning the souls of men for God, and who describe this as the work of reconciliation, though they may seem to the practical modern intelligence to be keeping close to reality, are doing all that can be done to make the Pauline, or rather the New Testament point of view, bewildering to a modern reader. Reconciliation, in the New Testament sense, is not something which is doing; it is something which is done. No doubt there is a work of Christ which is in process, but it has as its basis a finished work of Christ; it is in virtue

---

[1] Kaftan holds that nothing is to be called *Erlösung* or *Versöhnung* (redemption or reconciliation) unless as men are actually liberated and reconciled; Erlösung and Versöhnung are to be understood, as the Reformers rightly saw (?), as *Wirkungen Gottes in und an den Gläubigen*. But he overlooks the fact that whatever is to liberate or reconcile men must have qualities or virtues in it which, in view of their normal effect, whether that effect be in any given case achieved or not, can be called reconciling or liberative; and that the determination of these qualities or virtues—that is, as he calls it, an '*objective Heilslehre*'—is not only legitimate but essential in the interpretation of the work of Christ. See his *Dogmatik*, §§ 52 ff.

of something already consummated on His cross that Christ
is able to make the appeal to us which He does, and to win
the response in which we *receive* the reconciliation.   A
finished work of Christ and an objective atonement—a
καταλλαγή in the New Testament sense—are synonymous
terms : the one means exactly the same as the other ; and it
seems to me self-evident, as I think it did to St. Paul, that
unless we can preach a finished work of Christ in relation to
sin, a καταλλαγή or reconciliation or peace which has been
achieved independently of us, at an infinite cost, and to
which we are called in a word or ministry of reconciliation,
we have no real gospel for sinful men at all.   It is not in
something Christ would fain do that we see His love, it is in
something He has already done ; nay, it is only through
what He has already done that we can form any idea, or
come to any conviction, of what He would fain do.   He has
died for us all, and by that death—not His own, properly
speaking, but the death of the sinful race taken to Himself
—He has so demonstrated the reality and infinity of the
love of God to the sinful, as to make it possible for apostles
and evangelists to preach peace to all men through Him.

In the passage with which we are dealing, St. Paul appends
to the apostolic message, abruptly and without any conjunction, the statement of the great truth of Christ's finished
work which underlies it.   ' On Christ's behalf, then, we are
ambassadors, as though God were entreating you through
us : we beg of you on Christ's behalf, *Be* reconciled to God.
Him that knew no sin He made to be sin for us, that
we might become God's righteousness in Him ' (2 Cor. v.
20 f.).   The want of a conjunction here does not destroy the
connection ; it only makes the appeal of the writer more
solemn and thrilling.   There need not be any misunderstanding as to what is meant by the words, Him that
knew no sin He made to be sin for us.   To every one

who has noticed that St. Paul constantly defines Christ's death, and nothing but His death, by relation to sin, and who can recall similar passages in the Epistle to the Galatians or to the Romans, to which we shall presently come, it is obvious that these tremendous words cover precisely the same meaning as ' He died for our sins.' When the sinless one, in obedience to the will of the Father, died on the Cross the death of all, the death in which sin had involved all, then, and in that sense, God made Him to be sin for all. But what is meant by saying, ' in that sense '? It means, ' in the sense of His death.' And what that means is not to be answered *a priori,* or on dogmatic grounds. It is to be answered out of the Gospel history, out of the experience of our Lord in the Garden and on the Cross. It is there we see what death meant for Him; what it meant for Him to make our sin, and the death in which God's judgment comes upon sin, His own; and it is the love which, in obedience to the Father, did not shrink from *that* for us which gives power and urgency to the appeal of the Gospel. We ought to feel that moralising objections here are beside the mark, and that it is not for sinful men, who do not know what love is, to tell beforehand whether, or how far, the love of God can take upon itself the burden and responsibility of the world's sin; or if it does so, in what way its reality shall be made good. The premiss of the Gospel is that we cannot bear that responsibility ourselves; if we are left alone with it, it will crush us to perdition. The message of the gospel, as it is here presented, is that Christ has borne it *for* us; if we deny that He *can* do so, is it not tantamount to denying the very possibility of a gospel? Mysterious and awful as the thought is, it is the key to the whole of the New Testament, that Christ bore our sins. Of this, God made Him to be sin for us is merely another equivalent; it means neither more nor less.

The end contemplated—that we might become the righteousness of God in Him—is here stated religiously or theologically.   Christ takes our place in death, and in so doing
is identified with the world's sin; the end in view in this is
that we should take His place in life, and in so doing stand
justified in God's sight.   By what psychological process this
change in our position is mediated St. Paul does not here
tell.   What he does is to give a religious equivalent for the
ethical and psychological representation of ver. 14: ' He
died for all, that they which live should not live unto themselves, but to Him who died for them and rose again.'   It
took no less than His death for them to bring into their
life a motive of such creative and recreative power; and it
takes no less than His being made sin for them to open for
them the possibility of becoming God's righteousness in Him.
To say so is not to bring different things into an artificial
correspondence.   The two statements are but the ethical and
the theological representation of one and the same reality ;
and it confirms our interpretation of the passage, and our
conviction of the coherence of the apostolic gospel, that
under various and independent aspects we are continually
coming on the same facts in the same relation to each
other.

(III.) The closing verses of the fifth chapter of 2nd
Corinthians may fairly be called the *locus classicus* on the
death of Christ in St. Paul's writings.   Yet in proceeding
to the Epistle to the Galatians we are introduced to a docu-
ment which, more exclusively than any other in the New
Testament, deals with this subject, and its significance.
Even in the salutation, in which the apostle wishes his
readers grace and peace from God the Father and the Lord
Jesus Christ, he expands the Saviour's name by adding, in a
way unexampled in such a connection elsewhere, ' *who gave
Himself for our sins that He might redeem us from the*

present world with all its ills, according to the will of our God and Father ' (i. 4).   Reference has already been made to the vehement words in which he anathematises man or angel who shall preach a different gospel.[1]   At the end of the second chapter he puts again, in the strongest possible form, his conviction that Christianity, the new and true religion, is a thing complete in itself, exclusive of everything else, incapable of compromise or of supplement, and that it owes this completeness, and if we choose to call it so, this intolerance, to the supreme significance and power which belong in it to the death of Christ.   ' I have been crucified with Christ ; my life is no longer mine, it is Christ who lives in me ; the life I now live in flesh I live in faith, faith in the Son of God who loved me and gave Himself up for me ' (ii. 20).   The whole of the Christian religion lies in that.   The whole of Christian life is a response to the love exhibited in the death of the Son of God for men.   No one can become right with God except by making the response of faith to this love—that is, except by abandoning himself unreservedly to it as the only hope for sinful men.   To trust it wholly and solely is the only right thing a man can do in presence of it ; and when he does so trust it he is completely, finally, and divinely right.   To supplement it is, according to Paul, to frustrate the grace of God ; it is to compromise the Christian religion in its very principle ; and to such a sin St. Paul will be no party.   If righteousness is by law, as he sums it up in one of his passionate and decisive words, then Christ died for nothing (ii. 21). St. Paul knew by experience that all he was, or could ever become as a Christian, came out of the Cross.   This is why he could say to the Corinthians, ' I determined to know nothing among you save Jesus Christ and Him crucified ' (1 Cor. ii. 2) ; and why he repeats it in other words to the

[1] See above, p. 78.

Galatians, 'God forbid that I should glory save in the Cross of our Lord Jesus Christ, through which the world is cruci- fied to me and I to the world' (Gal. vi. 14).

Put positively, then, we may say that the aim of the Epistle to the Galatians is to show that all Christianity is contained in the Cross ; the Cross is the generative prin- ciple of everything Christian in the life of man. Put negatively, we may say its aim is to show that law, and especially, as it happened, the ritual side of the Jewish law, contributes nothing to that life. Now St. Paul, it might be argued, had come to know this experimentally, and independently of any theory. When it had dawned on his mind what the Cross of Christ was, when he saw what it signified as a revelation of God and His love, everything else in the universe faded from his view. Newman speaks, in a familiar passage of the *Apologia*, of resting in ' the thought of two, and two only, absolute and luminously self-evident beings, myself and my Creator ' ; in the relations and interaction of these two his religion consisted. A religion so generated, though it may be very real and powerful, is, of course, something far poorer than Chris- tianity ; yet in a somewhat similar way we might say of St. Paul that for him the universe of religion consisted of the soul and the Son of God giving Himself up for it ; all that God meant for him, all that he could describe as revelation, all that begot within him what was at once religion, life, and salvation, was included in this act of Christ. No law, however venerable ; no customs, however dear to a patriotic heart ; no traditions of men, however respectable in effect or intention, could enter into competi- tion with this. It was dishonouring to Christ, it was an annulling of the grace of God, to mention them alongside of it. To do so was to betray a radical misapprehension of Christ's death, such as made it for those who so misappre-

hended it entirely ineffective. 'Ye are severed from Christ,'
St. Paul cries, 'ye who would be justified by law ; ye are
banished from grace ' (v. 4).

But though St. Paul had learned this by experience, he
does not, in point of fact, treat this subject of law empirically.
He does not content himself with saying, 'I tried the law
till I was worn out, and it did nothing for me ; I made an
exhaustive series of experiments with it, resultless experiments, and so I am done with it ; through the law I have
died to the law (ii. 19) ; it has itself taught me, by
experience under it, that it is not the way to life, and
so it is to me now as though it were not.' He does not
content himself with giving this as his experience of the
law ; nor does he, on the other hand, content himself with
giving us simply and empirically his experience of Christ.
He does not say, ' Christ has done everything for me and in
me. The constraint of His love is the whole explanation of
my whole being as a Christian. By the grace of God, and
by nothing else, I am what I am, and therefore the law is
nothing to me : I am so far from finding myself obliged to
acknowledge its claims still, that it is my deepest conviction
that to acknowledge its claims at all is to frustrate the
grace of God, to make void the Cross of Christ.' Probably
if he had written thus—and he might truly have written
thus—it would have seemed attractive and convincing
to many who have misgivings about what he actually has
written. But St. Paul could not, and did not remain at
this empirical standpoint. He has a theory again—or let
us say an understanding—of the relations of Christ and
law, which enables him to justify and comprehend his
experience. But for the truths of which this theory is
the vehicle, the death of Christ would not be what it is, or
exercise over the soul the power which it does. It is some
dim sense of these truths, truths which the theory does not

import but only unfolds, which in every case gives the death of Christ its constraining influence upon sinful men. What, then, is the theory?

Briefly, it is summed up in the words, *Christ under the law.* This is the expression used in Galatians iv. 4, and its indefiniteness, in this form, makes it seem unobjectionable enough. It signifies that when He came into the world Christ came under the same conditions as other men : all that a Jew meant when he said 'Law' had significance for him ; the divine institutions of Israel had a divine authority which existed for him as well as for others. To say that the Son of God was made under the law would thus mean that He had the same moral problem in His life as other men ; that He identified Himself with them in the spiritual conditions under which they lived ; that the incarnation was a moral reality and not a mere show. But it is certain that this is not all that St. Paul meant ; and to the writer, at least, it is not certain that St. Paul ever had this as a distinct and separate object of thought present to his mind at all. What he really means by 'Christ under the law' comes out in its full meaning in chapter iii. 13 : *Christ redeemed us from the curse of the law by becoming curse for us.* 'Under the law,' in short, is an ambiguous expression, and it is necessary to be clear as to which of two possible interpretations it bears in this case. In relation to man in general, the law expresses the will of God. It tells him what he must do to please God. It is imperative, and nothing more. We may say, of course, that Christ was under the law in this sense ; it is self-evident. But as has just been hinted, it is doubtful whether St. Paul ever thought of this by itself. To be under the law in this sense did not to him at least yield the explanation of Christ's redeeming power. In the mere fact that Christ came to keep the law which was binding on all, there was no such demonstration of love to sinners as was sufficient, of itself, to make them new creatures. But this is not the only sense which can be assigned to the words, 'under the law.' The law has not only a relation to man as such, in which it expresses the will of God; it has a relation to men as sinners, in which it expresses the condemnation of God. Now Christ is our Redeemer, according to the apostle, because He was made under the law in this sense. He not only became *man*, bound to obedience—it is not easy to say where the omnipotent loving constraint is to be discovered in this; but He became *curse* for us. He made our *doom* His own. He took on Him not only the calling of a man, but our responsibility as sinful men; it is in this that His work as Redeemer lies, for it is in this that the measure, or rather the immensity, of His love is seen. To say, 'He became a curse for us,' is exactly the same as to say, 'He was made sin for us,' or 'He died for us'; but it is infinitely more than to say, 'He was made man for us'—or even man bound to obedience to the law—a proposition to which there is nothing analogous in the New Testament. The conception of obedience, as applicable to the work of Christ, will recur in other connections; here it is enough to say that if we wish to put the whole work of Christ under that heading, we must remember that what we have to do with is not the ordinary obedience of men, but the obedience of a Redeemer. Christ had an ethical vocation, as St. Paul reminds us in the very first reference to His death in this epistle: 'He gave Himself for our sins, to deliver us from the present evil world, *according to the will of our God and Father*'; but His vocation, in carrying out that redeeming will, was a, unique one; and, according to St. Paul, its uniqueness consisted in this, that one who knew no sin had, in obedience to the Father, to take on Him the responsibility, the doom, the curse, the death of the sinful.

And if any one says that this was morally impossible, may we not ask again, What is the alternative? Is it not that the sinful should be left alone with their responsibility, doom, curse, and death? And is not that to say that redemption is impossible? The obedience of the Redeemer transcends morality, if we will; it is something to which morality is unequal; from the point of view of ordinary ethics, it is a miracle.[1] But it is the very function of the Redeemer to do the thing which it is impossible for sinful men to do for themselves or for each other; and St. Paul's justification of the miracle is that it creates all the genuine and victorious morality—all the keeping of God's commandments in love—which the world can show.

There have been many attempts, if not to evade this line of argument, and this connection of ideas, then to find something quite different in Galatians, which shall dispense with the necessity of considering it. Thus it is argued that St. Paul in the whole epistle is dealing with Jews, or with people who wanted to be Jews, and with their relation to the ceremonial law—a situation which no longer has reality for us. But this is hardly the case. St. Paul nowhere draws any distinction in the law between ceremonial and moral; the law for him is one, and it is the law of God. It is owing to accidental circumstances that the ceremonial aspect of it is more prominent in this epistle, as the ethical aspect is in Romans. But we shall find the same line of argument repeated in Romans, where it is the moral law which is at stake; and when the apostle tells us that through the law he has died to the law (Gal. ii. 16), or that we have died to the law through the body of Christ (Rom. vii. 4), or that we are not under law but under grace (Rom. vi. 14), he has not the moral law any less in view than the ceremonial. He means that *nothing* in the Christian life is

[1] See *Expositor* for June 1901, p. 449 ff.

H

explained by *anything* statutory, and that everything in it
is explained by the inspiring power of that death in which
Christ made all our responsibilities to the law His own.
There is a sense, of course, in which the law is Jewish, but
St. Paul had generalised it in order to be able to preach the
Gospel to the gentiles; [1] he had found analogues of it in
every society and in every conscience; in his evangelistic
preaching he defined all sin by relation to it; in the utmost
extent of meaning that could be given to the term, 'law'
had significance for all men; and it was a gospel for *all*
men that St. Paul preached when he declared that Christ
redeemed us from the curse of the law by becoming curse for
us. No doubt when he wrote the words, 'Christ redeemed us
from the curse of the law by becoming curse for us,' he was
thinking, as his antecedents and circumstances compelled
him to think, of himself and his fellow-countrymen, who
had known so well the yoke of bondage; that is, it is an
exegetical result that ἡμᾶς means *us Jews*; but that does
not alter the fact that the universal gospel underlies the
expression, and is conveyed by it; it only means that here a
definite application is made of that gospel in a relevant case.

The same considerations dispose of the attempts that are
made to evacuate the 'curse' of meaning by identifying it
with the 'Cross.' No doubt Paul appeals in support of his
idea that Christ became a curse for us to the text in
Deuteronomy xxi. 23, which he quotes in the form 'Cursed
is every one who hangs upon a tree.' No doubt he avoids
applying to Christ the precise words of the text, Accursed
of God (κεκατηραμένος ὑπὸ τοῦ θεοῦ (LXX.) קִלְלַת־אֱלֹהִים).
So do we, because the words would be false and misleading.
Christ hung on the tree in obedience to the Father's will,
fulfilling the purpose of the Father's love, doing a work
with which the Father was well pleased, and on account of

---

[1] See *Expositor*, March 1901, p. 176 ff.

which the Father highly exalted Him; hence to describe Him as accursed of God would be absurd. It is not because St. Paul shrinks from his own logic that he says He became a curse for us, instead of saying He became a curse of God, or accursed of God, for us; it is because he is speaking in truth and soberness. Death is the curse of the law. It is the experience in which the final repulsion of evil by God is decisively expressed; and Christ died. In His death everything was made His that sin had made ours—everything in sin except its sinfulness. There is no essential significance in the crucifixion, as if it would have been impossible to say that Christ became a curse for us, if He had died in any other way. The curse, in truth, is only one of St. Paul's synonyms for the death of Christ—one which is relative, no doubt, to the conception of Christ as 'under the law,' but which for its meaning is entirely independent of the passage in Deuteronomy. The New Testament has many analogies to this use of the Old. Christ rode into Jerusalem on an ass, and declared Himself a King in doing so, but no one supposes that His sovereignty is constituted or exhausted in this; it is entirely independent of it, though in connection with a certain prophecy (Zech. ix. 9) it can be identified with it. So again He was crucified between two thieves, and an evangelist says that there the Scripture was fulfilled —He was numbered with transgressors; but we know that the Scripture was fulfilled in another and profounder sense, and would have been fulfilled all the same though Jesus had been crucified alone (Mark xv. 28 Rec., Luke xxii. 37). And so also with the Deuteronomic quotation in Galatians iii. 13. The Old Testament here gave Paul an expression— an *argumentum*, if we will; it did not give him his gospel. He had said already, *e.g.* in 2 Corinthians v. 21, and will say again in other forms, all he has to say here: that in His death Christ was made under the law, not merely as that which laid its imperative, but as that which laid its sentence, upon man; that He took to Himself in His death our responsibility, our doom, our curse, as sinful men, and not merely our obligation to be good men.   And though it is Christian, it is not illogical, to avoid such an expression as accursed of God.   For in so making the doom of men His own in death Christ was doing God's will.

The other passages in Galatians which deal with our subject bring to view the ethical rather than the theological import of the death of Christ.   One occurs at chapter v. 24 : 'They that are of Christ Jesus crucified the flesh with its passions and lusts.'   Ideally, we must understand, this crucifixion of the flesh is involved in Christ's crucifixion ; really, it is effected by it.   Whoever sees into the secret of Calvary—whoever is initiated into the mystery of that great death—is conscious that the doom of sin is in it ; to take it as real, and to stand in any real relation to it, is death to the flesh with its passions and desires.   So with the last passage in the epistle at which the subject recurs (vi. 14) : 'Never be it mine to boast but in the cross of our Lord Jesus Christ, through which the world has been crucified to me, and I to the world.'   Here the apostle reiterates with new emphasis at the end of his letter what he has enforced from the beginning, that the Cross is the explanation of everything Christian.   Of course it is the Cross interpreted as he has interpreted it ; apart from this interpretation, which shows it to be full of a meaning that appeals irresistibly to man, it can have no rational or moral influence at all.   But with this interpretation it is the annihilative and the creative power in Christianity ; the first commandment of the new religion is that we shall have no God but Him who is fully and finally revealed there.

(IV.) The Epistle to the Romans is not so directly controversial as that to the Galatians ; there are no personal

references in it, and no temper. But the Gospel is defined
in it in relation to law, in very much the same sense as in
Galatians; the completeness of the Christian religion, its
self-containedness, its self-sufficiency, the impossibility of
combining it with or supplementing it from anything else,
are assumed or proved in much the same way. The question
of religion for St. Paul is, How shall a man, a sinful man, be
righteous with God ? The Gospel brings the answer to that
question.   It is because it does so that it is a Gospel.   It
tells sinful men of a righteousness which is exactly what
they need.   It preaches something on the ground of which,
sinners as they are, God the Judge of all can receive them—
a righteousness of God, St. Paul calls it, naming it after
Him who is its source, and at the same time characterising
it as divinely perfect and adequate—a righteousness of God
which is somehow identified with Jesus Christ (iii. 22 ; cf.
1 Cor. i. 30).   In particular it is identified somehow with
Jesus Christ in His death (iii. 25), and therefore in Romans
as in Galatians this death of Christ is the source of all that
is Christian. All Christian inferences about God are deduced
from it.   Once we are sure of it and of its meaning, we can
afford a great deal of ignorance in detail. We know that it
covers everything and guarantees everything in which we are
vitally interested ; that it disposes of the past, creates the
future, is a security for immortal life and glory (v. 9 ff., viii.
31 ff.).   What, then, does St. Paul say of the righteousness of God, and of the death of Christ in relation
to it ?

The critical passage is that in ch. iii. 21 ff. To give a
detailed exegesis of it would be to do what has been perhaps
too often done already, and would raise questions to distract
as well as to aid intelligence.   As is well known, there are
two principal difficulties in the passage.   The one is the
meaning of ἱλαστήριον (propitiation) in v. 25.   The other

is that which is raised by the question whether the righteousness of God has the same meaning throughout, or whether it
may not have in one place—say in v. 22—the half-technical
sense which belongs to it as a summary of St. Paul's gospel ;
and in another—say in v. 26—the larger and more general
sense which might belong to it elsewhere in Scripture as a
synonym for God's character, or at least for one of His
essential attributes. Not that these two principal difficulties
are unrelated to each other : on the contrary, they are inex-
tricably intertwined, and cannot be discussed apart. It is
an argument for distinguishing two senses of δικαιοσύνη
θεοῦ (the righteousness of God) that when we do so we are
enabled to see more clearly the meaning of ἱλαστήριος. It
is the very function of Jesus Christ, set forth by God as a
propitiation in His blood, to exhibit these two senses (which
are equally indispensable, if there is to be a religion for
sinful men), in their unity and consistency with each other.
And, on the other hand, the term ἱλαστήριος, to say the
least, is relative to some problem created by sin for a
God who would justify sinners ; and the distinction of
two senses in which δικαιοσύνη θεοῦ is used enables us to
state this problem in a definite form.

Assuming, then, that both difficulties will come up for
consideration, there is a certain convenience in starting with
the second—that which is involved in the use of the expression ' the righteousness of God.' It is used in vv. 21, 22, 25,
and 26 ; and the use of it is implied in v. 24 : ' being
justified freely by His grace.' It seems to me a strong
argument for the double sense of this expression that when
the apostle brings his argument to a climax the two senses
have sifted themselves out, so to speak, and stand distinctly
side by side : the end of all God's action in His redeeming
revelation of Himself to men is ' that He may be just Him
self, and justify him who believes in Jesus ' (εἰς τὸ εἶναι αὐτὸ

δίκαιον καὶ δικαιοῦντα τὸν ἐκ πίστεως Ἰησοῦ, v. 26). The
first part of this end—God's being righteous Himself—might
quite fairly be spoken of as δικαιοσύνη θεοῦ (God's righteousness) ; it is, indeed, what under ordinary circumstances is
meant by the words.   Compare, for example, the use of
them in ch. iii. 5.   But God's appearance in the character
of ὁ δικαιῶν (he who justifies) is also the manifestation of a
righteousness of God, and indeed of the righteousness of
God in the sense in which it constitutes St. Paul's gospel—
a righteousness of God which stands or turns to the good of
the believing sinner.   Both things are there : a righteousness
which comes from God and is the hope of the sinful, and
God's own righteousness, or His character in its self-consistency and inviolability.   In virtue of the first, God is ὁ
δικαιῶν, the Justifier ; in virtue of the second, He is δίκαιος,
Just.   What St. Paul is concerned to bring out, and what
by means of the conception of Christ in His blood as
ἱλαστήριος (endued with propitiatory power) he does bring
out, is precisely the fact that both things *are* there, and
there in harmony with each other.   There can be no gospel
unless there is such a thing as a righteousness of God for
the ungodly.   But just as little can there be any gospel
unless the integrity of God's character be maintained.   The
problem of the sinful world, the problem of all religion, the
problem of God in dealing with a sinful race, is how to unite
these two things.   The Christian answer to the problem is
given by St. Paul in the words : ' Jesus Christ whom God
set forth a propitiation (or, in propitiatory power) in His
blood.'   In Jesus Christ so set forth there is the manifestation of God's righteousness in the two senses, or, if we prefer
it, in the complex sense, just referred to.   Something is done
which enables God to justify the ungodly who believe in
Jesus, and at the same time to appear signally and conspicuously a righteous God.   What this something is we

have still to consider; but meanwhile it should be noted that this interpretation of the passage agrees with what we have already seen—that justification of the ungodly, or forgiveness of sins, or redemption, or whatever we are to call it, is a real problem for St. Paul. *Gospel* is the last thing in the world to be taken for granted : before there can be any such thing a problem of tremendous difficulty has to be solved, and according to the apostle of the Gentiles it has received at God's hands a tremendous solution.

Before entering into this, it is only fair to refer to the interpretations of the passage which aim at giving the righteousness of God precisely the same force all through. In this case, of course, it is the technical, specifically Pauline sense which is preferred; the δικαιοσύνη θεοῦ is to be read always as that by which sinful man is justified. This is done by different interpreters with very various degrees of insight.

(1) There are those who seem unconscious that there is any problem, any moral problem, in the situation at all. The righteousness of God, they argue, is essentially self-imparting ; it 'goes out' and energises in the world ; it takes hold of human lives and fills them with itself; it acts on the analogy of a physical force, like light or heat, diffusing itself and radiating in every direction, indiscriminately and without limit. Legal religion, no doubt, conceives of it otherwise ; to legalism, God's righteousness is a negative attribute, something in which God, as it were, stands on the defensive, maintaining His integrity against the sin of the world ; but that is only a mistake. God's righteousness is effluent, overflowing, the source of all the goodness in the world ; and we see in Jesus Christ that this is so. The truth in all this is as obvious as the irrelevance. Of course all goodness is of God ; no man would less have wished to question this than St. Paul. But St. Paul felt that the sin of the world made a difference

to God; it was a sin against His righteousness, and His
righteousness had to be vindicated against it; it could not
ignore it, and go on *simpliciter* 'justifying' men as if nothing
had happened. Such an interpretation of the passage ignores
altogether the *problem* which the sin of the world (as St. Paul
looked at it) presented to God. It makes no attempt whatever to define the relation, on which everything in the
passage turns, between the divine righteousness and the death
of Christ as a ἱλαστήριον; and in missing altogether the
problem, it misses as completely the solution—that is, it
misses the Gospel. We cannot keep Christianity, or any
specifically Christian truth, if we deny its premises, nor can
we either state or solve a moral problem if we confine
ourselves to physical categories.

(2) There are those who assimilate the righteousness of
God in this passage to the δικαιοσύνη θεοῦ of the Psalms and
later Isaiah, those familiar passages in which it is so often
found as a parallel to σωτηρία (salvation). It is in these,
they argue, that the real antecedents are found both of
St. Paul's thoughts and of his language. What, for instance,
could be closer to his mind than Ps. xcvi. 2 : 'The Lord hath
made known His salvation; His righteousness hath He
openly shewed in the sight of the heathen'? In the Gospel
we have the manifestation of the righteousness of God in this
sense, a righteousness which is indistinguishable from His
grace, and in which He shows Himself righteous by acting
in accordance with His covenant obligations—receiving His
people graciously, and loving them freely.[1] There is some-

---

[1] This is the view of Ritschl, who decides that everywhere in Paul the
righteousness of God means the mode of procedure which is consistent with
God's having the salvation of believers as His end (*Rechtf. u. Vers.* ii[1]. 117).
In the same sense he argues that the correlative idea to the righteousness of
God is always that of the righteousness of His people (*ibid.* 108, 110). He
seems to forget here that the God of the Gospel is defined by St. Paul in terms
which expressly contradict this view, as ' He who justifies *the ungodly* ' (Rom.

thing attractive in this, and something true ; but it is as completely irrelevant to St. Paul's thought in the passage before us as the more superficial view already referred to. For one thing, St. Paul never refers to any of these passages in connecting his gospel with the Old Testament.   He must have been perfectly aware that they were written on another plane than that on which he stood as a sinful man and a preacher to sinners.   They were written for God's covenant people, to assure them that God would be true to the obligations of the covenant, and would demonstrate His righteousness in doing so ;   God's righteousness, in all these passages, is that attribute to which His people appeal when they are wronged. The situation which St. Paul has before him, however, is not that of God's people, wronged by their enemies, and entitled to appeal to His righteousness to plead their cause and put them in the right ; it is that of people who have no cause, who are all in the wrong with God, whose sins impeach them without ceasing, to whom God as Righteous Judge is not, as to a wronged covenant people, a tower of hope, but a name which sums up all their fears. The people for whom Isaiah and the Psalms were written were people who, being put in the wrong by their adversaries on earth, had a supreme appeal to God, before whom they were confident they should be in the right ; the people to whom St. Paul preaches are people who before God have no case, so that the assurances of the prophet and the psalmists are nothing to them. Of course there is such a thing as a New Covenant, and it is possible for those who are within it to

---

v. 5) ; and that a reference to sin rather than to righteousness in the people is the true correlative of the Pauline δικαιοσύνη θεοῦ.   Ritschl's treatment of the passage in Rom. iii. 3 ff., where God's righteousness is spoken of in connection with the judgment of the world, and with the infliction of the final wrath upon it, and where it evidently includes something other than the gracious consistency to which Ritschl would limit it, is an amusing combination of sophistry and paradox.

appropriate these Old Testament texts ; there is, for example, a clear instance of such appropriation in the First Epistle of John i. 9 : ' If we confess our sins, He is faithful and righteous to forgive us our sins, and to cleanse us from all unrighteousness.' In other words, He is true to the obligations of His covenant with us in Christ. These glorious Old Testament Scriptures, therefore, are not without their meaning for the New, or their influence in it ; but it is a complete mistake, and it has been the source of the most far-reaching and disastrous confusion, to try to deduce from them the Pauline conception of the righteousness of God. And it must be repeated that in such interpretations, as in those already referred to, there is again wanting any sense of a *problem* such as St. Paul is undoubtedly grappling with, and any attempt to define explicitly and intelligibly the relation between the righteousness of God, conceived as it is here conceived, and the propitiation in the blood of Christ. Indeed, it is not too much to say that for St. Paul there is no such thing as a δικαιοσύνη θεοῦ except through the propitiation ; whereas here the δικαιοσύνη θεοῦ is fully explained, with no reference to the propitiation whatever.

(3) It is worth while to refer to one particular construction of the passage, in which an attempt is made to keep the same sense of δικαιοσύνη θεοῦ throughout, and at the same time to do justice to the problem which is obviously involved. It is that which is given by Dr. Seeberg of Dorpat in his book, *Der Tod Christi*. Seeberg as a writer is not distinguished either by lucidity or conciseness, but, put briefly, his interpretation is as follows. Righteousness means acting according to one's proper norm, doing what one ought to do. God's proper norm, the true rule of action for Him, is that He should institute and maintain fellowship with men. He would not be righteous if He did not do so ; He would fail of acting in His proper character. Now, in setting forth

Christ as a propitiation, God does what the circumstances require if fellowship is to be instituted and maintained between Himself and sinful men ; and it is in this sense that the propitiation manifests or demonstrates His righteousness. It shows God not unrighteous, not false to Himself and to the true norm of His action, as He would have been if in the face of sin He had simply let the idea of fellowship with man go ; but manifesting Himself as a righteous God, who is true to Himself and to His norm most signally and conspicuously in this, that over sin and in spite of it He takes means to secure that fellowship between Himself and men shall not finally lapse.   This is ingenious and attractive, though whether the conception of the righteousness of God from which it starts would have been recognised by St. Paul or by any Scripture writer is another matter; but apart from this, it obviously leaves a question unanswered, on the answer to which a great deal depends.   That question is, What is the means which God takes to secure fellowship with *sinful* men, *i.e.* to act toward *them* in a way which does justice to Himself?   It is implied in Seeberg's whole argument that sin does create a problem for God ; something has to be *done*, where sinful men are concerned, before fellowship with God can be taken for granted ; and that something God actually *does* when He sets forth Christ a propitiation, through faith, in His blood.   The question, therefore, is—if we are going to think seriously at all—What is the propitiation, or more precisely, How is the propitiation to be defined in relation to the sin of the world, in view of which God provided it, that He might be able still to maintain fellowship with man ?

This is a question which, so far as I am able to follow him, Seeberg never distinctly answers.   He says that God set forth Christ in His blood as 'ein solches . . . welches durch den Glauben ein sühnhaft wirkendes ist' (a thing or power of such a sort that through faith it comes to have an atoning efficacy).[1] He refuses to explain the propitiatory character of Christ's death by regarding it as sacrificial; he refuses to explain it as in any sense vicarious; neither of these ideas, according to him, is supported by St. Paul. What St. Paul taught was rather this. Christ comprehended in Himself the whole human race, as Adam did (this idea St. Paul is supposed to have borrowed from the Jewish doctrine of original sin); and through the death of Christ humanity has suffered that which the holy God in grace claimed from it as the condition of its entering again into fellowship with Him.   As the Holy One, He has made this re-entrance dependent upon death, and as the Gracious One He has consented to be satisfied with that suffering of death which He has made possible for humanity in Christ.[2] It is not easy to regard this as real thinking. It does not set the death of Christ in any real relation to the problem with which the apostle is dealing. The suffering of death is that which God in His grace is pleased to claim from the sinful race as the condition of restored fellowship, and He has been further pleased to accept as satisfying this condition that particular suffering of death which Christ endured, and which can be reproduced in individuals through faith; but everything is of mere good pleasure, there is no rational necessity at any point. One can only repeat it: this is a medium in which thinking is impossible, and it is not the medium in which St. Paul's mind moved. It was not an arbitrary appointment of God that made the death of Christ ἱλαστήριον; it was the essential relation, in all human experience, of death and sin. Christ died for our sins, because it is in death that the divine judgment on sin is finally expressed. Once we put law and necessity out of the relations between Christ's death and our sin, we dismiss the very possibility of

---

[1] *Der Tod Christi*, p. 187.   [2] *Ibid.* p. 286.

thinking on the subject; we may use words about it, but they are words without meaning. It is a significant feature of all such explanations, to call them so, of Christ's death, that they do not bring it into any real relation to the Christian's freedom from the law, or to the controversies which raged round this in the Pauline churches; and this is only one of the ways in which it appears that though using certain Pauline words they have gone off the rails of Pauline thought. The passage in Romans becomes simple as soon as we read it in the light of those we have already examined in 2 Corinthians and in Galatians. It is Christ set forth in His blood who is a propitiation; that is, it is Christ who died. In dying, as St. Paul conceived it, He made our sin His own; He took it on Himself as the reality which it is in God's sight and to God's law: He became sin, became a curse for us. It is this which gives His death a propitiatory character and power; in other words, which makes it possible for God to be at once righteous and a God who accepts as righteous those who believe in Jesus. He is righteous, for in the death of Christ His law is honoured by the Son who takes the sin of the world to Himself as all that it is to God; and He can accept as righteous those who believe in Jesus, for in so believing sin becomes to them what it is to Him. I do not know any word which conveys the truth of this if ' vicarious ' or ' substitutionary ' does not, nor do I know any interpretation of Christ's death which enables us to regard it as a demonstration of love to sinners, if this vicarious or substitutionary character is denied.

There is much preaching *about* Christ's death which fails to be a preaching of Christ's death, and therefore to be in the full sense of the term gospel preaching, because it ignores this. The simplest hearer feels that there is something irrational in saying that the death of Christ is a great proof of love to the sinful, unless there is shown at the same time a rational connection between that death and the responsibilities which sin involves, and from which that death delivers. Perhaps one should beg pardon for using so simple an illustration, but the point is a vital one, and it is necessary to be clear. If I were sitting on the end of the pier, on a summer day, enjoying the sunshine and the air, and some one came along and jumped into the water and got drowned ' to prove his love for me,' I should find it quite unintelligible. I might be much in need of love, but an act in no rational relation to any of my necessities could not prove it. But if I had fallen over the pier and were drowning, and some one sprang into the water, and at the cost of making my peril, or what but for him would be my fate, his own, saved me from death, then I should say, ' Greater love hath no man than this.' I should say it intelligibly, because there would be an intelligible relation between the sacrifice which love made and the necessity from which it redeemed. Is it making any rash assumption to say that there must be such an intelligible relation between the death of Christ—the great act in which His love to sinners is demonstrated—and the sin of the world for which in His blood He is the propitiation? I do not think so. Nor have I yet seen any intelligible relation established between them except that which is the key to the whole of New Testament teaching, and which bids us say, as we look at the Cross, *He* bore *our* sins, *He* died *our* death. It is *so* His love constrains us.

Accepting this interpretation, we see that the *whole* secret of Christianity is contained in Christ's death, and in the believing abandonment of the soul to that death in faith. It is from Christ's death, and the love which it demonstrates, that all Christian inferences are drawn. Once this is accepted, everything else is easy and is secure. ' When we were yet sinners, Christ died for us ; *much more* then being justified now in His blood shall we be saved through Him from the wrath. For if when we were enemies we were reconciled to God through the death of His Son, *much more*, being reconciled, we shall be saved in His life' (Rom. v. 8 ff.). The *much more* implies that in comparison with this primary, this incredibly great proof of God's love, everything else may be taken for granted. It is the same argument which is employed again in chap. viii. 32: ' He that spared not His own Son, but delivered Him up for us all, how shall He not also with Him freely give us all things?' And as it includes everything else on the part of God, so does it also on the part of man. The propitiatory death of Christ, as an all-transcending demonstration of love, evokes in sinful souls a response which is *the whole of Christianity*. The love of Christ constraineth us: whoever can say that can say all that is to be said about the Christian life.

This is not the way in which St. Paul's gospel is usually represented now. Since Pfleiderer's first book on Paulinism was translated, some thirty years ago, it has become almost an axiom with many writers on this subject, that the apostle has two doctrines of reconciliation—a juridical and an ethico-mystical one. There is, on the one hand, the doctrine that Christ died for us, in a sense like that which has just been explained; and on the other, the doctrine that in a mystical union with Christ effected by faith we ethically die with Him and live with Him—this dying with Christ and living with Him, or in Him, being the thing we call salvation. What the relation of the two doctrines is to each other is variously represented. Sometimes they are added together, as by Weiss, as though in spite of their independence justice had to be done to both in the work of man's salvation: a doctrine of justification by faith alone in Christ who died for us finding its in-

dispensable supplement in a doctrine of spiritual regeneration through baptism, in which we are vitally united to
Christ in His death and resurrection. Weiss holds that
it is not Pauline to say that the fellowship of life with
Christ is established by faith; it is only established, according to his view, by baptism.[1] But Paul, it is safe to say,
was incapable of divorcing his thoughts so completely from
reality as to represent the matter thus. He was not
pedantically interpreting a text, he was expounding an
experience; and there is nothing in any Christian experience
answering to this dead or inert justification by faith, which
has no relation to the new life, nor again is there anything
in Christian experience like this new life which is added by
baptism to the experience of justification by faith, but
does not spring out of it. It is a moral wrong to any
serious-minded person to construe his words in this way.
Ritschl does not add the two sides of the Pauline gospel
together as Weiss does. For him they stand side by side
in the apostle, and though salvation is made equally
dependent on the one and the other they are never combined. Romans sixth has nothing to do with Romans
third. The conception of the new life, derived from union
to Christ in His death and resurrection, is just as indifferent to justification by faith, as the representation of
Christ's death in the sixth chapter of Romans is to the
sacrificial representation of the same thing in the third.
The new life or active righteousness of the sixth chapter
bears the same name as the divine righteousness of the
third, but materially they have nothing in common, and
the diversity of their contents stands in no relation to the
origination of the one from the other.[2] Ritschl says it is

---

[1] *Biblische Theologie des Neuen Testaments*, § 84 b. (English Translation,
i. p. 456 ff.).

[2] *Rechtf. u. Versöhnung*, ii. pp. 338 f.

for dogmatic, not biblical, theology to define the problem
created by these two ways of salvation and the apparent
contradiction between them—and to attempt its solution;
and Holtzmann is disposed to censure Weiss for over-
looking this, and attempting an adjustment in his *Biblical
Theology of the New Testament.*[1] But this is manifestly
unfair to St. Paul. The apostle knew nothing about the
distinctions which Theological Encyclopædia draws between
biblical and dogmatic; he was a man of intellectual force
and originality engaged in thinking out a redeeming and
regenerative experience, and the presumption surely is that
his thought will represent somehow the consistency and
unity of his experience. If it does so, it is for his interpreters to make the fact clear without troubling themselves
whether the result is to be labelled biblical or dogmatic.
There are too many people who refuse to take biblical
theology seriously, because it is incoherent, and who refuse
to take dogmatic seriously, because its consistency is arti-
ficially produced by suppressing the exuberant variety of the
New Testament. Perhaps if New Testament experience had
justice done to it, the incoherence of New Testament thinking would not be so obvious. Holtzmann himself attempts
to find points of contact, or lines of connection, or to borrow
from another field an expression of Dr. Fairbairn's, ' develop-
mental coincidences' between the two gospels, though in a
haphazard way; ideas like πίστις, πνεῦμα, and ἀπολύτρωσις,
it is pointed out, find a place in the unfolding of both.[2]

In spite of such high authorities, I venture to put in a
plea for the coherence of St. Paul. If we found the one
theory, as it is called, at one period of his life, and the
other at another, there might be a *prima facie* case for
inconsistency; but when both are set out in full detail, in
a definite sequence, in the same letter, and that the most

---

[1] *Neut. Theologie,* ii. p. 141.   [2] *Ibid.* ii. p. 137 ff.

systematic of all the apostle's writings, and one which aims unambiguously at exhibiting his gospel as a whole, the presumption is all the other way. There are cases in which it is fallacious to say *post hoc, ergo propter hoc,* but this is not one. There could not be a greater mistake than to assume that in the sixth chapter of Romans St. Paul makes a new beginning, forgetting all that he has said, and meeting objections to that gospel which we have been expounding by introducing ideas which have no relation to it, and which may indeed be described as a correction of it, or a supplement to it, or a substitute for it, but which are in no sense whatever a vindication of it. A vindication of it is clearly what St. Paul means to give, and we are bound to assume that he saw what he was doing. He had preached that sinful men are justified freely through faith in Jesus set forth by God as a propitiation in His blood, and his adversaries had brought against this gospel the accusation that it tempted to and even justified continuance in sin. What is his answer? To begin with, it is an expression of moral horror at the suggestion. μὴ γένοιτο! But, in the next place, it is a demonstration of the *inconsistency* of such a line of action with what is involved in justification. 'Men who like us *died* to sin, how shall we still live in it?' (Rom. vi. 2). Why should it be taken for granted that 'dying to sin' is a new idea here, on a new plane, an idea which startles one who has been following only that interpretation of justification which we find in Rom. chs. iii.-v.? It may be a new idea to a man who takes the point of view of St. Paul's opponents, and who does not know what it is to be justified through faith in the propitiation which is in Christ's death; but it is not a new idea to the apostle, nor to any one who has received the reconciliation he preaches; nor would he be offering any logical defence of his gospel if it *were* a new idea. But it is no new idea at all ; it is Christ dying for sin—St. Paul reminds the objectors to his doctrine— it is Christ dying our death on the tree, who evokes the faith by which we become right with God; and the faith which He evokes answers to what He is and to what He does : it is faith which has a death to sin in it. Of course, if Christ's death were not what it has been described to be, it would be nothing to us; it would evoke no faith at all ; but being what it has been described to be, the faith which is the response to it is a faith which inevitably takes moral contents and quality from it. The very same experience in which a man becomes right with God—that is, the experience of faith in Christ who died for sins—is an experience in which he becomes a dead man, so far as sin is concerned, a living man (though this is but the same thing in other words), so far as God is concerned. As long as faith is at its normal tension the life of sin is inconceivable. For faith is an attitude and act of the soul in which the whole being is involved, and it is determined through and through by its object. This, I repeat, is what is given in experience to the man who believes in Christ as St. Paul preaches Him in Rom. iii. 25 f., and this is the ethical justification of his gospel. What is fundamental here is Christ in the character of propitiation, Christ bearing our sin in His death ; it is this Christ and no other who draws us in faith to Himself, so that in and through faith His death and life become ours. The forensic theory of atonement, as it is called, is not unrelated to the ethico-mystical ; it is not parallel to it ; it is not a mistaken *ad hominem* or rather *ad Pharisaeum* mode of thought which ought to be displaced by the other ; it has the essential eternal truth in it by which *and by which alone* the experiences are generated in which the strength of the other is supposed to lie. I do not much care for the expression 'mystical union' with Christ, for it has been much abused, and in St. Paul especially has led to much hasty misconstruction of the New Testament; but if we are to use it at all, we must say that it is something which is not a substitute for, but the fruit of, the vicarious death of Christ. It owes its very being to that atonement outside of us, that finished work of Christ, which some would use it to discredit. And it is because this is so, that St. Paul can use it, so far as he does so, not to replace, or to supplement, or to correct, but to vindicate and show the moral adequacy of his doctrine of justification. Of course, in the last resort, the objection brought against St. Paul's gospel can only be practically refuted. It must be lived down, not argued down; hence the hortatory tone of Romans vi. But the new life is involved in the faith evoked by the sin-bearing death of Christ, and in nothing else; it is involved in this, and this is pictorially presented in baptism. Hence the use which St. Paul makes of this sacrament in the same chapter. He is able to use it in his argument in the way he does because baptism and faith are but the outside and the inside of the same thing. If baptism, then, is symbolically inconsistent with continuance in sin, as is apparent to every one, faith is really inconsistent with it. But faith is relative to the δικαιοσύνη θεοῦ, the divine justification which is St. Paul's gospel, and therefore that gospel in turn is beyond moral reproach.[1] The true connection of the apostle's ideas is perfectly put in the glorious lines of that great mystic, St. Bernard—

> *Propter mortem quam tulisti*
> *Quando pro me defecisti;*
> *Cordis mei cor dilectum*
> *In te meum fer affectum!*

---

[1] For a fuller treatment of this point, see article in *Expositor*, October 1901, 'The Righteousness of God and the New Life.'

As a comment on the connection between Romans iii.-v. and Romans vi.-viii. —on the relation of the substitution of Christ to ethical identification with Him—of Christ for us to Christ in us or we in Him—this for truth and power will never be surpassed.   But blot out the first two lines, and the inspiration of the third and fourth is gone.   Precisely so, if we blot out the 'forensic' gospel of St. Paul we shall find that the 'ethico-mystical' one has the breath of its life withdrawn.

It is possible to go more into detail here on lines suggested by St. Paul himself.   Christ died our death on the cross, and the faith which that death evokes has a death in it also. But how are we to interpret this?   By relation to what are we to define the death which is involved in faith?   We may define it by relation to anything by relation to which Christ's death has been defined.   Thus, following the apostle, we can say that the death involved in faith is (1) a death to sin. Christ's death on the cross was a death to sin, the apostle tells us, in the sense that it introduced Him to a condition in which He had no longer any responsibility in relation to it (Rom. vi. 10).   He had assumed the responsibility of it in love, but He had also discharged it, and sin had no claim on Him further.   For us, dying to sin may seem to have a different meaning ; it is not only a discharge from its responsibilities that is wanted, but a deliverance from its power. But this can only come on the foundation of the other ; it is the discharge from the responsibilities of sin involved in Christ's death and appropriated in faith, which is the motive power in the daily ethical dying to sin.   It really is such a motive power, and the only one in the world, when we realise what it is.   But just as death to the law—to anticipate for a moment another experience involved in faith in the death of Christ—needs to be realised by ceaseless vigilance against all that would enslave the conscience, and against everything in our nature that makes us seek external supports, and authorities to relieve us of the responsibility of becoming a law to ourselves under the constraint of the cross, so must death to sin also be realised by moral effort.   It is involved in faith, so far as the principle and the motive power are concerned ; the man who plants his whole hope in the revelation of God made in Christ the propitiation is a man who in the act and for the time is taking sin, death, the law, and the judgment of God, as all that they are to Christ ; that is, he is owning sin, and disowning it utterly ; acknowledging it as unreservedly in all its responsibility, and separating himself as entirely from it, as Christ did when He died.   Such faith, involving such a relation to sin as can be called a death to it, covers the whole life, and is a moral guarantee for it ; yet the death to sin which is lodged in it has to be carried out in a daily mortification of evil, the initial crucifixion with Christ in a daily crucifixion of the passions and lusts.

(2) It may even be said more specifically that the death involved in faith is a death to the flesh.   This is the point of the difficult passage in Romans viii. 3 f.   St. Paul is there describing the way of salvation from sin, and says that the law was impotent in the matter owing to the flesh. The flesh virtually means sin in its constitutional and instinctive character—sin as the nature or the second nature of man, it does not here matter which.   What the law could not do God took another way of doing.   He sent His Son in the likeness of flesh of sin, and as a sin-offering, and in so doing condemned sin in the flesh.   ὁμοίωμα here no doubt emphasises Christ's likeness to us : it is not meant to suggest difference or unreality in His nature.   He was all that we are, short of sin.   Yet He came in connection with sin, or as a sin-offering, and it is through this that we must interpret the expression ' condemned sin in the flesh.'

It does not mean that Christ showed sin to be inexcusable, by Himself leading a sinless life; there is no salvation, no emancipation from sin in that. The condemnation is the act of God, and in sending His own Son in connection with sin—which must mean in the one connection with it which St. Paul ever refers to, *i.e.* as a propitiation for it—God condemned it in the flesh. His judgment came on it in the death which Christ died in our nature, and with that judgment its right and its power in our nature came to an end. I say its right and its power, for the things are related. Until the responsibilities involved in sin have been fully acknowledged and met, as they are acknowledged and met in the death of Christ, its power remains; to express the truth psychologically, until sin is expiated, the sinner has a bad conscience, and as long as a man has a bad conscience, he cannot begin to be a good man. It is because Christ's death deals effectually with the responsibility of sin, and puts right with God the man who believes in Him, that it can do for our nature what law could never do—break sin's power. Weiss and others have argued that it is a mistake to find here the idea of expiation: the context is interested only in the moral deliverance from evil. But from the point of view of St. Paul, this is not a reasonable objection : it is setting the end against the means. He knew by experience that sin could only have its power broken by being expiated, and that is precisely what he teaches here. Only, he gives it a peculiar turn. The fact that expiation has been made through Christ's death for sin in the very nature which we wear, is used to bring out the idea that in that nature, at all events, sin can have no indefeasible right and no impregnable seat. The death involved in faith in Christ is a death not only to sin generally, but to sin in the constitutional and virulent character suggested by the flesh. But like the other 'deaths,' this one too needs to be morally realised. ' Mortify therefore your members which are upon the earth.'

(3) Further, the death involved in faith is repeatedly defined by St. Paul as a death to the law, or to law in general (Gal. ii. 19 ; Rom. vi. 14, vii. 4). There is undoubtedly something paradoxical in this, and it is the point at which St. Paul's gospel, from the beginning, was most misunderstood and most assailed. On the one hand, when Christ died, justice was done to the law of God, both as an imperative and as a condemning law, as it had never been done before. The will of God had been honoured by a life of perfect obedience, and the awful experience of death in which God's inexorable judgment on sin comes home to the conscience had been borne in the same obedience and love by His sinless Son. On the other hand, when this death evokes the faith for which it appeals, the righteous requirement of the law is fulfilled in the believer ; the law gets its due in his life also, or, as the apostle puts it, it is established by faith. How is it, then, that faith involves a death to the law ? It is through the assurance, given to faith at the cross, that so far as doing the will of God is concerned, a new and living way has been found. It is not the law in its old legal form—the law of statutory injunctions and prohibitions—which is to generate goodness in sinful man ; it is the law glorified in the atonement. The whole inspiration of the Christian life lies here, and it *is* an inspiration, not a statutory requirement. Nothing is to count in the life of a Christian which does not come with perfect freedom from this source. This explains the extraordinary emphasis which St. Paul everywhere lays on liberty. Liberty is the correlative of responsibility ; man must be perfectly free that the whole weight of his responsibilities may come upon him. But this weight of responsibility cannot be faced, and would not sanctify even if it

could be faced, *in vacuo* ; it can be faced only when we
know God in Christ crucified ; and it does sanctify, when
the constraint of the atonement, with its awful homage to
the holiness of God, descends upon the heart.   But this is
all that is required, for this is too great to be compromised
by alliance with anything else.   Perfect freedom, with entire
responsibility to the Redeemer—the obligation to be a law
to oneself, with the power of Christ's passion resting upon
the spirit—that is the death to law which St. Paul contemplates.   No statutes, no traditions of men, no dogmata,
intellectual or moral, no scruples in the consciences of
others, are to have legal obligations for us any longer.   Not
even the letters written by the finger of God on the tables
of stone constitute a legal obligation for the Christian.   *All*
that he is to be must come freely out of the atoning death
of Christ.   He is dead to the law—in the widest sense of
the word, he is dead to law—through the body of Christ.
From this freedom we are always being tempted to relapse.
We are always establishing for ourselves, or letting others
impose upon us, customs—whether intellectual, as creeds ;
or ethical, as the conventional ways of being charitable or
of worshipping God—which though good in themselves,
tend to corrupt the world just because they are customs :
in other words, we are always tacitly denying that the death
of Christ does full justice to law in every sense of the term,
and that for those who believe in it law exists henceforth
only in the divine glory of the atonement, and in the life
which it inspires.

It may seem astonishing that in all this no reference has
been made to the Spirit, but the omission, I think, can be
justified.[1]   For one thing, St. Paul himself discusses the
whole subject of the Christian's death with Christ, as

[1] For a fuller treatment of the Spirit and the New Life, see article in
Expositor, December 1901.

involved in Christ's death and the Christian's faith in it,
without reference to the Spirit. The Spirit is not
mentioned in the sixth chapter of Romans. I do not say
it is not implied—for instance, in the allusions to baptism ;
but it is implied *in* all that the apostle says ; it is not
implied as something to be *added* to it. Theologically, the
Spirit is the divine correlative of faith, and of the dying
with Christ and living with Christ, of which we have been
speaking ; it is the power of God which is manifested in
every Christian experience whatever. It is not something
specifically divine which comes in through baptism and has
no relation to faith and justification ; it is related in the
same way to all ; it is the divine factor in all that restores
man to, and maintains him in, the life of God. But the
Spirit does not work *in vacuo*. He glorifies Christ. He
works through the propitiation, interpreting, revealing,
applying it ; and when we talk of the Spirit as an abstractly
supernatural power, a power of God not working through
the gospel and its appeal to the reason, conscience, and will
of man, we are not on Christian ground. Without the
Spirit—that is, without God—all that has been said about
the meaning of Christ's death could not win upon men ; but
just because the action of the Spirit is implied as the correlative of faith at every point, it is illegitimate to call it in
to explain one Christian experience more than another—for
instance, to derive regeneration from it, or the new life, but
not justification. Either Spirit or Faith may truly be said
to be co-extensive with Christianity, and therefore they are
co-extensive with each other. But if we are speaking of the
new moral life of the Christian, and ask what we mean by
the Spirit psychologically—that is, what form it takes as an
experience- -I should say it is indistinguishable from that
infinite assurance of God's love, given in Christ's death,
through which the Christian is made more than conqueror

in all the difficulties of life, inward or external.   It is with
this assurance the Spirit is connected when St. Paul opens
his discussion of the subject in Romans v. 5 : ' The love of
God is shed abroad in our hearts through the Holy Spirit
given to us.'   It is with this same assurance he concludes
his discussion, ch. viii. 35 : ' Who shall separate us from the
love of God ? '   The triumphant certainty of this love, a
certainty always recurring to and resting on that miracle of
miracles, the sin-bearing death of Christ, is the same thing as
joy in the Holy Spirit, and it is this joy which is the Christian's
strength.   From the Spirit, then, or from the love of God
as an assured possession, the Christian life may equally be
explained.   And it is not another, but the same explanation,
when we say that it is begotten and sustained from beginning
to end by the virtue which dwells in the propitiatory death
of Jesus.

(V.) When we come to the epistles of the Imprisonment
a new range seems to be given to Christ's death, and to the
work of reconciliation which is accomplished in it.   This
holds, at least, of the Epistles to the Colossians and
Ephesians; so far as Philippians is concerned, we find
ourselves in the same circle of ideas as in Galatians and
Romans.   The close parallel, indeed, of Phil. iii. 9 f. with
the exposition of the apostolic gospel in these earlier letters
is a striking proof of the tenacity and consistency of
St. Paul's thought.   But in Colossians we are confronted with
a new situation.   ' The world' which is the object of
reconciliation is no longer as in 2 Cor. v. 19, or Rom.
iii. 19, the world of sinful men ; it is a world on a grander
scale.   ' God has been pleased through Him to reconcile all
things to Himself, having made peace through the blood of
His cross, through Him, whether they be things on earth or
things in heaven ' (Col. i. 20).   The reconciliation of sinful
men is represented as though it were only a part of this

vaster work. 'And you,' it is added, 'who were once
estranged, and enemies in mind by wicked works, He has
now reconciled in the body of His flesh through death'
(v. 21 f.). The same ideas are found in the Epistle to the
Ephesians (i. 7 ff.). Here we start with the historical
Christ, 'in whom we have our redemption through His
blood, even the forgiveness of our trespasses'; but when the
mystery of Christ's work is revealed to the Christian intelligence, it is seen to have as its end 'the gathering
together in one of all things in Him, both things in (or
above) the heavens and things on the earth' (v. 10). This
enlargement of the scope of Christ's death, or, if we prefer
to call it so, this extension of its virtue into regions where
we cannot speak of it from experience, has sometimes had a
disconcerting effect, and the bearings of it are not quite
clear. It is argued by some, who naturally wish to be as
precise as possible in interpreting their author, that 'the
things in heaven and the things on earth,' which are referred to in the passages just quoted, must be spiritual
beings; only such can be the objects of reconciliation, for
only such can have estranged themselves from God by sin.
But where do we find the idea of any such estrangement
in Scripture, except in the case of disobedient angels to
whom the idea of reconciliation is never applied? For
answer we are pointed to various passages in the Old and
the New Testament, not to mention Jewish literature
outside, in which there is the conception of spiritual beings
whose fortunes are somehow bound up with those of men.
Thus in Isaiah xxiv. 21, a late passage in which apocalypse
begins to displace prophecy, we read: 'It shall come to
pass in that day that the Lord shall punish the host of
the high ones on high, and the kings of the earth upon
the earth.' The two sets of persons here referred to
somehow correspond to each other; there is a counter-

part in the unseen world of the characters and fortunes visible on earth. Again, in the book of Daniel we hear of ' the prince of the kingdom of Persia ' (ch. x. 13), ' the prince of Grecia ' (x. 20), and ' your prince ' (x. 21), meaning the prince of the children of Israel : the princes, as the name Michael in x. 21 shows, being in all cases angelic beings, who in some way or other were identified with the nations, representing them in the unseen world, pleading their cause, fighting their battles, and mysteriously involved in their fortunes. It is something quite analogous to this that we find in the early chapters of Revelation, where the epistles of the risen Lord are addressed to the angels of the churches. The angel is not a bishop ; he is, so to speak, the personification of the church in the world unseen ; the spiritual counterpart of it, conceived as a person on whom its character and responsibilities will be visited somehow. It is the same idea, with an individual application, that we find in our Lord's word about the angels of the little ones, who in heaven do always behold the face of His heavenly Father (Matt. xviii. 10), and again in the book of Acts (xii. 15), where the people who would not believe that Peter had been released from prison said, ' It is his angel.' On such a background of Jewish belief the interpretation of these passages has been essayed. It is not man only, we are asked to believe, who has been involved in sin, and in the alienation from God which is its consequence ; the sin of man has consequences which reach far beyond man himself. It stretches downward through nature, which has been made subject to vanity because of it, and it stretches upward into a spiritual world which we may not be able to realise, but which, like nature, is compromised somehow by our sin, and entangled in our responsibility to God. For these higher beings, then, as well as for man, Christ has done His reconciling work, and when it is finished they as well as we will be gathered together in one in Him.

It would perhaps be going too far to say that there is nothing in this, and that no such ideas ever floated vaguely before the apostle's imagination. The people to whom he wrote believed in ' thrones and dominions and principalities and powers '; and although there is a touch of indifference, not to say scorn, in some of his own allusions to the high-sounding names—for instance, in Ephesians i. 22 f.—they had some sort of reality for him too. There are passages like Col. ii. 15, or those in which he refers to τὰ στοιχεῖα τοῦ κόσμου (Gal. iv. 3, Col. ii. 8), where he seems to connect the spiritual beings in question with the angels through whom the law was given (Gal. iii. 19, Acts vii. 53, Gal. ii. 2), and to represent the superseding of Judaism by Christianity as a victory of Jesus over these inferior but refractory powers to whom for a while the administration of human affairs, and especially of the immature, materialistic and legal stages of religion had been committed. But if he had definitely held such a view as has just been expounded, the probabilities are that it would have told more decidedly on his thinking, and found less ambiguous expression in his writings. He could not, for example, have given that complete account of his gospel—of the need for a righteousness of God, of the provision of it, and of the vindication of it—which he does give in Romans i.-viii., without so much as alluding to these vaguely conceived beings.[1] At best they could belong only to the quasi-poetical representation of his faith, not to the gospel which he preached on the basis of experience, nor to

[1] Rom. viii. 38 f. does not refute this, for the apostle's exposition of his thoughts is already complete, and this is an emotional utterance in which there is no more need or possibility of defining Christ's death by relation to angels and principalities and powers, than by relation to abstractions like height and depth. The only *thought* in the passage is that God's love in Christ is the final reality from which nothing can separate the believer.

the theology or philosophy which was its intellectual expression.   And when we look at the epistles of the Captivity
generally, our minds are rather drawn in another direction.
The enlarged scope of the work of reconciliation is part of that
expansion, so to speak, of Christ's person from a historical
to a cosmical significance which is characteristic of these
epistles as a whole.   Christ is no longer a second Adam,
the head of a new humanity, as in the earlier letters (Rom.
v. 12 ff., 1 Cor. xv. 45 ff.); He is the centre of the universe.
He is a person so great that St. Paul is obliged to reconstruct
His whole world around Him.   He is the primary source
of all creation, its principle of unity, its goal (Col. i. 15 ff.).
In consistency with this, the meaning and efficacy of what
He has done extends through it all.   His Person and work
have absolute significance; wherever we have to speak of
revelation or of reconciliation, in whatever world, in whatever
relations, it is of Him we have to speak.   Whether St. Paul
would have presented this genuinely Christian truth to his
imagination in the somewhat fantastic fashion just explained
may be more or less doubtful; in any case it is of little
consequence.   What is of consequence is his conviction that
in Jesus Christ dwelt all the fulness of the Godhead—all
that makes God in the full sense of the term God—bodily,
that is, in organic unity and completeness; and that the
same completeness and finality belong to His reconciling
work.   'The blood of His cross': it is in this we find the
resolution of all discords, not only in the life of man, but in
the universe at large.   It is in this we see a divine love which
does not shrink from taking on itself to the uttermost the
moral responsibility for the world it has made, and for all
the orders of being in it, and all their failures and fortunes.
The eternal truth of this different ages and circumstances
will picture to themselves in different ways; all we need
to care for is that ways of picturing it which are uncon-

genial to our imaginations do not deprive us of the truth itself.

It is a smaller but not a less attractive application of the idea of reconciliation, as accomplished in Christ's death, when we find it in the second chapter of Ephesians as the reconciliation of Jew and Gentile in the one body of Christ (vv. 11-22). The application may to us seem casual, but this is one of the great thoughts of St. Paul. 'Is God a God of Jews only?' he asks in Rom. iii. 29 as he contemplates Christ set forth as a propitiation in His blood. Is the great appeal of the Cross one which is intelligible only to men of a single race, or to which only those who have had a particular training can respond? On the contrary, there is nothing in the world so universally intelligible as the Cross; and hence it is the meeting-place not only of God and man, but of all races and conditions of men with each other. There is neither Greek nor Jew, male nor female, bond nor free, there. The Cross is the basis of a universal religion, and has in it the hope of a universal peace. But of all Christian truths which are confessed in words, this is that which is most outrageously denied in deed. There is not a Christian church nor a Christian nation in the world which believes heartily in the Atonement as the extinction of privilege, and the levelling up of all men to the same possibility of life in Christ, to the same calling to be saints. The spirit of privilege, in spite of the Cross, is obstinately rooted everywhere even among Christian men.

An examination of the pastoral epistles, quite apart from the critical questions that have been raised as to their authorship, does not introduce us to any new ideas on our subject. It is at all events genuinely Pauline when we read in 1 Tim. ii. 5, 'There is one God, one Mediator also between God and men, Himself man, Christ Jesus, who gave Himself a ransom for all (ἀντίλυτρον ὑπὲρ πάντων).' It is the ransoming death in virtue of which Jesus does mediate between God and sinners; but for it, He would not be a mediator in any sense relevant to man's situation. This, as Holtzmann has noticed, is in harmony with the use of 'mediator' in the Epistle to the Hebrews. There also Jesus is Mediator, but it is of a covenant which is characterised as κρείττων, καινή, and νέα; He is the means through which, at the cost of His death, sinners enter into the perfect religious relation to God. But though this idea is found in Hebrews, it does not follow that it is unpauline in itself, nor even (though ἀντίλυτρον is found here only in the New Testament) that it is unpauline in expression. The dying with Christ, referred to in 2 Tim. ii. 6, is akin rather to what we have found in 2 Cor. chs. i. and iv. than to Romans vi.: it is a share in martyr sufferings which is meant, not formally the mortification of the old man. In Titus there are two passages which require to be mentioned. The first is in ch. ii. 14, where we read of 'our Saviour Jesus Christ, who gave Himself for us that He might redeem us from all unrighteousness (ἀνομίας) and purify for Himself a people of His own, zealous of good works.' It is somewhat peddling to suggest, as Holtzmann does,[1] that Paul would rather have said we were redeemed from νόμος than from ἀνομία, and that even in touching on a Pauline thought an unpauline expression is used (λυτρώσηται for 'redeem'). The whole expression, λυτροῦσθαι as well as ἀνομία, comes from Ps. cxxx. 8, and St. Paul might have liberty to quote the Old Testament as well as anybody else. Nevertheless, the general impression one gets from the pastoral epistles is, that as a doctrine Christianity was now complete and could be taken for granted; it is not in process of being

[1] *Neut. Theologie*, ii. 265 f.

hammered out, as in the Epistle to the Galatians ; there is nothing creative in the statement of it ; and it is the combination of fulness and of something not unlike formalism that raises doubts as to the authorship. St. Paul was inspired, but the writer of these epistles is sometimes only orthodox. One feels this with reference to the second passage in Titus (iii. 4 ff.) : ' When the kindness of God our Saviour, and His love toward man, appeared, not by works done in righteousness which we did ourselves, but according to His mercy He saved us, through the washing of regeneration and renewing of the Holy Ghost, which He poured out upon us richly through Jesus Christ our Saviour : that, being justified by His grace, we might be made heirs according to the hope of eternal life.' St. Paul could no doubt have said all this, but probably he would have said it otherwise, and not all at a time. In any case, it adds nothing to the New Testament teaching on the death of Christ as we have already examined it.

CHAPTER IV

THE EPISTLE TO THE HEBREWS

THE Epistle to the Hebrews is in many ways one of the most perplexing books of the New Testament. It stands quite alone and is peculiarly independent, yet it has affinities with almost every strain of thought to be found elsewhere in primitive Christianity, and points of historical attachment for it have been sought all round the compass.[1] Thus there are those who think its true line of descent is to be traced to James, Cephas, and John—the three apostles who seemed to be pillars in the mother church of Jerusalem. It is the last and finest product of that type of Christian mind which we see at work in the fifteenth chapter of Acts. Perhaps this was the feeling of the person to whom the address—πρὸς Ἑβραίους—is due. When we examine the epistle closely, however, we discover that there is very little to be found in this direction to explain its peculiarities. Others, again, would trace it to the school of St. Paul. This, no doubt, has a greater plausibility. Discounting altogether the alleged Pauline authorship, the epistle has many points of contact with St. Paul in language, and some in thought. But we cannot fail to be struck with the fact that where the language coincides with St. Paul's, the thought does not; and that where the minds of the

[1] For a full discussion on this point, see Holtzmann, *Neut. Theologie*, ii. 281 ff.

authors meet, their language is independent.   Thus both
St. Paul and the writer to the Hebrews speak of the law,
of what the law cannot do (Rom. viii. 3 ; Heb. x. 1), of
the superseding of the law (Rom. x. 4 ; Heb. vii. 12), of
faith (Rom. iv. ; Heb. xi.), of a righteousness according to
faith (Rom. i. 17 ; Heb. xi. 7), and so on ; but when they
use the same words they do not mean the same thing.
The law to St. Paul is mainly the moral law, embodying
God's requirements from man ; in this epistle, it is the
religious constitution under which Israel lived, and which
gave it a certain though an imperfect access to God.   In
St. Paul and in this epistle alike the law is superseded in
the Christian religion, but the relation between them is
differently defined in the two cases.   St. Paul defines law
and gospel mainly by contrast ; in Hebrews they are set in
a more positive relation to one another.   It used to be
life under external statutory authority, now it is life under
inspiration, and the two are mutually exclusive—such is
St. Paul's conception : see Romans vi. and 2 Cor. iii.   It
used to be life under the shadowy, the unreal, that which
could bring nothing to perfection ; now it is life under the
real, the eternal, that which makes perfect for ever ; the
shadow is abandoned, because the coming good which cast
it is here : see Hebrews vii.-x.   No doubt such contrasts as
this (between St. Paul and the Epistle to the Hebrews)
require qualification, but broadly they are true, and they
could be illustrated at many other points.   At the present
moment the favourite tendency among critics is to explain
the peculiarities of the epistle by attaching it neither to
the primitive Christianity of Jerusalem, nor in the first
instance to the characteristic thoughts of St. Paul (though
both of course are implied), but to the quasi-philosophical
mind of Alexandrian Judaism.   It is there we find the
contrast of seen and unseen, of sensible and intelligible, of

this world and the world to come, of the transitory and the abiding, of earth and heaven, of which this epistle makes so much ; and there also the λόγος, which mediates between God and the world, is presented in many of the aspects (*e.g.* as Intercessor, as Mediator, as High Priest) in which Jesus figures here. But here again the differences outweigh the resemblances. The Son of God does exercise in this epistle many of the functions which in Philo are assigned to the Logos ; but in order to exercise them He must assume human nature and pass through all human experience—conceptions which are a direct contradiction of all that Logos in Philo means. Evidently the author of this epistle, whatever his intellectual affinities, combined with an extraordinary sensitiveness to all that was being thought and said in the world in which he lived an extraordinary power of holding fast his own thoughts, of living in his own mind, and letting it work along its own lines.

Of all New Testament writers he is the most theological—that is, he is most exclusively occupied with presenting Christianity as the final and absolute religion ; not *a* religion, in the sense in which it might concede a legitimate place to others, but religion *simpliciter*, because it does perfectly what all religion aims to do. This is what is expressed in his favourite word αἰώνιος (eternal). St. John in his gospel and epistles uses this word twenty-three times, but invariably to qualify *life*, and with him it is rather the combination than the adjective which is characteristic. But in Hebrews αἰώνιος is used far more significantly, though less frequently. Jesus is author of ' eternal ' salvation (v. 9), *i.e.* of final salvation, which has no peril beyond ; all that salvation can mean is secured by Him. The elements of Christianity include preaching on ' eternal ' judgment (vi. 2), *i.e.* a judgment which has the character of finality, from which there is no appeal, beyond which there is no fear

or no hope.   Christ has obtained 'eternal' redemption for
us (ix. 12) : not a redemption like that which was annually
achieved for Israel, and which had to be annually repeated,
as though its virtue faded away, but a redemption the
validity of which abides for ever.   Christ has offered
Himself through 'eternal' spirit (ix. 14), *i.e.* in Christ's
sacrifice we see the final revelation of what God is, that
behind which there is nothing in God ; so that the religion
which rests on that sacrifice rests on the ultimate truth of
the divine nature, and can never be shaken.   Those who are
called receive the promise of the 'eternal' inheritance
(ix. 15) : not an earthly Canaan, in which they are strangers
and pilgrims, and from which they may be exiled, but the
city which has the foundations, from which God's people go
no more out.   And finally, the blood of Christ is the blood
of an 'eternal' covenant (xiii. 20), *i.e.* in the death of
Christ a religious relation is constituted between God and
men which has the character of finality.   God, if it may be
so expressed, has spoken His last word ; He has nothing in
reserve ; the foundation has been laid of the kingdom which
can never be removed.   It is this conception of absoluteness
or finality in everything Christian which dominates the book.
The conception, of course, is involved in all Christian
experience, but to make it as explicit as it is in this epistle
does not come naturally to every one.   There are minds to
which a less reflective religion seems warmer and more
congenial : they miss in a writing like this the intimacy and
glow which pervade the epistles of St. Paul.   Those in whom
theological interest preponderates over religious may call
the Epistle to the Hebrews the high water-mark of inspiration ; those whose religion makes them averse to theology
can call it the high water-mark of uninspired writing.

Speaking generally, the epistle may be said to give a
description of the Person and Work of Christ as constituting

the perfect religion for men, and to define this religion in relation to the ancient religion of the Jews as embodied in the Tabernacle or Temple service. Curiously enough, the Person and Work of Christ thus interpreted have been looked at, so to speak, from both ends. Some theologians, of whom Westcott may be taken as a type, begin at the beginning, or rather at chap. i. 3. They start with the pre-existent, the eternal Son of God. They point to what He essentially is—the brightness of the Father's glory and the express image of His substance. They point to His providential action—He bears or guides all things by the word of His power. They point to the work He did as incarnate—He made purgation of sins. They point to the exaltation which followed—He sat down on the right hand of the Majesty in the Heavens. And then they draw the general conclusion that what Christ did, according to the epistle, was to fulfil man's destiny under the conditions of the fall. That destiny, it is assumed, He would have fulfilled in any case. The incarnation is part of the original plan of the world ; only, in the peculiar circumstances of the case in hand—that is, under the conditions of the fall—the incarnation had to be modified into an atonement. This is one way of construing the writer's ideas. Another is represented by writers like Seeberg, who begins, if one may say so, at the end. The Christ of the author is essentially Christ the High Priest, in the heavenly sanctuary, mediating between God and men, securing for sinful men access to God and fellowship with Him. Christ exercises His High Priestly function in heaven, but it rests upon the death which He died on earth. Though Seeberg does not include Christ's death in His priestly ministry, he frankly admits that His priestly ministry is based on His death, and that but for His death He could not be a priest at all. Hence his argument runs in exactly the opposite direction from

Westcott's.   Christ is essentially a priest, the work of
bringing sinners into fellowship with God is essentially the
work He has to do, and the work He does.   It is in that
work alone that we know Him.   But to do it He had to die,
and in order to die He had to have a body prepared for
Him, *i.e.* He had to become incarnate (ch. x. 5).   It is not
the incarnation which is taken for granted, and the atonement which in the peculiar circumstances of man's case is
wrought into it or wrought out of it to meet an emergency;
it is the actual fact of an atonement and a reconciling
priestly ministry which is made the foundation of everything; the incarnation is defined solely by relation to it.
The atonement, and the priestly or reconciling ministry of
Christ, are the end, to which the incarnation is relative as
the means.   That this last is the view of the epistle and of
the New Testament in general I do not doubt: it is the only
view which has an experimental, as opposed to a speculative,
basis; and I venture to say that the other shifts the centre
of gravity in the New Testament so disastrously as to make
great parts of it, and these most vital parts, unintelligible.
One could not go to the New Testament with a more misleading schematism in his mind than that which is provided
by the conception of the incarnation, and its relation to the
atonement, to which Westcott's influence has given currency
in many circles.   But leaving this larger question on one
side, we may start with the fact that both schools of
interpreters meet in the middle, and find the real content of
the epistle, religious and theological, in what it has to say
of the historical Christ.   And that, beyond a doubt, is
concentrated in what it has to say of His death.   It was
with ' the suffering of death ' in view that He became
incarnate; it is because of ' the suffering of death ' that He
is crowned with that glory and honour in which He appears
in the presence of God on our behalf.   Here then we come

to our proper subject again, and may ask, as in the case of
St. Paul, in what relations the death of Christ is defined by
the writer so as to bring out its meaning.

In the first place, it is defined by relation to God, and
especially, as in St. Paul, by relation to His love. It is by
the grace of God that Jesus tastes death for every man
(ii. 9). God is not conceived in this epistle, or in any part
of the New Testament, as a malignant or hostile being who
has to be won by gifts to show His goodwill to man : whatever the death of Christ is or does, it is and does in the
carrying out of His purpose. It is the grace of God to
sinners which is demonstrated in it. This is involved also
in two other ideas emphasised in the epistle. One is the
idea that no man takes the honour of priesthood to himself
of his own motion : he must be called of God, as Aaron was
(v. 4). Christ has had this call ; we hear it in the 110th
Psalm, which He Himself applied to Himself (Mark xii.
35 ff.). 'Thou art a priest for ever, after the order of
Melchisedec.' It is true that the priest represents the
people toward God, but he can only do so by God's
appointment, and consequently it is a work of God which
he does, a gracious work, in which he is not persuading God,
as it were, against His will, but on the contrary carrying out
His will for the good of men. The other idea used in the
interpretation of Christ's work, and especially of His death,
which connects them in a similar way with God, is the idea
of obedience. Jesus, though He were Son, yet learned
obedience through the things which He suffered (v. 8).
When He appeared in the body which God had prepared
for Him, it was with the words on His lips, 'Lo, I come to
do *Thy will*, O God' (x. 7). There is nothing in Christ's
life and death of irresponsibility or adventure. It is all
obedience, and therefore it is all revelation. We see God
in it because it is not His own will but the will of the

Father which it accomplished. Even when we come to consider its relation to sin, this must be borne in mind. Atonement is not something contrived, as it were, behind the Father's back; it is the Father's way of making it possible for the sinful to have fellowship with Him. The author introduces one idea, not very easy to define, in this connection. In speaking of the actual course of Christ in life and death, he says, ' It became Him (ἔπρεπεν γὰρ αὐτῷ) for whom are all things and through whom are all things, in bringing many sons unto glory, to make the Captain of their salvation perfect through sufferings ' (ii. 10). What ἔπρεπεν suggests is not so much the kind of necessity we have found in other places in the New Testament as moral congruity or decorum. Suffering and death are our lot; it is congruous with God's nature—we can feel, so to speak, the moral propriety of it—when He makes suffering and death the lot of Him who is to be our Saviour. He would not be perfect in the character or part of Saviour if He did not have this experience. What this suggests is the interpretation of Christ's death by moral æsthetics rather than by moral law, by a rule to be apprehended in feeling rather than in conscience. It is moving and impressive, this action in congruity with God's nature and our state, whether we see a more inevitable necessity for it or not. In all these ways, at all events, the writer attaches Christ's death to the grace, the will, and the character of God; and in all these ways, therefore, he warns us against setting that death and God in any antagonism to each other.

But besides defining it by relation to God, the writer defines Christ's death also by relation to sin. At the very beginning, in the sublime sentence in which He introduces the Son, His earthly work is summed up in the phrase: ' having made purgation of sins ' (i. 3). How this is done, he does not tell at this point, but the sequel makes it indubitable. It was done by His sacrificial death. So, again, he speaks of Christ as being once offered to bear the sins of many (ix. 28); as having been once manifested at the end of the world to put away sin by the sacrifice of Himself (ix. 26); as being a merciful and faithful high priest in our relations to God to make propitiation for the sins of the people (ii. 17); as having offered one sacrifice for sins for ever, and having perfected for ever by that sacrifice those who are being sanctified (x. 12-14). There is the same sacrificial conception in all the references in the epistle to the blood of Christ. He entered into the most holy place with ($\delta\iota\grave{a}$) His own blood (ix. 12). The blood of Christ shall purge your conscience from dead works (ix. 14). We have boldness to enter into the holiest in the blood of Jesus (x. 19). His blood is the blood of the covenant with which we are sanctified, and to lapse from the Christian religion is to be guilty of the inconceivable, the unpardonable sin, of counting that blood a profane thing (x. 29). In all these ways the death of Christ is defined as a sacrificial death, or as a death having relation to sin: the two things are one. It is quite possible to lose ourselves here by trying to give to details in the sacrificial language of the epistle an importance which they will not bear. The writer refers to sacrifices of different kinds in his interpretation of the death of Christ. Sometimes he speaks of it in connection with the Old Testament sin offerings; at others in connection with the covenant sacrifices at Sinai, on which the ancient relation of God to His people was based; more than all, in connection with the annual sacrifices on the great day of atonement, when the earthly sanctuary was purged of its defilement, and the high priest entered into the most holy place, representing and embodying Israel's access to God and fellowship with Him. But no emphasis is laid on the distinguishing features of these various sacrifices: they are

looked at simply in the expiatory or atoning significance
which is common to them all.   They represent a divinely
appointed way of dealing with sin, in order that it may not
bar fellowship with God; and the writer thinks of them
broadly in this light.   I do not feel at liberty to belittle
this, as is sometimes done, and to say with Holtzmann that
the convincing power of the writer's arguments reaches
precisely as far as our conviction of the divine origin of the
Mosaic cultus, of the atoning power of sacrificial blood, and
of the typical significance of the sacrificial ritual ; the tacit
assumption being that in regard to all these things rational
conviction can reach but a very little way.   As we have seen
already, the death of Christ is defined by relation to sin in
many places in the New Testament where no use, at least
no explicit use, is made of sacrificial phraseology.   Such
phraseology is not essential either to reach or to express the
truth held by Christian faith as to the relation of Christ's
death to sin.   Neither is it forced by the author of the
epistle : he only expresses by means of it, and that, as we
have seen, with the greatest freedom, the conviction of all
New Testament Christians, that in the death of Christ God
has dealt effectually with the world's sin for its removal.   It
is easy to disparage too lightly what Wellhausen has called
the pagan element in the religion of Israel ; but it is
probably truer to hold with this writer that the sacrificial
system had something in it which trained the conscience and
helped man to feel and to express spiritual truths for which
he had no adequate articulate language.

Important, however, as his reference to sacrifice may be, it
is not so much through the idea of sacrifice that we are
initiated into the writer's mind as through the idea of priesthood.   Now in relation to the priest the various conceptions
of sacrifice are unified ; the distinctions of sin offerings, burnt
offerings, peace offerings, and so forth, disappear ; sacrifice

is reduced to this—it is the characteristic function of the
priest, the indispensable means to the fulfilment of his calling.
A priest is the essential figure in religion as it is conceived
in the Epistle to the Hebrews ; when the priesthood is
changed there is necessarily also a change of law—the whole
religious constitution is altered (vii. 12) ; in other words, the
priest determines what the religion is.   Hence if we wish to
know what Christianity is, in which Christ is priest, we must
investigate the priesthood as it is discharged by Him.

The priest's function, speaking generally, is to establish and
to represent the fellowship of God and man.   That fellowship must exist, it must be incorporated and made visible, in
the priest's own person ; and through his ministry it must
be put within reach of the people for whom he acts as priest.
Through his ministry they must be put in a position to draw
near to God themselves, to worship, to have fellowship with
God ; in a word, to become God's people.   If we ask why a
priest and a priestly work of mediation are necessary, why
men cannot immediately and in their own right, as it were,
draw near to God, the answer is self-evident.   It is because
their sin stands in the way, and cannot be ignored.   In the
Epistle to the Hebrews, as everywhere in the New Testament,
sin is a problem, and the burden of the book is that God
has dealt with the problem in a way answering to its magnitude.   He has instituted a priesthood to deal with it.   He
has appointed His Son a priest with this very end in view,
that He should make propitiation for the sins of the people
(ii. 17).   If we ask how this priest deals with sin in order
to make propitiation for it, the answer, as has already been
observed, is given in Old Testament terms.   He deals with
it by the way of sacrifice.   This is the only method of propitiation, known to the Old Testament, which is of a piece
with the idea of priesthood.   It is irrelevant to argue, as is
sometimes done by persons who are anxious that the grace

of the gospel should not be abused, that the Old Testament only provides propitiation for certain kinds of sin, and these not the more serious ; such thoughts are not present to the writer's mind.   Propitiation must be made for sin, if sinful men are to have fellowship with God at all ; the only propitiation known to scripture, as made by a priest, is that which is made through sacrifice (apart from shedding of blood there is no remission, ix. 22) ; and the writer has no conception beforehand of sins with which the priest and the sacrifice present to his mind are unable to deal.   He does recognise the possibility that men may contemn the gospel altogether, and even after they have known its power may trample under foot the blood of the covenant with which they were sanctified, and so commit a sin for which in the nature of the case there can be no further propitiation—as he puts it, for which there is no more a sacrifice in reserve (x. 26) ; but that is another matter. His position, speaking generally, is that in Christ and His death we have a priest and a sacrifice capable of dealing effectively with sin as the barrier between God and man, and actually dealing with it in such a way that in despite of it God has a worshipping people among sinful men.

Can we, now, get any way under the surface here ? Sacrifice is not a familiar nor a self-interpreting idea to us, whatever it may have been to the author and to those whom he addressed ; can we penetrate or explain it at all, so as to make intelligible to ourselves any relation which the death of Christ had to sin, or to the will of God in regard to sin ?

Sometimes the attempt is made to do this by looking immediately at the effect of Christ's work in the souls of men, and deducing its relation to sin, as a secondary thing, from this.   The epistle, of course, does not ignore the effect of Christ and His sacrifice upon men : it has, indeed, a variety of words to describe it.   Sometimes the word employed is

ἁγιάζειν (to sanctify).   The priestly Christ and His people
are He who sanctifies, and they who are sanctified (ii. 11).
Christians have been sanctified through the offering of the
body of Jesus Christ once for all (x. 10).   By one offering
He has perfected for ever those who are being sanctified
(x. 14).   It was Christ's object in dying to sanctify the people
through His own blood (xiii. 12).   There has been much
discussion as to what sanctification in such passages means,
and especially as to whether the word is to be taken in a
religious or an ethical sense.   Probably the distinction would
not have been clear to the writer ; but one thing is certain,
it is not to be taken in the sense of Protestant theology.
The people were sanctified, not when they were raised to
moral perfection—a conception utterly strange to the New
Testament as to the Old—but when, through the annulling
of their sin by sacrifice, they had been constituted into a
people of God, and in the person of their representative had
access to His presence.   The word ἁγιάζειν, in short, in the
Epistle to the Hebrews, corresponds as nearly as possible to
the Pauline δικαιοῦν ; the sanctification of the one writer is
the justification of the other ; and the προσαγωγή or access
to God, which St. Paul emphasises as the primary blessing of
justification (Rom. v. 2 ; Eph. ii. 18, iii. 12), appears everywhere in Hebrews as the primary religious act of ' drawing
near ' to God through the great High Priest (iv. 16, vii. 19-
25, x. 22).   It seems fair then to argue that the immediate
effect of Christ's death upon men is religious rather than
ethical ; in technical language, it alters their relation to God,
or is conceived as doing so, rather than their character.
Their character, too, alters eventually, but it is on the basis
of that initial and primary religious change ; the religious
change is not a result of the moral one, nor an unreal
abstraction from it.

A similar result follows if we consider another of the words used to explain the effect of Christ's priestly and sacrificial work upon men—the word τελειοῦν, rendered 'to make perfect.' It is widely used in the epistle in other connections. Christ Himself was made perfect through sufferings (ii. 10); that is, He was made all that a high priest, or a captain of salvation, ought to be. It does not mean that suffering cured Him of moral faults; but that apart from suffering and what He learned in it He would not have been completely fitted for His character of representing, and succouring, mortal men. So again when we read, the law made nothing perfect (vii. 19); the meaning is, that under the ancient religion of Israel nothing reached the ideal. The sanctuary was a worldly or material sanctuary (ix. 1); the priests were sinful mortal men, ever passing on their unsatisfactory functions to their successors (vii. 23); the sacrifices were of irrational creatures—the blood of bulls and goats, which could never make the worshipper perfect as touching the conscience (ix. 9.); that is, they could never completely lift the load from within, and give him παρρησία and joy in the presence of God; the access to the holiest of all was not abiding; as represented in the High Priestly ministry of the day of atonement, the way to God was open only for a moment, and then shut again (ix. 7 f.). There was nothing perfect there, nothing in that religious constitution which could be described as τέλειον or αἰώνιον. But with Christ, all this is changed. By one offering He has perfected for ever those who are being sanctified (x. 14). The word cannot mean that He has made them sinless, in the sense of having freed them completely from all the power of sin, from every trace of its presence; it means obviously that He has put them into the ideal religious relation to God. Because of His one offering, their sin no longer comes between them and God in the very least; it does not exclude them from His presence or intimidate them; they come with boldness to the throne of grace;

they draw near with a true heart and in full assurance of faith ; they have an ideal, an unimpeachable standing before God as His people (iv. 16, x. 22). In Pauline language, there is now no condemnation ; instead of standing afar off, in fear and trembling, they have access to the Father; they joy in God through the Lord Jesus Christ, through whom they have received the atonement (Rom. viii. 1, v. 2-11).

Once more, if we examine the passage in which the verb καθαρίζειν is used to express the result of Christ's work in relation to man, we shall be led to the same conclusion. It is in ix. 14, and occurs in the sentence contrasting the efficacy of the ancient sacrifices with that of the sacrifice of Christ. 'For if the blood of goats and bulls and ashes of a heifer sprinkling the defiled sanctifies to the purification of the flesh, how much more shall the blood of Christ, who through eternal spirit offered Himself without spot to God, purify your conscience from dead works to serve the living God.' The Old Testament sacrifices had an outward efficacy ; they removed such defilements as excluded a man from the communion of Israel with God in its national worship. The New Testament sacrifice has an inward efficacy ; it really reaches to the conscience, and it puts the man in a position to offer religious service (λατρεύειν) to a living God. In some way it neutralises or annuls sin so that religious approach to God is possible in spite of it.

The examination of these words justifies us in drawing one conclusion. The writer of the Epistle to the Hebrews does not conceive of a regenerating, or, in the modern sense of the term, sanctifying, effect of Christ's death upon the soul as immediate or primary. He does not conceive it as directly emancipating the soul from sin, as an immoral power operative in it ; nor does he regard this experience of emancipation as the only reality with which we have to deal. It is a reality, but it is an effect, and an effect to be traced to a cause. That cause is not simply Christ's death ; it is Christ's death as a reality capable of being so interpreted as to yield the rational explanation of such an effect. It is often argued that the idea of an antecedent relation of Christ's death to sin—antecedent, that is, to the emancipation of the soul from sin's power—is essentially unreal, nothing more than the *caput mortuum* of this great experience. This is certainly not the view of the writer to the Hebrews. On the contrary, he has, like St. Paul and others to whom reference has been, and will yet be made, the conception of a *finished work* of Christ, a work finished in His death, something done in regard to sin once for all, whether any given soul responds to it or not. As he puts it at the beginning of the epistle, He made purgation of sins—the thing was done—before He sat down at the right hand of the Majesty in the Heavens. As he puts it later, He has offered one sacrifice for sins for ever, and by the one offering He has brought for ever into the perfect relation to God those who are being sanctified. And though the epistle does not use the once familiar language about the risen Saviour pleading the merits of His sacrifice, it does undoubtedly represent this sacrifice, offered through eternal spirit, as the basis on which the eternal priest-hood of Christ is exercised, and the sinner's access to God assured. Now, a finished work of Christ and an objective atonement are the same thing, and the question once more presents itself: What is it, in Christ's death, which gives it its atoning power ? Why is it that, on the ground of this death, God, with whom evil cannot dwell, allows sinners unimpeded, joyful, assured access to Himself, and constitutes them a people of His own ?

It is possible to answer this question too vaguely. It is too vague an answer when we look away from Christ's death, and its specific relation to sin, and emphasise broadly Christ's identification of Himself with us as laying the basis for our identification of ourselves with Him, in which acceptance with God is secured. No doubt the epistle does give prominence to Christ's identification of Himself with those whose priest He is to become. He who sanctifies and they who are being sanctified—He who constitutes others into a people of God, and they who are so constituted—are all of one (ii. 11). He is not ashamed to call them brothers. He takes their nature on Him, becoming with them a partaker of flesh and blood (ii. 14). He takes their experience to Himself, being tempted in all things like as they are (iv. 15). Even in death He does not stand aloof from them; He dies because they have to die; He dies that through death He may destroy him who has the power of death, and free them who through fear of death were all their lifetime subject to bondage (ii. 14). But all this, not excepting the death itself in this aspect, belongs, from the point of view of the epistle, rather to the preparation for priesthood than to the discharge of priestly functions. The priest must undoubtedly be kindred to the people for whom he acts; he must know their nature and life; he must be taught by experience like theirs to have compassion on the ignorant and erring; nay, he must have sounded the tragic depths of mortal fear if he is to bring weak, sinful, dying men to God. All this Christ has done. He has qualified Himself by the immeasurable condescension of the Incarnation and the life in the flesh to be all that a priest should be. But when we come to the supreme act of His priesthood, the offering of Himself to God in death, the entering into the holiest of all through His own blood, the question recurs : What is it which gives this in particular its efficacy in regard to sin?

The one hint of an answer to this question offered by the epistle itself is that which we find in the words of ix. 14 : ' Christ who through eternal spirit offered Himself without spot to God.' The sinlessness of Jesus entered into the

Atonement: only one who knew no sin could take any responsibility in regard to it which would create a new situation for sinners. But more important even than this is the suggestion contained in the words ' through eternal spirit.' This is not the same as through 'indissoluble life' (vii. 16), as though the idea were that the life offered to God on the Cross was one which death could not hold, but was rather by death ' liberated ' and ' made available ' for others. Neither is it the same as ' through His divine nature,' as though the idea were that the divine nature or the divine personality through which Christ surrendered His human life to God gave the sacrifice an immeasurable value. These are forms of words rather than forms of thought, and it is difficult to attach to them any intelligible or realisable meaning. If we follow the line of thought suggested by the use of αἰώνιος (eternal) in other passages of the epistle, we shall rather say that what is meant here is that Christ's offering of Himself without spot to God had an absolute or ideal character ; it was something beyond which nothing could be, or could be conceived to be, as a response to God's mind and requirements in relation to sin. It was the final response, a spiritual response, to the divine necessities of the situation. Something of what is included in this may be suggested by the contrast which is here drawn in the epistle between Christ's offering of Himself through eternal spirit and the sacrifices of the Old Testament. As opposed to these, His sacrifice was rational and voluntary, an intelligent and loving response to the holy and gracious will of God, and to the terrible situation of man. But what we wish to understand is why the holy and gracious will of God, and the terrible situation of man, demanded and were satisfied by this particular response of Christ's death, and not by anything else.

So far as I can see, there is no explanation of this whatever, unless we can assume that the author shared the view of St. Paul and of primitive Christianity generally, that sin and death were so related to one another—were in some sense, indeed, so completely one—that no one could undertake the responsibility of sin who did not at the same time submit to death.   As has been already said, it is not necessary to suppose that this relation of sin and death was established arbitrarily ; if it existed for the human conscience, as part of the actual order of the world, the situation would be before us which required Christ to die in order to take really upon Him our responsibility in this relation.   That it does thus exist, the New Testament elsewhere, and something in human experience as well, combine to prove ; and that the writer to the Hebrews was conscious of this is shown by the fact that he, like other New Testament writers, makes the death of Christ the very thing by which sin is annulled as a power barring man's approach to God.   His idea is not that Christ by His death, or in virtue of it, acts immediately upon the sinful soul, turning it into a righteous one, and in that sense annulling sin ; it is rather that sin is annulled and, in its character as that which shuts man out from God's presence and makes worship impossible, ceases to be, through the once for all accomplished sacrifice of Christ.   And though his dominant thought may be said to be that Christ by His death removes sin, as an obstacle standing in our path—bears it away, so that it blocks our road to God no longer—still He does not do this except by dying ; in other words, He bears sin *away* because He *bears* it ; He removes the responsibility of it from us because He takes it upon Himself.

The connection of ideas which is here suggested is often controverted by appeal to the passage at the beginning of the tenth chapter.   There the writer is contrasting the sacrifices of the old covenant with that of the new.   'The law,' he says, 'having a shadow of the good things to come, not the very image of the things, could never with the same sacrifices which they offer year by year continually make perfect those who draw near. Otherwise would they not have ceased to be offered, owing to the worshippers, having been once purged, having no longer conscience of sins? So far from this being the case, sins are brought to mind in them year by year. It is impossible for blood of bulls and goats to remove them. Accordingly, at His entrance into the world, He says, " Sacrifice and offering Thou didst not desire, but a body didst Thou prepare for me. In whole burnt offerings and offerings for sin Thou hadst no pleasure." Then I said, " Behold I come ; in the volume of the Book it is written concerning Me ; to do Thy will, O God." Above, in saying " sacrifices and offerings, and whole burnt offerings, and offerings for sin Thou didst not desire nor take pleasure in"—that is, God had no delight in such sacrifices as are offered according to the law—then His Word stands, " Lo, I come to do Thy will." He removes the first to establish the second.' This passage is often read as if it signified that sacrifice was abolished in favour of obedience, and the inference is drawn that no use can be made of the conception of sacrifice in the interpretation of Christ's death, or as it is sometimes put, that no significance can be assigned to His death which does not belong equally to every part of His life. His obedience is what atones, and His obedience is the same from first to last. But to argue thus is to ignore the very words with which the writer proceeds : ' *in which will*— that is, the will of God which Christ came to do—we have been sanctified, *i.e.* constituted a worshipping people of God, *through the offering of the body of Jesus Christ once for all.*' We cannot here, any more than in other passages of the New Testament, make the original sense of Old Testament words a key to their meaning when they are quoted in the New.

What is contrasted in this passage is not sacrifice and
obedience, but sacrifice of dumb creatures, of bulls and goats
and suchlike, with sacrifice into which obedience enters, the
sacrifice of a rational and spiritual being, which is not passive
in death, but in dying makes the will of God its own. The
will of God, with which we are here concerned, is not satisfied by an obedience which comes short of death.   For it is
not merely the preceptive will of God, His will that men
should do right and live according to His holy law, which
Christ came to fulfil; it is His gracious will, a will which
has it in view that sinful men should be constituted into a
people to Himself, a will which has resolved that their sin
should be so dealt with as no longer to keep them at a
distance from Him ; a will, in short, that sinners should find
a standing in His sight.   And in that will we are sanctified,
not merely by Christ's fulfilment of the law of God as it is
binding on man in general, but by His fulfilment of the law
as it is binding on sinful men, by His obedient suffering of
death as that in which God's mind in relation to sin finds its
final expression : to use the words of the writer himself,
' through the offering of the body of Jesus Christ once for all.'
There is an ambiguity in saying that obedience is the
principle of the atonement, or its spiritual principle, or that
which gives the work of Christ its value.[1]   It is no doubt
true to say so, but after we have said so the essential question remains—that question the answer to which must show
whether, when we say ' obedience,' we have seen any way
into the secret of the Atonement : viz. obedience to what ?
It is not enough to say, Obedience to the will of God ; for
the will of God is one thing when we think of man abstractly,
another when we think of man under the definite conditions
produced by sin.   It is one thing when we conceive of it as
an imperative will, having relation only to man as God's

[1] Cf. *Non mors sed voluntas placuit sponte morientis* (Bernard).

creature ; it is another when we conceive it as a redeeming, restorative, gracious will, of which the human race is in reality the object, not the subject, the subject by whom the will is carried out being Christ. In both cases, of course, obedience, the free fulfilment of the divine will, is that which has moral value. But just because, in both cases, the attitude of the human will is formally the same—just because we can say 'obedience,' whether we are thinking of God's will generally, or thinking of it as a will specially directed to the redemption of the sinful—just for this reason it is inadequate, ambiguous, and misleading to speak of obedience as the principle of the Atonement. Christ's obedience is not merely that which is required of all men, it is that which is required of a Redeemer ; and it is its peculiar content, not the mere fact that it is obedience, which constitutes it an atonement. He had a moral vocation, of course ; but it was not this — and this is all that obedience means—which made Him a Redeemer : it was something unique in His vocation, something that pertained to Him alone. Christ did not come into the world to be a good man : it was not for this that a body was prepared for Him. He came to be a great High Priest, and the body was prepared for Him that by the offering of it He might put sinful men for ever into the perfect religious relation to God.

In determining the meaning of obedience, and of the will of God, in this passage, we touch the quick of the great question about the relations of Incarnation and Atonement. If we have read it correctly, it confirms what has been already said about the ideal priority of the latter. It is the Atonement which explains the Incarnation : the Incarnation takes place in order that the sin of the world may be put away by the offering of the body of Jesus Christ. The obedience of the Incarnate One, like all obedience, has moral value—that is, it has a value for Himself ; but its redemptive value, *i.e.*

its value for us, belongs to it not simply as obedience, but as obedience to a will of God which requires the Redeemer to take upon Himself in death the responsibility of the sin of the world. That this is done obediently implies that in dying the Son of God acknowledges the justice of God in connecting death and sin, as they are connected for the human conscience; He does right, as it has been put, by the divine law which is expressed in that connection. And in doing so He does perfectly, and therefore finally and once for all, something through which sinful men can enter into fellowship with God. He lays the basis of the new covenant; He does what sinners can look to as a finished work; He makes an objective atonement for sin—exactly what St. Paul describes as καταλλαγή or reconciliation. There is peace now between God and man; we can draw near to the Holy One.

The Epistle to the Hebrews does not make as clear to us as the Pauline epistles how it is that Christ's death becomes effective for men. The author was not an evangelist so much as a pastor, and it is not the initiation of Christianity but its conservation with which he deals throughout. But the answer to the question is involved in the conception of Christ as Priest. The priest is a person who acts as the representative of a people: he does something which it properly falls to them to do, but which they cannot do for themselves; by God's grace he does it, and on the strength of it they draw near to God. The epistle lays great stress on the fact that Christ has identified Himself with man; in substance, therefore, it may be said, His work must be appropriated by men's identifying themselves with Him. The writer never uses the Pauline expression 'in Christ' to express this identification or its result; he has the vaguer conception of being 'partakers of Christ,' μέτοχοι τοῦ Χριστοῦ, which so far answers to it (iii. 14, cf. iii. 1, vi. 4,

xii. 8). Christ is not represented, as He is by St. Paul, as the object of faith ; He is rather the great exemplar of faith. Yet He is the object of the Christian confession, both as apostle and High Priest (iii. 1) ; it is to those who obey Him that He is the author of eternal salvation (v. 9) ; and He is the centre to which the eyes and hearts of Christians are steadily directed.   It does not, therefore, exhaust the meaning of the writer to say that He is our representative, and that He does nothing for us which it is not for us to do over again.   It is true that He is our representative ; but He not only acts in our name, and in our interest ; in His action He does something for us which we could never have done for ourselves, and which does not need to be done over again ; He achieves something which we can look to as a finished work, and in which we can find the basis of a sure confidence toward God.   He achieves, in short, ' purgation of sins ' (i. 3).   This is the evangelical truth which is covered by the word ' substitute,' and which is not covered by the word ' representative ' ; and it is the consciousness of this truth that makes the Evangelical Church sensitive and even jealous of a too free and easy use of the ideas that Christ becomes one with us in all things, and we in all things one with Him.   There is an immense qualification to be made in this oneness on both sides—Christ does not commit sin, and we do not make atonement.   The working in us of the mind of Christ toward sin, which presumably is what is meant by our identification with Him in His death, is not the making of atonement, nor the basis of our reconciliation to God ; it is the fruit of the Atonement, which is Christ's finished work. Seeberg's elaborate essay on the death of Christ in Hebrews is an admirable illustration of the confusion which results from the hazy use of words like ' identification,' *Zusammenschluss*, etc., or the idea (to call it an idea) that Christ and the Christian are one person, and that this is what makes access to God and forgiveness of sins possible. It leads to expressions like this: 'Forgiveness of sins therefore presupposes that the life of him who has experience of it comes to have the standing of a life which has passed sinless through death.'[1] The forgiveness of sins may come to this in the end; it may beget a life which shares in Christ's victory over sin and death; but it is surely a subversion of the very idea of forgiveness to say that it presupposes it. A life that has passed sinless through death, whatever else it may know, knows nothing of forgiveness; and therefore forgiveness, whatever it may be, is not a participation in any part of such a life's experience, whether by the method of 'identification' or by any other. Or again, from another side, the hazy use of such language leads to utterances like this: 'The thing Christ has done (*die Leistung Christi*), though it has not been done by the sinner, is yet a thing which he might or would fain have done, and is therefore in principle his doing.'[2] This is not wrestling with mysteries, or sounding great deeps; it is trifling with words, or trying to say Yes and No in the same breath. Let the Passion of Christ draw us to the utmost to share in His mind toward God and toward sin, and the fact remains that its power to do so is dependent on the clear recognition of the truth that Christ did something for us in His death which we could not do for ourselves, and which we do not need to do after Him. By His one offering He put us for ever in the perfect relation to God. This is the vital point in Christianity, and to deny the debt to Christ at this point is eventually to deny it altogether. The process which starts with rejecting the objective Atonement—in other words, the finished work of Christ and the eternal dependence on Him and obligation to Him which this involves—has its inevitable and natural issue in the denial that Christ has any essential place in the

---

[1] *Der Tod Christi*, p. 92 f.   [2] *Ibid.* p. 99.

Gospel. We can only assent to such a view by renouncing the New Testament as a whole.

Although faith is not defined in the epistle directly by relation to Christ, it is nevertheless faith which saves (x. 22, 38 f., xiii. 7), and the well-known description or definition in the eleventh chapter can easily be applied in the Christian religion. Faith is there said to be the assurance of things hoped for, the proof of things not seen (xi. 1). It is to the invisible world what sight is to the visible; it is the means of realising it, so that its powers and motives enter into the life of men, and enable them after patient endurance and fulfilment of God's will to inherit the promises. What, then, is the unseen world which is realised by Christian faith? It is a world in which Christ holds the central place, and in which, in the virtue of that death in which He made purgation of sins, He appears perpetually in the presence of God on our behalf. It is a world in which everything is dominated by the figure of the great High Priest, at the right hand of the Majesty in the Heavens, clothed in our nature, compassionate to our infirmities, able to save to the uttermost, sending timely succour to those who are in peril, pleading our cause. It is this which faith sees, this to which it clings as the divine reality behind and beyond all that passes, all that tries, daunts, or discourages the soul; it is this in which it finds the *ens realissimum*, the very truth of things, all that we mean when we speak of God. It is holding fast to the eternal realities revealed in Christ, and not some indefinable 'identification' with Him, on which all that is Christian depends. And it is this, more than anything, which, in spite of differences of form, makes the writer akin to St. Paul. For he too builds everything on Jesus Christ, crucified and exalted.

CHAPTER V

THE JOHANNINE WRITINGS

By the Johannine writings are meant the Apocalypse and the fourth gospel, as well as the three catholic epistles to which the name of John is traditionally attached. It is not possible to enter here into a review of the critical questions connected with them, and especially into the question of their authorship. The most recent criticism, while it seems to bring the traditional authorship into greater uncertainty, approaches more nearly than was once common to the position of tradition in another respect: it ascribes all these writings to the same locality, to pretty much the same period, and to the same circle of ideas and sympathies. This is a nearer approach than would once have been thought probable to ascribing them all to the same hand. When a writer like Weizsäcker concludes that the Apocalypse and the fourth gospel have so many points of contact that they must have come from one school, while they are nevertheless so distinct that they must have come from different hands,[1] it is probably quite legitimate to treat the two in connection, if not to regard them as at one. Thirty years ago it would have been uncritical to speak of them except as the extremest opposites to each other. As for the connection between the gospel and the epistles, or at least the first epistle, with which alone we shall be concerned, that seems to me indubitable. No doubt there are differences between them, and a difference

[1] *Das apostolische Zeitalter*, p. 484.

touching closely on our subject—the epistle, like all epistles
in contrast with all gospels, having more of what may be
called reflection upon Christ's death, or interpretation of
it, than the kindred gospel. But that does not prove, as
J. Réville argues,[1] that they were due to different hands; it
only proves that the gospel, however much it may be sub-
dued in form to the style of the writer's own thoughts, is
true to its character as a gospel, and the epistle to its
character as an epistle. If these two books cannot be ascribed
to the same pen, literary criticism is bankrupt. The whole
of the Johannine writings, it may be safely assumed, belongs
to the region of Asia Minor, to a school, let us say, which had
its headquarters in Ephesus, and to the last quarter, or
perhaps the last decade, of the first century of our era.

The opening words of the Apocalypse carry us at once to
the heart of our subject. John interweaves with the address
of his book to the seven churches a sudden doxology: 'To
Him that loveth us, and loosed us from our sins in His blood,
and He made us a kingdom, priests to His God and Father,
to Him be the glory and the dominion for ever and ever'
(i. 5 f.). What is before his mind as he speaks is Christ in
His exaltation—the faithful witness, the firstborn of the
dead, the prince of the kings of the earth; but he cannot
contemplate Him, nor think of the grace and peace which he
invokes on the churches from Him, without recurring to the
great deed of Christ on which they ultimately depend.
Christ's love is permanent and unchanging, and John thinks
of it as such (τῷ ἀγαπῶντι ἡμᾶς, to Him that *loveth* us);
but the great demonstration of it belongs to the past (καὶ
λύσαντι ἡμᾶς ἐκ τῶν ἁμαρτιῶν ἡμῶν ἐν τῷ αἵματι αὐτοῦ).
He does not say, 'who liberates us from our sins,' as though
a progressive purification were in view; but 'who liberated

---

[1] *Le quatrième Évangile*, p. 51 ff. See also Moffatt, *Introduction to the Literature of the New Testament*, 589 ff.

us,' pointing to a finished work. It seems to me far the most probable interpretation of ἐν τῷ αἵματι to make ἐν represent the Hebrew בְּ of price : Christ's blood was the cost of our liberation, the ransom price which He paid. This agrees with the word of our Lord Himself in the Gospel about giving His life a ransom for many (Matt. xx. 28), and with other passages in the Apocalypse in which the notion of 'buying' a people for God finds expression (v. 9, xiv. 3 f.). Sin, or rather sins, held men in bondage; and from this degrading servitude Christ purchased their freedom at no less a cost than that of His own life. It is not any undefined goodwill, it is the love revealed in this dear-bought emancipation of the sinful, which inspires the doxology, 'to Him that loveth us.' Redemption, it may be said, springs from love, yet love is only a word of which we do not know the meaning till it is interpreted for us by redemption.[1]

The result of the liberty, bought by Christ's blood, is that those who were once held by sin are made a kingdom, even priests, to His God and Father. These words are borrowed from the fundamental promise of the Old Covenant in Exodus xix. 6. ' He made us a kingdom ' does not mean ' He made us kings ' (so some MSS. and A.V.). It means, ' He constituted us a people over whom God reigns ': the dignity conferred on us is not that of sovereignty, but of citizenship. ' He made us priests ' means that in virtue of His action we are constituted a worshipping people of God ; on the ground

---

[1] λούσαντι (*washed*) is the reading familiar to us from the Received Text and the Vulgate. It also, as well as λύσαντι, has analogies in the book : cf. vii. 14 and the Text. Rec. at xxii. 14 ; and Bousset calls attention to the frequent mention of white robes without any particular reference to the blood of Christ. The sacrament of baptism made the figure of washing an obvious one to Christians, quite apart from such suggestions as are given by Ps. l. 4, Isa. i. 16, 18, and its influence is apparent in 1 Cor. vi. 11, Tit. ii. 14. On the whole, λύσαντι is much the better-supported reading : for the meaning which would go with λούσαντι ἐν see below on vii. 14, p. 178.

of it we have access to the Father. Both words together imply that it is the action of Christ, who died for our redemption, to which we owe our standing in God's sight, and our whole relation to Him so far as it is anything in which we can rejoice. All dignity and all privilege rest on the fact that He set us free from our sins at the cost of His blood. A doxology is not the place at which to seek for the rationale of anything, and we do not find the rationale of these things here. It is the fact only which is brought into view. The vision of Christ calls out the whole contents of the Christian consciousness; the Christian heart is sensible of all it owes to Him, and sensible that it owes it all in some way to His death.

Next in significance to this striking passage come the frequent references in the Apocalypse to the Lamb, and especially to the Lamb as it had been slain. In all, this name occurs twenty-nine times. The most important passages are the following: (1) ch. v. 6-14. Here the Lamb is represented as sovereign—the object of all praise; as a Lamb which had been sacrificed—$\dot{\epsilon}\sigma\phi\alpha\gamma\mu\acute{\epsilon}\nu o\nu$ means 'with the throat cut'; as living and victorious—$\dot{\epsilon}\sigma\tau\eta\kappa\acute{o}\varsigma$ (standing). It has the character which sacrifice confers, but it is alive; it is not dead, but it has the virtue of its death in it. It is on the ground of this death, and of the redemption (or purchase of men for God) effected by it, that all praise is ascribed to the Lamb, and the knowledge and control of all providence put into His hands. 'Worthy art Thou to take the book and to open the seals of it, for Thou wast slain and didst purchase to God by Thy blood ($\dot{\epsilon}\nu\ \tau\hat{\omega}\ a\H{\iota}\mu\alpha\tau\acute{\iota}\ \sigma o\nu$) out of every tribe and tongue and people and nation, and didst make them to our God a kingdom and priests, and they shall reign upon the earth.' Here we have the ideas of i. 5 repeated, with the further thought that love like that displayed in Christ's death for man's redemption is worthy not only of all praise, but of having all the future committed to its care. It is really a pictorial way of saying that redeeming love is the last reality in the universe, which all praise must exalt, and to which everything else must be subordinate. (2) The next passage is that in vii. 14, about the martyrs in the Neronic (or Domitianic?) persecution. 'One of the elders answered me, saying, These that are clothed in the white robes, who are they, and whence did they come? and I said to Him, My Lord, Thou knowest. And He said to me, These are they that come out of the great tribulation, and they washed their robes and made them white ἐν τῷ αἵματι τοῦ ἀρνίου (in the blood of the Lamb).' Here what is referred to is evidently the power of Christ's death to sanctify men, though how it is exercised we are not told. The people seen in this vision, the endless procession coming out of the great tribulation, were martyrs and confessors. They had taken up their cross and followed Jesus to the end. They had drunk of His cup, and been baptized with His baptism. They had resisted unto blood, striving against sins, and now they were pure even as He was pure. But the inspiration to all this, and the strength for it, was not their own: they owed it to Him. They washed their robes and made them white in the blood of the Lamb; it was the power of His Passion, descending into their hearts, which enabled them to do what they did. Once more, the rationale is wanting. Some may feel that none is needed—that the Cross acts immediately in this way on those who are of the truth: none, at all events, is given. We can only feel that the Cross must have some divine meaning in it when it exercises so overwhelming a constraint. (3) The third passage has also a relation to martyrdom, or at least to fidelity in a time of terrible persecution. 'And they overcame him because of the blood of the Lamb, and because of the word of their testimony, and they loved not their life unto death' (xii. 11).

It is implied in this that but for the blood of the Lamb
they would not have been able to overcome ; the pressure
put on them would have been too great, and they would
inevitably have succumbed to it.[1]   But with a motive behind
them like the blood of the Lamb they were invincible.   Now
nothing can be a motive unless it has a meaning ; nothing
can be a motive in the line and in the sense implied here
unless it has a gracious meaning.   To say that they overcame, because of the blood of the Lamb, is the same as to
say that the love of Christ constrained them.   They dared
not, with the Cross on which He died for them before their
eyes, betray His cause by cowardice, and love their own lives
more than He had loved His.   They must be His, as He
had been theirs.   It is taken for granted here that in the
blood of the Lamb there had been a great demonstration of
love to them ; in other words, that the death of Christ was
capable of being defined in such a way, in relation to their
necessities, as to bear this interpretation.   It is because
it is an incomparable demonstration of love that it is an
irresistible motive.   And though the relation is not thought
out nor defined here—where it would have been utterly out
of place—it is not forcing the language in the least to assume
that it must have existed in fact for the author.

There are two other passages which might be brought
into connection with our subject—xiii. 8, and xxi. 27—in
which reference is made to ' the Lamb's book of life.'   In
this book the names are written of those who are to inherit
life everlasting : those whose names are not found there die
the second death.   Nothing could express more strongly the
writer's conviction that there is no salvation in any other

---

[1] Compare Moffatt *ad loc.* in *Expositor's Greek Testament* : ' In opposition
to the contemporary Jewish tradition (Ap. Bar. ii. 2, xiv. 12 ; 4 Esd. vii.
77 etc.), it is not reliance on works but the consciousness of redemption
which enables them to bear witness and to bear the consequences of their
witness.'

than the Lamb: that in Jesus Christ and Him crucified is the whole hope of a sinful world.   It is very common to take the first of the two passages just quoted as though it spoke of 'the Lamb slain from the foundation of the world,' and to argue from it that atonement is no afterthought, that redemption belongs to the very being of God and the nature of things; but though these are expressions upon which a Christian meaning can be put, they find no support in this passage.   The words 'from the foundation of the world' are not to be construed with 'slain,' but with 'written,' as the parallel passage proves; it is the names of the redeemed that stand from eternity in the Lamb's book of life, not the death or sacrifice of the Lamb which is carried back from Calvary and invested with an eternal, as distinct from its historical, reality.   An apostle would probably have felt that the historical reality was compromised by such a conception, or that something was taken away from its absolute significance. But even discounting this, it has no exegetic support.[1]

If we try to put together the various lights which the Apocalypse casts on the death of Jesus, we may say: (1) That death is regarded as a great demonstration of love

---

[1] The use of this text which is here rejected is found *e.g.* in *Contentio Veritatis*, p. 298, where Mr. Inge writes : ' These [the death and resurrection of Christ] are eternal acts, even as the generation of the Son of God is an eternal act.   They belong to the unchangeable and ever-operating counsels of God.   So it is possible for the New Testament writers to say that the Lamb was slain for us from the foundation of the world, and that the rock which followed the Israelites through the wilderness was Christ.   The passion of Christ was itself (as the Greek Fathers called it) a sacrament or mystery of an eternal truth : it was the supreme sacrament of human history; the outward and visible sign of a great supra-temporal fact.'   This point of view, whatever its legitimacy or illegitimacy, is certainly much more characteristic of the Greek Fathers than of the New Testament writers.   To the latter Christ is the equivalent of absolute spiritual reality.   They never raise the abstract question of the relation of time to eternity ; and though the eternal import of the historical, in the life and death of Jesus, is the foundation of all their thinking, they never describe the Passion as the sacrament or symbol of any reality beyond itself.

(i. 5). (2) It is a death which once for all has achieved something—the aorists λύσαντι (i. 5), ἐσφάγης καὶ ἠγόρασας ἐν τῷ αἵματι (v. 9), prove this. There is a finished work in it. (3) It is a death which has an abiding power—ἀρνίον ὡς ἐσφαγμένον (v. 6), not σφαγέν.[1] (4) This abiding power is exercised in this, that it enables men to be faithful to Christ under persecution, to suffer with Him rather than sin, finally, rather to die than sin (xii. 11). Christ Himself was a martyr, and the typical Christian is a martyr too. To be a martyr is to furnish the decisive proof that the abiding power of Christ's blood is being exercised over one's life. (5) Hence the blood of Christ both does something once for all—in breaking the bond which sin holds us by, and bringing us into such a relation to God that we are a people of priests—and does something progressively, in assuring our gradual assimilation to Jesus Christ the faithful witness. In both respects the Christian life is absolutely indebted to it ; without it, it could neither begin nor go on. There is the same experience, it may be said, of Christ's death, the same practical appreciation of it, and the same exultant and devout utterance of that appreciation in the language of worship, which we find in St. Paul ; but, as we might expect, when the nature of the composition is taken into account, we do not find any such dialectic treatment of this Christian experience, and of the ideas it involves, as in the writings of the apostle of the Gentiles.

We may now proceed to the examination of the gospel. The general conception of the fourth gospel is that what we owe to Christ is life, eternal life ; and this life, it may further be said, we owe to the Person rather than to anything He does. This is true without any qualification of the prologue (ch. i. 1-18), and it is true of the gospel

---

[1] Compare St. Paul's use of the perfect participle ἐσταυρωμένον, I Cor. i. 23, 2 Cor. ii. 2, Gal. iii. 1.

so far as the influence of the prologue can be traced through it. If we use the word redemption at all—and it occurs naturally to us as we come from the Apocalypse— we must say that redemption is conceived in the gospel as taking place through revelation. Jesus redeems men, or gives them life, by revealing to them the truth about God. The revelation is made in His own Person—by His words and deeds, no doubt, but supremely by what He is. 'This is life eternal, that they should know Thee, the only true God, and Him whom Thou didst send, Jesus Christ' (xvii. 3). The work of redemption, to borrow the dogmatic category, is interpreted through the prophetic office of Christ almost exclusively. It is on this basis that the ordinary contrasts are drawn between the theology of St. Paul and that of the fourth gospel, and if we do not look too closely they can be drawn in very broad lines ; to change the figure, they can be put in epigrammatic and striking forms. Thus it may be said that in St. John the great and fundamental idea is revelation ; God makes Himself known to men, and in making Himself known He redeems them; to see Him in His true nature is to be withdrawn from the world of sin. In St. Paul, on the other hand, revelation is through redemption. It is because God in Jesus Christ takes the responsibilities of the sinful world upon Himself, so reconciling the world to Himself, that we know what He is: the relation of revelation and redemption is reversed. It agrees with this, again, that as Schultz has put it,[1] in St. John the death of Jesus only comes, though it comes inevitably, because of the flesh ; the Word was made flesh, and there-

---

[1] *Die Gottheit Christi*, 447. ' Also nicht als ein *Einzelereigniss*, nicht in Beziehung auf *das Gesetz*, nicht als *Opfer* in gewöhnlichem Sinne hat der Tod Christi seine Bedeutung (sc. in John). Nicht *um des Todes willen ist das Fleisch Christi nöthig gewesen*, sondern *der Tod ist nöthig gewesen um des Fleisches willen.*

fore must share the fate of all flesh, fulfil the destiny of
man by a perfect death as by a perfect life.   In St. Paul,
on the contrary, it is the death which is the primary thing ;
except for the purpose of dying for man's redemption
Christ would never have been here in the flesh at all.   It
agrees with this further, so it is said, that whereas in
St. Paul (as in the synoptic gospels) the people in whom
Jesus is most interested, and who are most interested in
Him, are the sinners who need redemption and whom He
died to redeem, in St. John the sinners have practically
disappeared, and the persons who have an interest in Jesus
are the relatively good people who are prepared to appreciate the revelation He has brought.   'He that doeth the
truth cometh to the light' (iii. 21).   'Every one that is
of the truth heareth My voice' (xviii. 37).   A sentence
like x. 26, 'Ye do not believe, because ye are not of My
sheep,' would, according to Holtzmann, have been exactly
reversed in the synoptics ; it would have been, ' You are
not of My sheep, because you do not believe.' [1]   The trick
of such contrasts is easily learned, but does not strike one
as very valuable.   It depends for its plausibility on those
generalities in which there is always some delusion hidden.
It depends in this case, for example, on taking the somewhat abstract and speculative standpoint of the prologue,
and allowing that to dominate the historical parts of the
gospel.   But if we turn from the prologue to the gospel
itself, in which Jesus actually figures, and in which His
words and deeds are before us, we receive a different impression.   There is a great deal which resists the speculative solvent supposed to be contained in the Logos
theory.   There is, in particular, a great deal bearing
upon the death of Christ and its significance, which goes
to discredit those abstract contrasts which have just been

[1] *Neut. Theologie*, ii. p. 492.

illustrated.   When we do take such a closer look at the gospel, what do we find ?

We find that the death of Christ in a great variety of ways comes to the front, as something which is of peculiar significance for the evangelist.   (1) The first allusion to it is that which is put into the lips of John the Baptist in i. 29 : 'Behold the Lamb of God which taketh away the sin of the world.'   If these are not the words of the Baptist, they are all the more the words of the evangelist, and define his standpoint from the outset.   That they refer to the death of Jesus does not seem to me open to question.   Granting that ὁ αἴρων τὴν ἁμαρτίαν τοῦ κόσμου is rightly rendered *qui tollit* or *qui aufert peccatum mundi*— *who takes away*, not *who takes on him*, the sin of the world —we have to take the subject of the sentence into consideration, the Lamb.   When sin is taken away by a lamb, it is taken away sacrificially ; it is borne off by being in some sense—in the case of an unintelligent sacrifice, only a figurative sense—borne.   It is not too much to say that the conception of Christ's death as a sacrifice for sin, put thus, at the very beginning of the gospel, into the lips of the great witness to Jesus, is meant to convey decisively the evangelist's own conception of Jesus and His work.   He is here to put away sin—that sums up His vocation ; and He does not put it away by the method of denunciation, like the Baptist, but by the sacrificial method, in which it has to be borne.[1]

(2) There is a further allusion to the death of Jesus in ii. 19 : 'Destroy this temple, and in three days I will build it up.'   This, according to the evangelist, He spoke concerning the temple of His body.   The evangelist's interpretation has been treated with very little respect by critics of all schools.   It is not necessary to defend it ; but I

---

[1] On this passage, see Garvie, *Studies in the Inner Life of Jesus*, p. 125.

repeat, that if this is not what Jesus meant, all the more must we recognise the preoccupation of the evangelist himself with the idea. He drags it in, we must believe, where it is out of place, only because it is the centre of all his thoughts about Jesus ; it is in it he instinctively seeks the key to anything mysterious in the Master's words.

(3) The third reference is indisputable, though the terms in which it is expressed may not be free from ambiguity. It is that in ch. iii. 14 in which Jesus is represented as comparing Himself to the brazen serpent : 'Even so must the Son of Man be lifted up.' The expression 'lifted up' occurs in one or two other places, and the same happy or unhappy ambiguity attaches to it in all. Thus in ch. viii. 28 Jesus says to the Jews : 'When ye have lifted up the Son of Man, then shall ye know that I am He,' etc. In xii. 32 we have : 'And I, if I be lifted up from the earth, will draw all men to Myself.' Here the evangelist again has a note which has excited the contempt of critics. 'This He said, indicating by what kind of death He was to die' (xii. 33). All that the Jews seem t have taken out of the word was the idea of 'removal' ; for they contrast the inevitable 'uplifting' of the Son of Man with the 'abiding of the Christ for ever.' Here it is by no means necessary to join in the common censure of the evangelist. Where the 'uplifting' is spoken of indefinitely, it may be conceived, properly enough, to include the exaltation ; but where it is spoken of as the act of the Jews (viii. 28), and compared to the elevation of the brazen serpent on a pole (iii. 14 f.), the allusion to the Cross is unmistakable. There is, indeed, an exact parallel to it in Ezra vi. 11 (R.V.), though the word ὑψοῦν is not used : 'Also I have made a decree that whosoever shall alter this word, let timber be pulled down from his house, and let him be lifted up and fastened thereon.' That was the death which Jesus

died, and to such a death the evangelist understood Him to refer when he used the word which he represents by ὑψοῦν. The word had the advantage—for no doubt it was counted an advantage—of carrying a double meaning, of raising the mind at once to the cross and to the heavenly throne. But nothing is more characteristic of the writer, or of Jesus as He is set before us in this gospel, than the unification of these two things. They are inseparable parts of the same whole. Hence the peculiar use of the term 'glorify' (*e.g.* 'Now is the Son of Man glorified,' xiii. 31) to express what happens to Christ in His death. There is no conception of a humiliation in death followed and rewarded by an exaltation; on the contrary, Christ is lifted up and ascends through His death : His glory is revealed in that whole experience which death initiates, and into which it enters, more than in all His miracles. The mere fact that words like ὑψωθῆναι and δοξασθῆναι are the evangelist's chosen words to describe Christ's death shows how thought had been preoccupied with it, and how, the prologue notwithstanding, the Christian soul felt itself here at the heart of the revelation and of the redeeming power of God.

(4) The death of Christ is again alluded to, in all probability, in chap. vi., and that in close connection with the life which is His supreme gift to men ; He speaks there of His flesh, which He will give for the life of the world, and of eating the flesh and drinking the blood of the Son of Man (vi. 51-53). If it were possible, as I do not think it is, to deny that there is any reference in this chapter to the sacrament of the Lord's Supper, it might be possible also to deny that it contained any reference to Christ's death. Verses like those just quoted would merely be an enigmatic and defiant manner (such as we frequently find at the close of a discussion in the

fourth gospel) of putting the general truth of v. 57 : ' He that eateth Me, he it is who shall live because of Me.' ' My flesh' and ' My blood' would in this case only be a more concrete and pictorial ' Me'; there would not of necessity be any reference to the death. But when we remember the period at which the gospel came into use, the sacramental allusion (see below, p. 200 ff.), both here and in the third chapter, seems to me quite indisputable; and this carries with it the allusion to Christ's death as in some way or other the life of the world.

(5) In the tenth chapter we again come upon passages in which there is nothing equivocal. ' I am the Good Shepherd : the Good Shepherd layeth down His life for the sheep' (x. 11). This, it might be said, is only an ideal way of putting it; it is what the Good Shepherd would do if the situation emerged which required it. But it is not put so by the evangelist. The need has emerged, and the laying down of His life with a view to its resumption is made the sum and substance of the vocation of Jesus. ' Therefore doth My Father love Me, because I lay down My life that I may take it again. No one taketh it from Me, but I lay it down of Myself. I have authority to lay it down, and I have authority to take it again. This commandment have I received from My Father ' (x. 17 f.). Christ's death is not an incident of His life, it is the aim of it. The laying down of His life is not an accident in His career, it is His vocation ; it is that in which the divine purpose of His life is revealed.

(6) A peculiar solemnity attaches in the gospel to a sixth allusion to Christ's death, that which is made in the unconscious prophecy of Caiaphas. A prophecy is that which a man speaks under the impulse of the Holy Spirit, and the evangelist means us to understand that a divine authority attaches for once to the words of this bad man. ' Being

high priest that fateful year, he prophesied that Jesus was to die for the nation, and not for the nation only, but also to gather together in one the children of God who were scattered abroad.' Some interest of the nation, and this great interest of the family of God, were conditioned by the death of Jesus, however that death may be related to the ends it was to achieve.

(7) In the twelfth chapter there are several significant allusions. There is the corn of wheat which, unless it fall into the ground and die, abides alone, but if it die, bears much fruit (xii. 24)—a similitude in which the influence of Jesus is made to depend directly on His death ; and in close connection with this there is the anticipation of the near and awful future, the shadow of which struck dark and cold upon the Saviour's soul. ' Now is My soul troubled, and what shall I say ? Father, save Me from this hour. But for this cause came I unto this hour ' (xii. 27). ' This hour ' is the great crisis in the life of Jesus, the hour which no one could anticipate (vii. 30, viii. 20), but from which, now that it has come, He will not shrink. It has come, in the sense already explained, as the hour in which the Son of Man is to be *glorified* : the hour in which He is to drink the cup which the Father gives Him to drink, and to crown the work the Father has given Him to do. The way in which He is moved by it, shrinks from it, accepts it, reveals the place it holds in His mind, and in that of the evangelist also.

(8) Just as the Lamb of God at the beginning of the gospel (i. 29) connected it with Isa. liii., so does the quotation in chap. xii. 38 give us the same key to its interpretation at the end. ' Though He had done so many signs before them, they did not believe on Him, that the word of Isaiah the prophet might be fulfilled which he said : Lord, who hath believed our report, and to whom is the arm of the Lord revealed ? ' Taken alone, this passage

could not be made to bear any special reference to the death of Christ or to its interpretation; but occurring as it does after the triple and unmistakable references of the corn of wheat, the dreaded hour, and the lifting up from the earth (vv. 24, 27, 32), it seems to me rather probable than otherwise that it is meant to bring before the reader's mind, by a sufficient hint, the fifty-third chapter of Isaiah, as the Old Testament, and therefore the divine, solution of the mysteriously disappointing career of Jesus.

(9) If this instance is reckoned doubtful, there can be no doubt about the one in the fifteenth chapter: 'Greater love hath no man than this, that a man lay down his life for his friends' (xv. 13). It is characteristic of St. John, we are told, as opposed to St. Paul, that in St. John Jesus died for His friends; St. Paul thinks of Him as dying for His enemies (Rom. v. 10). It is an inept remark. Jesus at the moment is speaking to His friends, and about the supreme pledge of love He is going to give them. In other places, St. John, like St. Paul, represents Him as giving His flesh 'for the life of *the world*' (vi. 51), and lays stress on the fact that it is God's love for *the world*, in its all-inclusive yet individualising intensity, which explains His 'lifting up' (iii. 14). This is the great thing on which they agree: the highest revelation of love is made in the death of Jesus.

(10) A singular and striking allusion to His death has been found in our Lord's intercessory prayer: 'For their sakes I sanctify Myself that they also may be sanctified in truth' (xvii. 19). The meaning of this will be considered presently (see below, p. 194).

And finally (11) there is the story of the Passion itself. A peculiar significance attaching to the death of Jesus is implied (*a*) by the fulness with which the story is told; (*b*) by the references in it to the fulfilment of prophecy, which mean that a divine purpose was being carried out by it

(xix. 24 = Ps. xxii. 19 ; xix. 28 f. = Ps. lxix. 22 ; xix. 36 f. = Ex. xii. 46, Zech. xii. 10) ; and (c) by the peculiarly emphatic attestation given to some mysterious circumstances attendant on it, the sense of which might have remained hidden from us but for the interpretation of them provided in the first epistle. 'One of the soldiers with a spear pierced His side, and there came out immediately blood and water. And he that hath seen hath borne witness, and his witness is true, and he knoweth that he saith true, that ye also may believe. For these things took place that the Scripture might be fulfilled : A bone of Him shall not be broken. And again, another Scripture says : They shall look on Him whom they pierced' (xix. 36 f., cf. 1st epistle, v. 6).

This series of passages has not been cited at random, but to dissipate the impression which many people have, and which some writers on New Testament theology propagate, that the death of Christ has no place in the fourth gospel corresponding to that which it has elsewhere in the New Testament. I think they are sufficient to dissipate such an impression. No doubt there is much in the fourth gospel which makes it plausible to say, St. Paul deals with the work of Christ, St. John with His person ; for St. Paul, Christ only lives to die ; for St. John, He dies because death is the only issue from life ; but such contrasts do as much to mislead as to illumine. As soon as we are past the prologue, into the scenery of what Jesus actually said, did, thought, feared, and suffered, we see that His death really fills the place it does everywhere in the New Testament, and has the same decisive importance. Indeed, the constant complaint of commentators is that the evangelist drags it in at inappropriate places, a complaint which, so far as it is justified, only shows how completely his mind was absorbed and dominated by the Cross.

But does this prominence of the death of Jesus in the

gospel throw any light upon its meaning? Is it defined by
St. John (or by Jesus in the fourth gospel) in any such
relations as by St. Paul? Allowing for the fact that the
writer's mind is not of a dialectical turn like that of St. Paul,
but given rather to intuition than to reflection—in other
words, to the contemplation of results rather than of pro-
cesses, of ends rather than of means or conditions—we must
answer these questions in the affirmative.

In St. John, as in St. Paul, Christ's death is set in
relation to the love and saving will of God. 'God so
loved the world that He gave His only begotten Son, that
whosoever believeth in Him should not perish, but have
eternal life' (iii. 16). Again, in St. John as in St. Paul,
Christ's death is related to His own love: 'Greater love
hath no man than this, that a man lay down his life for
his friends' (xv. 13). This is the favourite text of Abaelard,
quoted again and again as having the whole secret of the
atonement in it: everything, according to Abaelard, lies in
this, that there is love in Christ's death, with power in it
to evoke love, the response of love being the whole experience of salvation. The more fully Christ's love wins from
us the answer of love, the more fully are we justified and
saved; that is all.[1] Without raising the question whether
the act of Christ in laying down His life must not be
related in some real way to our real necessities before it can
either be or be conceived to be an act of love at all, we may
notice that its character as connected with His love is again

---

[1] See Abaelard in *Migne*, vol. 178, p. 836: 'Justior quoque, id est
amplius Dominum diligens, quisque fit post passionem Christi quam ante,
quia amplius in amorem accendit completum beneficium quam speratum.
Redemptio itaque nostra est illa summa in nobis per passionem Christ
dilectio quae non solum a servitute peccati liberat, sed veram nobis
libertatem filiorum Dei acquirit, ut amore ejus potius quam timore cuncta
impleamus, qui nobis tantam exhibuit gratiam qua major inveniri ipso
attestante non potest.' He then refers to John xv. 13, Luke xii. 49,
Rom. v. 5.

emphasised in the allegory of the Good Shepherd. The perfect freedom with which Christ acts the shepherd's part, on to the final sacrifice which it demands, is apparently the characteristic of His work to which He attaches the greatest importance. And it is so because it is through the freeness with which the surrender of life is made that the love which is its motive is revealed. 'I lay down My life of Myself. No one taketh it from Me. I have authority to lay it down, and I have authority to take it again' (x. 17 f.). This spontaneity on the part of Jesus, when it is put in relation to the love of the Father in giving the Son, appears as obedience. The authority or liberty He has to lay down His life and to take it again is a commandment He has received from the Father. Equally with St. Paul or with the writer to the Hebrews, St. John could use the term 'obedience' to describe the whole work of Christ; but just as with them, with him too it is loving obedience to a will of love, an attitude at once to God's purpose and to man's need which makes the Passion the sublimest of actions, and justifies the paradox of the gospel that the Cross is a 'lifting up' or a glorifying of Jesus.

It is possible, however, to go further in defining the death of Christ in the fourth gospel. Proceeding as it does from the love of the Father and the Son, it is nevertheless not conceived as arbitrary. It is free, but there is a rational necessity for it. The Son of Man *must* be lifted up if He is to save those who believe. The corn of wheat *must* fall into the ground and die if it is not to abide alone. Not much, indeed, is said to explain this. The various ends secured by Christ's death—the advantage of the flock for which as the Good Shepherd He lays down His life (x. 11), the eternal life of those who believe in Him (iii. 14 f.), the rallying round Him as a centre of the scattered children of God, so that He becomes the head of a new humanity

(xi. 52) : these, no doubt, are all dependent upon it somehow ; but how, the evangelist is at no pains to tell. But
we do no violence to his thought when we put this and
that in the gospel together in order to discern what he
does not explicitly say. Everything, we have seen, comes
from the love of God ; the death of Christ is to be construed
in harmony with this, not in any antagonism to it. But
the love of God to the world is never conceived in Scripture
abstractly. It is not manifested in some evolutionary process which is necessarily determined *a priori*, as might be
hastily inferred from the prologue to the fourth gospel ; to
conceive it so would be to deny its grace. It is conceived,
practically, in relation to definite needs of man which it
meets ; it is manifested not on the analogy of natural forces,
which simply are what they are, but on the analogy of the
free actions of men, which are determined by specific
motives. To deny this is to lose the living and gracious
God of revelation, and to take in His place a metaphysical
phantom. God so loved the world that He gave His only
begotten Son. The giving of the Son at least includes the
giving of Him to that death which, as we have seen, pervades the gospel from beginning to end ; indeed, the death
is emphasised in the immediate context (iii. 14 f.). Nor
are we left without sufficiently clear hints as to the necessity
which determined the gift. In the passage just referred to
(iii. 16), we see that apart from it men are lost ; they perish,
instead of having eternal life. St. John's mind revolves
round these ultimate ideas, death and life, rather than
their moral equivalents or presuppositions, sin and righteousness ; but we cannot suppose that he did not include in
' death ' and ' life ' all that we mean by these latter words.
That he did include all this we see when the consequence of refusing the gift of God is presented in the
terrible word of Jesus, ' If ye believe not that I am He,

N

ye shall die in your sins ' (viii. 24); or when the evangelist himself writes, ' He that believeth on the Son hath eternal life; he that disobeyeth the Son shall not see life, but *the wrath of God abideth on him* ' (iii. 36). The love of God, then, represented in the gift of Christ, has in view, according to the fourth gospel, the sin of the world, its exposure to the divine wrath, its perishing if left to itself; and the gift in which that love is embodied, if it is to be intelligently apprehended at all, must also have a definite relation to this concrete case. If it delivers men from perishing under the wrath of God, and from the sin by which that wrath is evoked, then an intelligible relation to sin and to the divine wrath is implicit in the writer's consciousness of it, whether he has given articulate expression to such a relation or not. It is quite legitimate here to emphasise such passages as i. 29, where, as has been already shown, a sacrificial deliverance from sin is represented as the sum and substance of the gospel; and xx. 23, where the power which the Risen Lord confers on His disciples in virtue of all that He has achieved is a power connected with the forgiveness of sins. It may seem to some a less obvious instance, but the striking word of Jesus in xvii. 19 points in the same direction: 'For their sakes I sanctify Myself, that they also may be sanctified in truth.' What men needed was to be sanctified, that is, to be consecrated to God. It was not in their power—surely no reason can be conceived for this but that which lies in their sin—to consecrate themselves, and what they were not able to do for themselves Christ did for them in His own Person. He consecrated Himself to God in His death. That the reference is to His death does not seem open to question; the present tense, ἁγιάζω, which suggests something going on at the moment, and the circumstances of the Speaker, whose mind is full of what is at hand, put out of court the

idea that the word is intended to describe His life as a
whole. His life was past, and now, in His own Person,
through death, He is about to establish between God and
man a relation which men could never have established for
themselves, but into which they can truly enter, and into
which they will be drawn once it is established by Him.
This seems to me the exact equivalent of the Pauline doctrine
that Christ dies our death that we may be drawn into the
fellowship of His death, and so put right with God. He
acts—'I sanctify Myself'; men are acted on—'that they
also may be sanctified.' He establishes the reconciliation ;
they, to use Pauline language, receive it (Rom. v. 11).

I have spoken of the gospel throughout as if it expressed
the mind of the writer rather than that of the Subject.
The necessity of such a concession to the current criticism is
shaken when we pass to the epistle, for there we find the
death of Christ and its significance put in a light which
more imperatively recalls the other New Testament epistles,
and which differentiates this one to a considerable extent
from the gospel. The contrast with the epistle on this
very point is one of the evidences that the gospel is truer to
its assumed historical position than many would admit ; it is
not his own mind the writer wishes to impart, but the mind
of Christ ; and though it is certainly by the same hand as
the epistle, he does not feel at liberty to say everything in
it that the epistle allows him to say.

For example, we frequently find in the epistle explicitly
stated, what we have as a rule to infer in the gospel, the
connection between the death of Christ and sin. Thus in
i. 7 : 'The blood of Jesus His Son cleanseth us from all sin.'
In ii. 1 f. : 'These things write I unto you, that ye sin not.
And if any one sin, we have an advocate with the Father,
Jesus Christ the righteous. And He Himself is a propitiation for our sins : and not for ours only, but also for the

whole world.'   In ii. 12: 'I write unto you, little children, because your sins are forgiven you for His name's sake.'   In iii. 5: 'Ye know that He was manifested to take away sins.'   In iv. 10: 'Not that we loved God, but that He loved us, and sent His Son a propitiation for our sins.'   The whole Person and Work of Christ, we see here, His whole manifestation in the world, but in some signal way His death, are set in relation to sin.   It is characteristic of the writer, here as in the gospel, that his interest is in the end or result, the actual cleansing of the soul from sin, its sanctification not in the sense of 1 Cor. vi. 11, or of Heb. x. 29, but in the sense of modern Protestant theology.   This sanctification is dependent on the death of Christ.   If we walk in the light as God is in the light, the blood of Jesus His Son continuously and progressively cleanses us from all sin: our sanctification is gradually achieved under its influence (i. 7).   It is the removal of sin in this sense which is referred to also in iii. 5: 'He was manifested, that He might put sins away.'   It is by no means necessary, for the understanding of the evangelist here, that we should adopt the strange caprice which fascinated Westcott, and distinguish with him in the blood of Christ (1) His death, and (2) His life; or (1) His blood shed, and (2) His blood offered; or (1) His life laid down, and (2) His life liberated and made available for men.[1]   No doubt these distinctions were meant to safeguard a real religious interest: they were meant to secure the truth that it is a living Saviour who saves, and that He actually does save, from sin, and that He does so in the last resort by the communication of His own life; but I venture to say that a more groundless fancy never haunted and troubled the interpretation of any part of Scripture than that which is introduced by this distinction into the Epistle

[1] See Westcott, *The Epistles of St. John*, p. 34 ff. ; *Epistle to the Hebrews*, p. 293 ff.

to the Hebrews and the First Epistle of John. The New
Testament writers, though they speak often of Christ's death,
never think of a dead Christ: their Christ is One who
became dead and is alive for evermore, and in His immortal
life the virtue of His death is present. He did something
when He died, and that something He continues to make
effective for men in His Risen Life ; but there is no meaning
in saying that by His death His life—as something other
than His death—is 'liberated' and 'made available' for
men : on the contrary, what makes His risen life significant
and a saving power for sinners is neither more nor less than
this, that His death is in it ; it is the life of one who by
dying has dealt with the fatal necessities of man's situation,
and in doing so has given a supreme demonstration of His
love.

This connection of ideas becomes apparent when we notice
that St. John uses a word akin to St. Paul's ἱλαστήριον in
describing the relation of Christ to sin. Jesus Christ the
righteous, he says, is the ἱλασμός for our sins (ii. 2); and
again, he says, God of His own accord loved us, and sent
His Son a propitiation for our sins (iv. 10). It is impossible
to suppose that St. John used this word in any other
relations than those in which it is found (or in which the
cognate terms are found) in Hebrews or in St. Paul. The
characteristic words of religion cannot be applied in new
ways at will. Now the idea of ἱλασμός or propitiation is
not an insulated idea—indeed there cannot be any such
thing. It is part of a system of ideas, which we have to
reconstruct with the means at our disposal. It is related,
for one thing, to the idea of sin. It is sin, according to the
uniform teaching of the New Testament, which creates the
necessity for it, and which is in some sense the object of it.
In other words, sin is the problem with which ἱλασμός deals.
St. John agrees with all New Testament writers in regarding

sin as a problem.   It cannot simply be ignored or suppressed; something has to be done with it, and the effective something (when its removal is in view) has been done by Christ the ἱλασμός.   Again, the idea of ἱλασμός is related to the ideas of sacrifice and intercession.   When St. John says that Jesus Christ the righteous is the propitiation for our sins, this is implied.   He has spoken almost immediately before about the *blood* of Jesus cleansing from all sin ; he speaks further on with significant emphasis about His coming in *blood* as well as in water (v. 6); and he no doubt conceived Jesus as set forth, as St. Paul has it (Rom. iii. 25), in His blood in this propitiatory character.   Further, the idea of ἱλασμός by being related to sin is related also to some divine law or order which sin has violated, and which is acknowledged in its inviolable rights by the ἱλασμός.   This is what is meant when the propitiation is described as Jesus Christ *the Righteous.*   All that is divine, all the moral order of the world, all that we mean by the Law of God, has right done by it in the death of Christ.   Sin, in that sense, is neutralised by the propitiation, and if men could enter into it, or if the benefit of it could come to them, sin would no more be a barrier to their fellowship with God.   The propitiation would draw them to God and put them right with Him, and as it held their hearts more closely it would more effectually and thoroughly cleanse them from every taint of sin.   The power of sanctification is lodged in it as well as the condition of the sinner's primary acceptance with God.   The first of these—the power of sanctification—preponderates in the epistle ; but it would be as complete a negation of its teaching, as of that of every New Testament writing, to say that the second—the sinner's acceptance with God—is dependent upon it.   The very reverse is the case.   The sin of *the whole world* has been atoned for, as the apostle expressly asserts (ii. 2); and it is on the basis of this work finished for all, and assumed to underlie everything, that the progressive purification of the Christian proceeds. It is the virtue of the ἱλασμός, in which all sin has been dealt with for its removal, and dealt with according to the realities of the divine law involved in the case, which eventually effects sanctification.

Perhaps the most striking thing in the first Epistle of St. John is the manner in which the propitiation of Christ is related to the love of God. The connection of the two things is, as we have seen, universal in the New Testament. No one could teach more emphatically than St. Paul, for example, that it is to the love of God we owe the presence of Jesus in the world and His work for men. No one could contrast what the love of God has done for us in Christ more emphatically than St. Paul does with the utmost which men will do from love for each other. But St. John rises above all comparisons to an absolute point of view at which propitiation and love become ideas which explain each other, and which have no adequate illustration apart from each other. He not only defines the propitiation by relation to love—God Himself loved us and sent His Son a propitiation for our sins (iv. 10); He defines love by relation to the propitiation—in this have we come to know what love is, that He laid down His life for us (iii. 16). The emphasis in this last sentence is on the expressly contrasted words ἐκεῖνος ὑπὲρ ἡμῶν. It is the contrast of what He is and of what we are, of the sinless Son of God and the sinful sons of men, in which the nerve of the proposition lies. So far from finding any kind of contrast between love and propitiation, the apostle can convey no idea of love to any one except by pointing to the propitiation—love is what is manifested there; and he can give no account of the propitiation but by saying, Behold what manner of love. For him, to say ' God is love ' is exactly the same as to say ' God has in His

Son made atonement for the sin of the world.' If the propitiatory death of Jesus is eliminated from the love of God,
it might be unfair to say that the love of God is robbed
of all meaning, but it is certainly robbed of its apostolic
meaning. It has no longer that meaning which goes deeper
than sin, sorrow, and death, and which recreates life in the
adoring joy, wonder, and purity of the first Epistle of
St. John.

In speaking of the death of Christ, it would not be just
either to the gospel or to the Epistle of St. John to ignore
the place held in both by the sacraments. That place has
been ignored by some and disputed by others; but if we
realise the date at which both documents were written, the
place which the sacraments had in Christian worship at the
time, and the inevitableness with which ordinary Christians
must have thought, and as we know did think, of the sacraments when they read, it seems to me indisputable. Baptism
and the Lord's Supper, it is no exaggeration to say, were full
in the writer's view at many points. He must have thought
of baptism when he wrote in the third chapter of the gospel
the words about being born of water and spirit; he must
have thought of the Supper as he wrote in the sixth about
eating the flesh of the Son of Man and drinking His blood.
I cannot doubt that he thought of both when he told in xix.
34 of the blood and water that issued from the pierced side
of Jesus, and again in the epistle (v. 6 f.) urged that Jesus
Christ came through water and blood, adding, with unambiguous emphasis, not in the water only, but in the water
and in the blood. The water and the blood were always
present in the church in the form of the sacraments, and the
evangelist uses the sacraments here as witnesses to the
historical reality of the life and experiences of Jesus.
Christian baptism answers to His baptism; the Christian
feast in which faith partakes of His body and blood is a

perpetual testimony to His passion.   It is in this last that
St. John is peculiarly interested as he writes the epistle.
There were teachers abroad, of whom Cerinthus is a type,
who preached a Christ that had come in the water only, not
in the blood.   The redeeming love and power of God, they
held, had descended on Jesus at His baptism, and been with
Him in His ministry of teaching and healing : there is a
divine reality in this, therefore, on which we can depend.
But they had withdrawn from Him before the Passion : there
is therefore no corresponding divine reality there.   It is
against such a view that the apostle makes the elaborate and
emphatic protest of v. 6 f. : 'not in the water only, but in
the water and in the blood.'   To deny the divine reality and
saving significance of the Passion was to rob the most sacred
rite of the Christian religion at once of its basis and its
import ; it was to abolish the Lord's Supper.   The apostle
appeals to the Lord's Supper against such a view.   A Christ
who did not come by blood—a Christ whose flesh was not
the true meat and His blood the true drink, as the celebra-
tion of the Supper and the liturgical language used at it
implied—a Christ who did not by His death bring life to
men—was not the Christ known to the faith and acknowledged in the worship of the church.   The sacraments, but
especially the sacrament of the Supper, are the stronghold
of the New Testament doctrine concerning the death of
Christ.

But there is another side to this.   While the apostle sees
in the sacraments a testimony to the historicity of the
baptism and death of Christ, and to the perpetual presence
in the church of the saving power of the Lord's Passion, and
while he insists upon their historicity as against those who
denied that Jesus Christ had come in flesh, and who made
the life on earth, and especially the death, phantasmal, so
far as a revelation of God was concerned, he protests on the

other hand against those who would materialise the history. He checks them at every point by introducing and emphasising the Spirit. Thus in the gospel, chap. iii., he speaks once of being born of water and spirit, but from that point onward the water is ignored : we hear of the Spirit alone ; of its breathing where it will, of being born of the Spirit, of every one who is so born. So also in the sixth chapter, after using the strongest language about eating the flesh and drinking the blood of the Son of Man—language in which enigmatic defiance to antipathetic minds is carried to the furthest point—he precludes all possibility of religious materialism by the words : ' It is the Spirit which gives life ; the flesh is of no use for this ; the words that I have spoken to you are spirit and are life ' (vi. 63). Words and speech address man on the spiritual side of his nature, and it is on this side that everything included in Christ—' he that eateth *Me*,' He says—finds access to us. And finally, in the epistle, after laying the stress we have seen on the water and the blood, he concludes : ' And the Spirit is that which beareth witness, for the Spirit is the truth. For three are they that bear witness, the Spirit and the water and the blood, and the three agree in one.' In every case the historical is asserted, but care is taken that it shall not be materialised : a primacy is given to the spiritual. On the other hand, there is no such spiritualising as would leave to the historical merely a position of vanishing or relative importance. There is no sublimation of Christianity into ' ethical ' or ' spiritual principles,' or into ' eternal facts,' which absolve us from all obligation to a Saviour who came in blood. Except through the historical, there is no Christianity at all, but neither is there any Christianity till the historical has been spiritually comprehended.

This is closely connected with our subject. Christianity is as real as the blood of Christ : it is as real as the agony in the garden and the death on the Cross. It is not less real than this, nor more real; it has no reality whatever which is separable from these historical things. Yet it is not in their mere externality, as events in past time, that they establish Christianity or save men from their sins. It is as their spiritual meaning is recognised, and makes a spiritual appeal to men, and awakes a spiritual response. It is when that awful experience of Jesus is revealed as a propitiation for sins, an assumption of our responsibilities by One who does right by the eternal law which we have wronged, and does it for us at this tremendous cost ; it is then that the soul of man is reached by the divine love, and through penitence and faith drawn away from evil, and born again of God. It is then that the blood of Jesus, God's Son, cleanses from all sin. It is then that in His death the Son of Man is glorified, and God is glorified in Him.

A friendly critic of this book pointed out what he regarded as a serious omission in it—the want of any reference to the death of Christ as a victory over Satan. This is a point of view which is principally found in the fourth gospel. Thus it is with His death and its consequences in view that Jesus says, 'Now is the judgment of this world ; now shall the prince of this world be cast out ; and I, if I be lifted up from the earth, will draw all men unto Myself' (ch. xii. 31 f.). As His hour comes nearer He says again, ' I shall no longer speak much with you, for the prince of the world cometh, and in Me he hath nothing ' (ch. xiv. 30). And finally, in the description of the work and power of the Spirit, who is to take His place in the hearts of the disciples after His departure, the same conception recurs. ' He when He is come will convict the world . . . of judgment, because the prince of this world has been judged ' (xvi. 11). A mind which does not naturally personalise the principle of evil— turning the principle into a prince—has the same embarrassment in dealing with these passages as with the Pauline ones referred to at p. 143. Possibly we get out too easily with our abstract nouns. The evil in the world may be represented as a principle, or an atmosphere, or an abstraction of some kind, by a spectator who is not engaged in conflict with it; but for One whose life is spent in conflict, for One who resists unto blood in the strife against it and finds it impossible not to do so, evil may assume a more malignant, and therefore a more personal aspect. It is not an unconscious but a wilful and wicked force. It is not a *vis inertiæ* in the moral world, but an awful Enemy of God. It reveals the intensity of the conflict, the stress of the battle which Jesus fought, that the power which He vanquished is represented thus. There is no suggestion in the fourth gospel that the Prince of this World had any rights in it—even relative and temporary rights, such as might be supposed to belong to the angels who gave the law, and who were superseded in their authority by Christ; the Prince of this World has no rights at all, and that is what Jesus demonstrates by His death. He has nothing in Christ; he is judged, he is cast out; through the death on the Cross the kingdom of this world is taken from him, and becomes the kingdom of God and of His Christ.

CHAPTER VI

THE IMPORTANCE OF THE DEATH OF CHRIST IN PREACHING AND IN THEOLOGY

If the series of studies which we have now completed has reproduced with any adequacy or accuracy the mind of the New Testament writers, certain conclusions of importance may fairly be deduced from it. One is that there really is such a thing as the New Testament. There is, as we were disposed to assume, a real and substantial unity of thought in the books which we call by that name. They were not written with a view to incorporation in a canon ; to repeat the paradox referred to in the introduction, New Testament theology is the theology of the Church at a time when as yet it had no New Testament. But the New Testament books have a unity, nevertheless, which is not external or imposed, nor due to the accident of their being approximately contemporary, but which is inward, essential, and spiritual, and which qualifies them to be canonical. Another conclusion to which we are led is that the death of Christ is the central thing in the New Testament, and in the Christian religion as the New Testament understands it. And when we say the death of Christ, we include, of course, the significance which the New Testament ascribes to it. Apart from that significance the death of Christ has no more right to a place in religion than the death of the penitent or the impenitent thief. The Cross and the word of the Cross—the

Cross and the rationale of it in relation to the love of God
and the sin of Man—are for religion one thing. This being
so, it is apparent that both for the propagation and for the
scientific construction of the Christian religion the death of
Christ is of supreme importance. Not that I should draw
too abstract a distinction. The propagation of Christianity
and its interpretation by intelligence—in other words,
preaching and theology—should never be divorced. At the
vital point they coincide. The simplest truth of the gospel
and the profoundest truth of theology must be put in the
same words—He bore our sins. If our gospel does not
inspire thought, and if our theology does not inspire preaching, there is no Christianity in either. Yet vitally related
as they are, there is a sufficiently clear distinction between
them, and in considering some consequences, for preaching
and theology, of New Testament teaching on Christ's death,
it will be convenient to take preaching first.

It is an immediate inference, then, from all that we have
seen in the New Testament, that where there is no Atonement there is no gospel. To preach the love of God out of
relation to the death of Christ—or to preach the love of God
in the death of Christ, but without being able to relate it
to sin—or to preach the forgiveness of sins as the free gift
of God's love, while the death of Christ has no special
significance assigned to it—is not, if the New Testament is
the rule and standard of Christianity, to preach the gospel
at all. Many ministers have suffered from the charge of not
preaching the gospel, and have resented it as an injustice.
In any given case it may quite well have been so. There
are those who are unable to separate form from substance in
thinking, and who are only too ready to believe that if the
familiar form in which the truth has been expressed is
varied, the substance is being injured or dissipated. But it
is not saying a hard or unjust thing to say that in some

cases the charge may not be groundless. It may be made
not merely by the unintelligent, who fail to distinguish form
from substance, but by the simple Christian spirit which
has the anointing from the Holy One, and knows instinctively
whether that by which it lives is present in the message it
hears or not.   There is such a thing as preaching in which
the death of Christ has no place corresponding to that which
it has in the New Testament.   There is preaching in which
the New Testament interpretation of Christ's death is ignored,
or carped at, or exploded.   We do not need to argue that no
man can preach the gospel until he has absorbed into his mind
and heart the whole significance of Christ's death as the New
Testament reveals it ; in that case, who could preach at all ?
But it is not unjust to say that no man will so preach as to
leave the impression that he has the Word of God behind him
if he is inwardly at war with the idea of atonement, constantly engaged in minimising it, maintaining an attitude of
reserve, or even of self-defence, in relation to it.   We may take
it or leave it, but it is idle to attempt to propagate the Christian religion on the basis and with the authority of the New
Testament, unless we have welcomed it with our whole heart.

It is proper to remember in this connection that very
often it is the simplest expressions, and those most open
to abstract criticism, in which the profoundest truth is
most tellingly expressed and most really apprehended ; and
that when this is the case, if we are compelled to criticise,
we should be careful that we do not discredit the essential
truth as well as the inadequate form.   It is easy, for
instance, to criticise the insufficiency of any commercial
figure, like that of ' debt,' to exhibit the personal and
spiritual relations subsisting between man and God ; yet
Christ used this figure habitually, and the whole impression
which it makes upon the conscience is sound.   The words
of the revival hymn, ' Jesus paid it all, All to Him I owe,'

have the root of the matter in them; and, however inadequate they may be to the interpretation of Christ's work and of Christian experience as a whole, they are infinitely truer than the most balanced, considerate, or subtle statement which denies them. Hence, whatever the motive which prompts criticism of such forms, we should be sensitive to the meaning they bear. Even if we think they are morally inadequate, and leave the new life unprovided for, we should remember that in the New Testament the new life is the immediate response to the very truth which such forms convey. The new life springs out of the sense of debt to Christ. The regenerating power of forgiveness depends upon its cost : it is the knowledge that we have been bought *with a price* which makes us cease to be our own, and live for Him who so dearly bought us. And we should remember also that it is not always intellectual sensitiveness, nor care for the moral interests involved, which sets the mind to criticise statements of the Atonement. There *is* such a thing as pride, the last form of which is unwillingness to become debtor even to Christ for forgiveness of sins ; and it is conceivable that in any given case it may be this which makes the words of the hymn stick in our throats. In any case, I do not hesitate to say that the sense of debt to Christ is the most profound and pervasive of all emotions in the New Testament, and that only a gospel which evokes this, as the gospel of Atonement does, is true to the primitive and normal Christian type.

Not only must Atonement by the death of Christ be preached if we would preach the New Testament gospel, but the characteristics of the Atonement must be clearly reflected in the preaching if justice is to be done to the gospel. As the finished work of Christ the Atonement is complete, and the perfection which belongs to it belongs also to the new relation to God into which we enter when the Atonement is appropriated by faith. There is *no* condemnation to them that are in Christ Jesus. Their relation to God is not determined now in the very least by sin or law, it is determined by Christ the propitiation and by faith. The position of the believer is not that of one trembling at the judgment seat, or of one for whom everything remains somehow in a condition of suspense; it is that of one who has the assurance of a divine love which has gone deeper than all his sins, and has taken on itself the responsibility of them, and the responsibility of delivering him from them. A relation to God in which sin has nothing to say, but which is summed up in Christ and His perfect Atonement for sin— in John Wesley's words, *full salvation now*—is the burden of the gospel. If it is not easy to believe this or to preach it, it is because, as the heavens are higher than the earth, so are God's thoughts higher than our thoughts, and His ways than our ways. In the New Testament itself there is always something startling, something almost incredible, which breaks again and again on the soul with a sense of wonder, in the experience of reconciliation through the death of Christ. But it is this great gospel which is the gospel to win souls—this message of a sin-bearing, sin-expiating love, which pleads for acceptance, which takes the whole responsibility of the sinner unconditionally, with no preliminaries, if only he abandon himself to it. Only the preaching of full salvation now, as Wesley tells us— and who knew better from experience than he?—has any promise in it of revival.

Further, preaching which would do justice to the Atonement must hold out in the gospel an assurance corresponding to the certainty of Christ's death and to the sin-bearing love demonstrated in it. Nothing is more characteristic

o

of churches than their attitude to assurance, and the place they give it in their preaching and in their systems of doctrine. Speaking broadly, we may say that in the Romish church it is regarded as essentially akin to presumption ; in the Protestant churches it is a privilege or a duty ; but in the New Testament religion it is simply a fact. This explains the joy which, side by side with the sense of infinite obligation, is the characteristic note of apostolic Christianity. The great invincible certainty of the reconciling love of God, which even when we were enemies made peace for us, this underlies all things, embraces all things, makes all things work together for good to those who love God, makes us more than conquerors in all things ; take away the certainty of it, and the New Testament temper expires. Joy in this certainty is not presumption ; on the contrary, it is joy in the Lord, and such joy is the Christian's strength. It is the impulse and the hope of sanctification ; and to deprecate it, and the assurance from which it springs, is no true evangelical humility, but a failure to believe in the infinite goodness of God, who in Christ removes our sins from us as far as the east is from the west, and plants our life in His eternal reconciling love. The New Testament spirit is not meant for our despair, but for our inspiration ; that assurance of sin-bearing love, that sanctifying strength and gladness, are the type of genuine Christian life.

We can understand and appreciate the motive which, both in the Romish and in the Protestant churches, has fostered in relation to assurance a temper which is not that of the New Testament, and which does not answer to the completeness and certainty of Christ's finished work. The motive is in both cases a desire to safeguard moral interests and to put a check upon self-deception. The Romish church safeguards moral interests by making justification and the new life identical : men are justified as, and only in proportion as, they are actually and morally renewed. The objection to this method is that the security is too good.   An absolute justification is needed to give the sinner a start. He must have the certainty of ' no condemnation,' of being, without reserve or drawback, right with God through God's gracious act in Christ, before he can begin to live the new life. As Chalmers put it with magnificent simplicity, ' What could I do if God did not justify *the ungodly* ? '   It is not by denying the gospel outright, from the very beginning, that we are to guard against the possible abuse of it.   In the Protestant churches, on the other hand, the attempt to check presumption and to safeguard moral interests was usually made by laying stress on the proper kind of faith.   The German Pietists, in opposition to a dead orthodoxy, in which faith had come to mean no more than the formal recognition of sound doctrine, spoke with emphasis of penitent faith, living faith, true faith, obedient faith, and so on.   It is somewhat against qualifications like these that they are foreign to the New Testament. What they come to in practice is this : Before the mercy of God in Christ the propitiation can be available for you, O sinful man, you must have a sufficient depth of penitence, a sufficiently earnest desire for reconciliation and holiness, a sufficient moral sincerity ; otherwise grace would only minister to sin.   But such qualifications do infringe upon the graciousness of the gospel—I mean on its absolute freeness—as something to be explained out of the love of God and the necessity, not the merits, of men. Christ did not die for those who were sufficiently penitent. He is the propitiation for the whole world, and He bore the sins of all that all might believe and receive through Him repentance and remission.   To try to take some preliminary security for the sinner's future morality before you make the gospel available for him is not only to strike at the root of assurance, it is to pay a very poor tribute to the power of the gospel. The truth is, morality is best guaranteed by Christ, and not by any precautions we can take before Christ gets a chance, or by any virtue that is in faith except as it unites the soul to Him. Now the Christ who is the object of faith is the Christ whose death is the Atonement, and the faith which takes hold of Christ as He is held out in the gospel conducts, if we may use such a figure, the virtue of the Atonement into the heart. The mercy of God which we welcome in it, and welcome as the first and last of spiritual realities with invincible assurance, is a mercy which has deep in the heart of it God's judgment upon sin ; and such a mercy, absolutely free as it is, and able to evoke in sinful men a joy unspeakable and full of glory, can never foster either immorality or presumption. But when its certainty, completeness, and freeness are so qualified or disguised that assurance becomes suspect and joy is quenched, the Christian religion has ceased to be.[1]

There is one other characteristic of the Atonement which ought to be reflected in gospel preaching as determined by

[1] I venture to quote two sentences in illustration of this paragraph. Dr. Dale (*Life*, p. 666), who read Pusey's life ‘with a deep impression of the nobleness and massiveness of his nature, and feeling more than ever that the power of God was with him,’ had nevertheless to add : ‘The absence of joy in his religious life was only the inevitable effect of his conception of God's method of saving men ; in parting with the Lutheran truth concerning justification (it might equally well be said with the New Testament truth of Christ's finished work) he parted with the springs of gladness.’ It is in the same line that Dr. Fairbairn has said of Pusey, that the sense of sin was ‘more a matter for himself to bear than for grace to remove’ (*Philosophy of the Christian Religion*, p. 333). The other sentence is from Chalmers, a great nature who had an original experience of the New Testament religion and often found original utterance for it : ‘Regaled myself with the solidity of the objective part of religion, and long to enter a field of enlargement in preaching on the essential truths of the gospel’ (*Life*, by Hanna, vol. ii. p. 417).

it, and which may for want of a better word be described as
its finality.   Christ died for sins once for all, and the man
who believes in Christ and in His death has his relation to
God once for all determined not by sin but by the Atonement.   The sin for which a Christian has daily to seek
forgiveness is not sin which annuls his acceptance with
God, and casts him back into the position of one who has
never had the assurance of the pardoning mercy of God
in Christ; on the contrary, that assurance ought to be
the permanent element in his life.   The forgiveness of sins
has to be received again and again as sin emerges into act;
but when the soul closes with Christ the propitiation, the
assurance of God's love is laid at the foundation of its
being once for all.   It is not to isolated acts it refers,
but to the personality; not to sins, but to the sinner; not
to the past only, in which wrong has been done, but to
time and eternity.   There will inevitably be in the Christian
life experiences of sinning and being forgiven, of falling and
being restored.   But the grace which forgives and restores
is not some new thing, nor is it conditioned in some new
way.   It is not dependent upon penitence, or works, or
merit of ours; it is the same absolutely free grace which
meets us at the Cross.   From first to last, it is the blood of
Jesus, God's Son, which cleanses from sin.   The daily
pardon, the daily cleansing, are but the daily virtue of
that one all-embracing act of mercy in which, while we
were yet sinners, we were reconciled to God by the death
of His Son.

To say that there is no gospel without Atonement, and
that the characteristics of the Atonement must be impressed
upon Christian preaching and reflected in the completeness,
assurance, and joy of the Christian life which is the response
to it, does not mean that the preacher is always to be
expressly and formally engaged with the death of Christ,

nor does it determine in what way that death in its redeeming significance is to be presented to men. It is impossible to forget the example of our Lord, though we are bound to remember that what was natural and inevitable before the Passion and the Resurrection may not be either wise or natural now. But looking to the gospels, we cannot but see that our Lord allowed His disciples every opportunity to become acquainted with Him, and to grow into confidence in Him, before He began to teach them about His death. He allowed them to catch the impression of His Personality before He initiated them into the mystery of His Passion. As for outsiders, He seems not to have spoken to them on the subject at all. Yet it would be a mistake, as we have seen, to suppose that the death of Jesus was not present—in His mind and in His life—even where nothing was said of it. The more we study the gospels, and the more thoroughly we appreciate such incidents as the Baptism, the Temptation, and the Transfiguration, with the heavenly voices attendant on them—not to mention the occasions on which His death rises even in early days to the surface of our Lord's mind—the more we shall be convinced that the sense and the power of it pervade everything we know of Him. He lived in the same spirit in which He died, and in a true sense we are in contact with the Passion and the Atonement whenever we are in contact with the soul of Jesus. To preach the gospels, therefore, it may be said, is to preach the gospel. On the other hand we must remember, and allow the remembrance its full weight as a directory for teaching and preaching, that a time came when Jesus set Himself deliberately, systematically, and with unwearied reiteration to bring home to His disciples the meaning of His death. Everything conspires to make us see how deeply it moved Him, and how deeply He was concerned

to have it apprehended by the disciples as what it was.   The
very names by which He names it—My baptism, My cup ;
the profound virtue He ascribes to it as a ransom, and as
the basis of a new covenant between God and man ; the
striking ordinances of baptism and the Supper which He
associated with it, and which in spite of intelligible yet
misconceived protests will guard its meaning while the
world stands ; all these separately, and still more in
combination, warn us that whatever method may be
prescribed in any given case by pedagogic considerations,
it must not be one which leaves it optional to us to give
the death of Christ a place in our gospel or not, as we
please.   It is as certain as anything can be that He meant
us to be His debtors and to feel that we are so.   He meant
to represent Himself as the mediator between God and
sinners, and to evoke in sinners an infinite sense of obligation
to Himself as they realised that they had peace with God.
And it always comes to this in the long-run.   Men may
come into contact with Christ at different places ; they may
approach Him from all quarters of the compass, under
various impulses, yielding to a charm and constraint in Him
as manifold as the beatitudes or as the gracious words and
deeds of the gospel.   But if they are in dead earnest as He
is, they will come sooner or later to the strait gate ; and
the ultimate form the strait gate assumes—for it is a gate
that goes on straitening till the demand for death is made
as the price of life—is that to which Jesus leads up His
disciples in His last lessons : are you willing to humble
yourselves so as to owe to Me, and to My death for you,
the forgiveness of sins and the life which is life indeed ?
There is a straight line from every point in the circumference
of a circle to the centre, and when we get to the quick of
almost anything in the relations of men to Jesus, it leads
with wonderful directness to this decisive point.

A striking passage from Kierkegaard's diary may help to reconcile in our minds what seem to be conflicting assertions : the one, that there is no preaching of the gospel unless the Atonement is preached ; the other, which, as we have seen, has a superficial support in the life and practice of Jesus, that the Atonement is the last thing in Christ to which the mind can be opened or reconciled. In general, Kierkegaard says,[1] the relation between God and man is represented thus : Christ leads us to God ; man requires a mediator in order to have access to the Father. But this, he argues, is not how the New Testament puts it. Nor can this by any possibility be the true way of putting it if, as he further argues, our relation to God is to become continually higher and more real ; for it can only become such through a continual experience on our part of being more deeply humbled in God's presence. But there is no sense of being deeply humbled in the first stages of our religion. We begin, in short, with the Father, quite easily and naturally, and without any mediator. This and nothing else is the childlike way of beginning. For the child nothing is too high ; he says *Du* to the Kaiser just as he does to his nurse, and finds it perfectly intelligible and proper that God should be his Father. It would have no meaning to him if he heard a voice which said, ' No man cometh unto the Father but by Me.' But as soon as man has attained to a certain degree of maturity, God's greatness or sublimity, moral as well as metaphysical, becomes so overwhelming to him that it is no longer natural or easy to call Him Father. There is something presumptuous in it, or something quite unreal. Now this sense of the relation between himself and God, which grows upon man as his moral consciousness matures, is true, and there is that which answers to it in the mind of God

---

[1] *Aus den Tiefen der Reflexion :* aus Sören Kierkegaards Tagebüchern 1833-1855 : aus dem Dänischen übersetzt von F. Venator.

Himself. Hence at this stage God points us to His Son, the
Mediator. 'It is written in the prophets,' says Jesus (John
vi. 45), 'And they shall all be taught of God. Every one
who has heard from the Father and has learned comes to
Me.' This is the remedy for the presumption and unreality
just referred to. It is as though God said: You must not
assert or claim sonship in your own right; you must not
take Fatherhood for granted; but through the Mediator I
can be your Father. This, however, is not all. The
Mediator also, like the Father at first, is apt to be taken for
granted with the assurance of youth, if not of childhood.
For the Mediator is at first conceived as example; it is in
imitation of Him, in likeness to Him—to use the phrase
which is most popular in our own day, and is charged to the
full with this unreflecting youthful assurance, it is in self-
identification with Him—that we must realise the Fatherhood of God. There is an amiable youthfulness, says
Kierkegaard, the token of which is that it finds nothing too
high for it. It seems to it quite natural and becoming that
it should have such an infinitely lofty example as Jesus, the
Son of God; among its amiable illusions is to be counted a
pious conviction that it is within its power to attain to this
example; it takes for granted that the example and he who
is striving to follow it are in such a sense of one kind that
nothing can really come between them. But once more, as
the moral consciousness matures, a change comes. The
example towers to such a height before man's eyes—the
sinless Son of God is so remote and inaccessible in His
sinlessness and sonship—that man can no longer think of
imitating it, or of trying to do so, in the independent style
of good comradeship. He cannot take it for granted that
he can make himself what Christ is: that he can 'identify'
himself with Christ offhand, simply because he wants to do
so. And Christ, too, is of this opinion; it is another and a

more dependent relation, with a deeper sense of obligation in it, which He requires from His followers. The example has another side, of which amiable and aspiring youth is at first ignorant : He is also the Reconciler.   This it is which brings us to the point.   Partly, Kierkegaard argues, there is a stage in life—the stage of amiable and aspiring youth—which is without the moral categories necessary for appreciating the example ; it does not see, feel, nor understand how Christ transcends all that it is, and how He must in some profound way be of another as well as of the same nature ; partly, he thinks, it has an illusory conception of its own powers, and of what it is in it to be.   But whatever the reason, the fact remains ; experience reveals to one who is trying to imitate Jesus, or to identify himself with Him, that he needs reconciliation first : he must become debtor to Jesus for this one thing needful before he can have a sound start in the filial life.   He must owe it to Christ as Reconciler, and owe it from the very beginning, if he is ever to stand in the relation of a son to the Father.   He may think at first that he can identify himself with the Son of God at any point over the whole area of his life, but he discovers experimentally that this is not so.   He finds out in a way surer than any logical demonstration that Christ is in the last resort as inaccessible to him as the God to whom he would draw near by imitating Christ, and that the only hope he has of getting to God in this way depends upon Christ's making Himself one with him in that responsibility for sin which separates him from the Father.   His one point of contact with Christ, when his whole situation is seriously taken, is Christ's character as a propitiation for sin ; and sooner or later he is driven in upon that.

The type of experience here described may be common enough in Christian lands, but what, it may be asked, is its relation to such a practice as St. Paul describes in 1 Cor.

xv. 3: 'I delivered unto you *first of all* that which I also received, that Christ died for our sins according to the Scriptures?' Is this consistent with what has just been said, or with what we have seen of our Lord's method of teaching? Is there a rule in it for all evangelistic preaching?

St. Paul's expression, ἐν πρώτοις, is not quite so pointed as 'first of all.' It is certainly to be taken, however, in a temporal sense: among the first things the apostle transmitted to the Corinthians were the fundamental facts of the Christian religion, the death and resurrection of Jesus in the significance which belonged to them 'according to the Scriptures,' that is, in the light of the earlier revelation. And among these first things the death of Christ in its relation to sin had a foremost place. It is, I think, a fair inference from this that in preaching the gospel the main appeal is to be made to the conscience, and that it cannot be made too soon, too urgently, too desperately, or too hopefully. It is because the Atonement is at once the revelation of sin and the redemption from sin, that it must inspire everything in preaching which is to bring home to the conscience either conviction of sin or the hope and assurance of deliverance from it. 'Eternity,' Halyburton said, 'is wrapt up in every truth of religion'; the Atonement, it is not too much to say, is wrapt up in every truth of the Christian religion, and should be sensible through every word of the Christian preacher. In this sense at least it must be delivered ἐν πρώτοις. We may begin as wisely as we please with those who have a prejudice against it, or whose conscience is asleep, or who have much to learn both about Christ and about themselves before they will consent to look at such a gospel, to say nothing of abandoning themselves to it; but if we do not begin with something which is essentially related to the Atonement, presupposing it or presupposed by it or involved in it, something which

leads inevitably, though it may be by an indirect and unsus-
pected route, to the Lamb of God that taketh away the sin
of the world, we have not begun to the gospel at all.   This
may seem a hard saying to those who have listened to
weariness to the repetition of orthodox formulæ on this
subject, and have realised that even under the New Covenant
there are conditions which compel us to say, The letter
killeth.   But it is not because the formulæ are orthodox
that they weary, it is because they are formal; the vital
interest of the great realities which they enshrine has
slipped from an unbelieving grasp, and left the preacher
with nothing to deliver but words.   A fresh realisation of
the truth which they embody would bring new words or
put new life into the old; and in any case the fact remains
that there is nothing which is so urgently and immediately
wanted by sinful men, nothing which strikes so deep into the
heart, which answers so completely to its need, and binds it
so irrevocably and with such a sense of obligation to God, as
the atoning death of Jesus.   Implicit or explicit, it is the
Alpha and Omega of Christian preaching.

Most preachers in any sympathy with this line of thought
have deplored in the present or the last generation the
decay of the sense of sin.[1]   Now, the Atonement is addressed
to the sense of sin.   It presupposes the bad conscience.
Where there is no such thing, it is like a lever without a
fulcrum; great as its power might be, it is actually power-
less, and often provokes resentment.   The phenomenon is a
curious one, and though it cannot be permanent, it calls for
explanation.   Possibly the explanation is partly to be found
in the circumstance that the Atonement itself was once
preached too much as though it had relation only to the
past, and had no assurance or guarantee in it for man's
future.   It contained the forgiveness of sins, but not the new

_____
[1] For a typical illustration, see Dale's *Christian Doctrine*, pp. 251 ff.

life. Where this was the case we can understand that it ceased to be interesting to those whose hearts were set on holiness. We can understand how Bushnell could speak of the forgiveness of sins as 'only a kind of formality, or verbal discharge, that carries practically no discharge at all.' But it is not easy to understand how this could be brought into any kind of relation to the New Testament. There, as we have seen, the forgiveness of sins, and the Atonement which is its ground, are no formality. They are the supreme miracle of revelation, the hardest, most incredible, most wonderful work of the God who alone does wondrous things; the whole promise and potency of the new life are to be found in them alone. The Atonement, or God's justification of the ungodly, which takes effect with the acceptance of the Atonement, regenerates, and there is no regeneration besides. But while a defective appreciation of the New Testament may have done something to discredit the Atonement, and to make men think of forgiveness, and of the sense of sin which demands it, as alike 'formalities' in contrast with actual sanctification, the deadening of conscience is probably to be traced on the whole to other causes. It is due in great part to the dominance in the mind for the last forty or fifty years of the categories of natural science, and especially of a naturalistic theory of evolution. All things have been 'naturalised,' if we may so speak; the spiritual being no longer retains, in the common consciousness, his irreducible individuality; he has lapsed to some extent into the vast continuity of the universe. Even to speak of the individual is to use language which is largely unreal, and with individuality individual responsibility has lost credit. It is the race which lives, and it is the qualities and defects of the race which are exhibited in what we call the virtues and vices of men. When we look at the lives of others, the last thing we now think of is the responsibility

which attaches to each of them for being what he is ; and it
is apt to be the last thing also which we think of when we
look at ourselves.   Heredity and environment—these are the
dominant realities in our minds ; and so inevitable, so impor-
tunate is their pressure, that what was once known as freedom
passes out of view.   We are afraid to speak as the Bible
speaks about personal responsibility—we are afraid to say
the tremendous things it says about sin and sinful men—
both because we would not be unjust to others, and because
we wish to be considerate to ourselves.   For the same reason
we are afraid to give that decisive importance to the atoning
death of Christ which it carries in the New Testament.
But of one thing we may be certain : sooner or later there
will be a reaction against this mental condition.   When our
sense of the unity of the race in itself, and of its unity with
the ' nature ' which is the theatre of its history, has done its
work—when the social conscience has been quickened—when
the feeling of corporate responsibility has attained adequate
intensity, so that the duties of society to the individual shall
be no longer overlooked, the responsibility of the individual
will come back in new strength.   The naturalistic view of
the world cannot permanently suppress the moral one.
Even while it has seemed to threaten it, it has been prepar-
ing for its revival in a more profound and adequate form.
The sense of personal responsibility, when it does come back,
will be less confined, more far-reaching and mysterious ; it
will be more than ever such a sense of responsibility as will
make the doctrine of a divine atonement for sin necessary,
credible, and welcome.

   Meanwhile, surely, the preaching of the atonement has
something to do with producing the very state of mind on
which its reception depends.   It is the highest truth of
revelation ; and the highest truth is like the highest poetry
—it has to generate the intellectual and moral atmosphere

in which alone it can be appreciated and taken to the heart. To say that there is no sense of sin, or that the sense of sin is defective, is only to say in other words that there is no repentance, or no adequate repentance ; no returning of the mind upon itself deeply enough, humbly enough, tenderly and hopefully enough, to have any healing or restoring effect. But how is this spiritual condition to be altered ? What is the cure for it ? There are those who cannot be convinced that any cure is necessary. In spite of all Christian confession to the contrary, they cling to the idea that such a returning of the mind upon itself as would constitute repentance unto life and be the proper condition of pardon and acceptance with God, is an experience which the sinful soul can produce out of its own resources, and clothed in which it can come hopefully to meet God. But true repentance—that is, repentance which is not self-centred, but which realises that sin is something in which God has an interest as well as we ; repentance which is not merely a remorseful or apathetic or despairing regret, but a hopeful, healing, sanctifying sorrow—such repentance is born of the knowledge of God, and of what God has done for us in our sins. It is not a preliminary to the Atonement, nor a substitute for it, nor a way in which we can be reconciled to God without being indebted to it ; it is its fruit. It is born at the Cross where we see sin put away, not by our own regret, however sincere and profound, but by the love of God in the Passion of His dear Son. Hence we lose the only chance of seeing it, and of seeing in its true intensity the sense of individual responsibility which is part and parcel of it, if we give the Atonement anything less than the central place in our preaching. No one is really saved from sin until he has in relation to it that mind which Christ had when He bore our sins in His own body on the tree. And no motive is potent enough to generate that mind in sinful men but the love with which Christ loved us when He so gave Himself for us. It is true to say that the Atonement presupposes conscience and appeals to it, but it is truer still to say that of all powers in the world it is the supreme power for creating and deepening conscience. One remembers again and again the story of the first Moravian missionaries to Greenland, who, after twenty years of fruitless toil in indirect approaches to the savage mind, found it suddenly responsive to the appeal of the Cross. Probably St. Paul made no mistake when he delivered to the Corinthians ἐν πρώτοις the message of the Atonement. No one can tell how near conscience is to the surface, or how quickly in any man it may respond to the appeal. We might have thought that in Corinth much preliminary sapping and mining would have been requisite before the appeal could be made with any prospect of success; but St. Paul judged otherwise, and preached from the very outset the great hope of the gospel, by which conscience is at once evoked and redeemed. We might think that in a Christian country conscience would be nearer the surface, more susceptible, more conscious of its needs, more quickly responsive to the appeal of the atonement; and if we do not always find it so, it is only, as St. Paul himself puts it, because all men have not faith. We cannot get behind this melancholy fact, and give the rationale of what is in itself irrational. Yet all experience shows that the gospel wins by its magnitude, and that the true method for the evangelist is to put the great things in the forefront. If this is not the way to the conscience, this sublime demonstration of the love of God in Christ, in which our responsibility as sinful men is taken by Him in all its dreadful reality and made His own, what is? In what, if not in this, can we find the means of appealing to all men, and to that which is deepest in all?

One other characteristic ought to distinguish evangelical

preaching, as preaching determined by the Atonement : it ought to have a deep impression of the absoluteness of the issues in faith and unbelief, or let us say in the acceptance or rejection of the reconciliation. In one way, it may be said, this is always the note of religion. It is a form of the absolute consciousness, and deals not with a sliding scale but with the blank, unqualified antithesis of life or death, weal or woe, salvation or perdition, heaven or hell. This is true, yet of no religion is it more emphatically true than of that which is exhibited in the New Testament. It is a life and death matter we are concerned with when we come face to face with Christ and with what He has done for us. It is quite possible to preach with earnestness, and even with persuasiveness, from another standpoint. It is quite possible to have a very sincere admiration for goodness, and a very sincere desire to be better men than we are and to see others better ; it is quite possible even to see the charm and beauty of Christ's goodness, and to commend it in the most winning way to men, and yet to want in preaching the very note which is characteristic both of Christ and the apostles. Christ knew that He was to give His life a ransom ; the apostles knew that He had done it, and had made peace through the blood of His Cross ; and their preaching, though it is never overbearing or unjust, though it never tries to intimidate men, or (as one may sometimes have been tempted to think in a mission service) to bully them into faith, is as urgent and passionate as the sense of the atoning death can make it. To receive the reconciliation, or not to receive it —to be a Christian, or not to be a Christian— is not a matter of comparative indifference ; it is not the case of being a somewhat better man, or a man, perhaps, not quite so good ; it is a case of life or death. It is difficult to speak of this as it ought to be spoken of, and to urge it in any given situation may easily expose the preacher to the charge of intolerance, uncharitableness, or moral blindness ; but difficult as it may be to preach the gospel in the spirit of the gospel, with a sense at the same time of the infinite love which is in it, and the infinite responsibility which it puts upon us, it is not a difficulty which the preacher's vocation will allow him to evade. He may easily be represented as saying that he is making the acceptance of his own theology the condition of acceptance with God, and arrogating to himself the right to judge others ; but while he repudiates such charges as inconsistent with his whole relation both to God and man, he will not abandon his conviction that the apostolic sense of the infinite consequences determined by man's relation to the gospel is justified, and that it is justified because it is in harmony with all that the New Testament teaches about the finished work of Christ. God has spoken His last word in His Son ; He has done all that He can do for men ; revelation and redemption are complete, and the finality on which the Epistle to the Hebrews lays such emphasis as characteristic of everything belonging to the new covenant ought to have an echo in every proclamation of it. If therefore we are conscious that this note is wanting in our preaching—that it fails in urgency and entreaty—that it is expository merely, or attractive, or hortatory—that it is interpretative or illuminative, or has the character of good advice, very good advice indeed, when we come to think of it,—it is probably time to ask what place in it is held by the Atonement. The proclamation of the finished work of Christ is not good advice, it is good news : good news that means immeasurable joy for those who welcome it, irreparable loss for those who reject it, infinite and urgent responsibility for all. The man who has this to preach has a gospel about which he ought to be in dead earnest : just because there is nothing which concentrates in the same way the judgment and the mercy of God, there is nothing which has the same power to evoke seriousness and passion in the preacher.

Leaving out of account its importance to the sinner, the supreme interest of the doctrine of the Atonement is, of course, its interest for the evangelist ; without a firm grasp of it he can do nothing whatever in his vocation.   But what is central in religion must be central also in all reflection upon it, and the theologian no less than the evangelist must give this great truth its proper place in his mind.   I have no intention of outlining a system of theology in which the atonement made in the death of Christ should be the determinative principle ; but short of this, it is possible to indicate its bearing and significance in regard to some vital questions.

For example, if we have been correct in our appreciation of its place in the New Testament, it is not too much to say that as the focus of revelation it is the key to all that precedes.   It may not always be historically true, but it will always be divinely true—that is, it will answer to God's mind as we can see it now, if not as it was apprehended from stage to stage in the history of revelation—if we let the light of the final revelation of the New Testament fall all along upon the Old.   The nature of the unity which belongs to Scripture has always been a perplexing question—so perplexing, indeed, that the very existence of any unity at all has been denied ; yet there is an answer to it.   Scripture converges upon the doctrine of the Atonement ; it has the unity of a consentient testimony to a love of God which bears the sin of the world.   How this is done we do not see clearly till we come to Christ, or till He comes to us ; but once we get this insight from Him, we get it for revelation as a whole. To Him bear all the Scriptures witness ; and it is as a testimony to Him, the Bearer of sin, the Redeemer who gave His life a ransom for us, that we acknowledge them.   This is the burden of the Bible, the one fundamental omnipresent truth to which the Holy Spirit bears witness by and with the word in our hearts. This, at bottom, is what we mean when we say that Scripture is inspired.

It is worth while to insist on this in view of the widespread confusion which prevails in regard to inspiration; the apparent readiness, on the part of some, to give it up as an insignificant or irrelevant idea, if not an utterly discredited one; and the haphazard attempts, on the part of others, to save it piecemeal, after abandoning it as a whole. The truth is, the unity of the Bible and its inspiration are correlative terms. If we can discover a real unity in it—as I believe we can and do when we see that it converges upon and culminates in a divine love bearing the sin of the world —then that unity and its inspiration are one and the same thing. And it is not only inspired as a whole, it is the only book in the world which is inspired. It is the only book in the world to which God sets His seal in our hearts when we read in search of an answer to the question, How shall a sinful man be righteous with God? It is mere irrelevance and misunderstanding to talk in this connection of the 'inspiration' of great minds like Æschylus or Plato, not to speak of those who have been born and bred in the Christian atmosphere, like Dante or Shakespeare. We do not believe in inspiration because we find something in Isaiah which we do not find in Æschylus—though we do; nor because we find something in St. Paul which we do not find in Plato—though again, and more emphatically, we do; we believe in inspiration because in the whole Bible, from Isaiah to St. Paul, and earlier and later, there is a unity of mind and spirit and purpose which shines out on us at last in the atoning work of Christ. When we approach the greatest of human minds with the problem of religion, How shall a sinful man be just with God? we shall, no doubt, find sympathy, for the problem of religion is a universal problem; we find sympathy, for instance, of the profoundest in writers like Æschylus and Sophocles. But when we approach Scripture with this problem, we not only find sympathy, but a solution; and with the solution is identified all that we mean by inspiration. All the suggestions of the Bible with reference to this problem converge upon the Cross. The Cross dominates everything. It interprets everything. It puts all things in their true relations to each other. Usually those who are perplexed about the inspiration of the Bible discuss their difficulties with no consideration of what the Bible means as a whole; and yet it is only as a whole that we can attach any meaning to its being inspired. There is no sense in saying that every separate sentence is inspired: we know that every separate sentence is not. There are utterances of bad men in the Bible, and suggestions of the devil. Neither is there any sense in going through the Bible with a blue pencil, and striking out what is not inspired that we may stand by the rest. This may have the apologetic or educational advantage of compelling some people to see that after all abatements are made there is a great deal which retains its authority, and imposes responsibility; but it is precarious and presumptuous in the highest degree. And though it may have the appearance of greater plausibility, it is just as futile to attempt to graduate the inspiration of Scripture, to mark the ebb and flow of the divine presence in the heart of a writer, or the gradual rise of the tide from the remote beginnings of revelation till it reaches its height in Christ. No doubt it is a task for the historian to trace the gradual progress of revelation and to indicate its stages, but the historian would be the first to acknowledge that the questions so often raised about the inspiration of persons or books or sentences or arguments are mostly unreal. We will never know what inspiration is until Scripture has resolved itself for us into a unity. That unity, I venture to say, will be its testimony to a love in God which we do not earn, which we can never repay, but which in our sins comes to meet us with mercy, dealing, nevertheless, with our sins in all earnest, and at infinite cost doing right by God's holy law in regard to them ; a love which becomes incarnate in the Lamb of God bearing the sin of the world, and putting it away by the sacrifice of Himself. It is in its testimony to this that the unity of Scripture and its inspiration consists, and whoever believes in this believes in inspiration in the only sense which can be rationally attached to the word.

The doctrine of the atonement, in the central place which Scripture secures for it, has decisive importance in another way : it is the proper evangelical foundation for a doctrine of the Person of Christ. To put it in the shortest possible form, Christ is the person who can do this work for us. This is the deepest and most decisive thing we can know about Him, and in answering the questions which it prompts we are starting from a basis in experience. There is a sense in which Christ as the Reconciler confronts us. He is doing the will of God on our behalf, and we can only look on. It is the judgment and the mercy of God in relation to our sins which we see in Him, and His Presence and work on earth are a divine gift, a divine visitation. He is the gift of God to men, not the offering of men to God, and God gives Himself to us in and with Him. We owe to Him all that we call divine life. On the other hand, this divine visitation is made, and this divine life is imparted, through a life and work which are truly human. The presence and work of Jesus in the world, even the work of bearing sin, does not prompt us to define human and divine by contrast with each other : there is no suggestion of incongruity between them. Nevertheless, they are both there, and the fact that they are both there justifies us in raising the question as to Jesus' relation to God on the one hand, and to men on the other. We become sensible, as we contemplate this divine visitation, this achievement of a work so necessary to man yet so transcending his powers, that Jesus is not in the human race one man more to whom our relation may be as fortuitous as to any other. Rather does the whole phenomenon justify us in putting such a question as Dale's : What must Christ's relation to men be in order to make it possible that He should die for them ?— a question leading to an essentially evangelical argument, that Christ must have had an original and central relation to the human race and to every member of it. Whether this is the best way to express the conclusion need not here be considered, but that this is the final way to approach the problem is not open to doubt.

In this connection I venture to emphasise again a point referred to at the close of the first chapter. It is the doctrine of the Atonement which secures for Christ His place in the gospel, and which makes it inevitable that we should have a Christology or a doctrine of His Person. Reduced to the simplest religious expression, the doctrine of the Atonement signifies that we owe to Christ and to His finished work our whole being as Christians. We are His debtors, and it is a real debt ; a debt infinite, never to be forgotten, never to be discharged. The extraordinary statement of Harnack—as extraordinary, perhaps, in its ambiguity as in its daring— that in the gospel as Jesus preached it the Son has no place but only the Father, owes whatever plausibility it has under the most favourable construction to the assumption that in the gospel as Jesus preached it there is no such thing as an atoning work of Jesus. Jesus *did* nothing in particular by which men become His debtors ; He only showed in His own life what the state of the case was between God and men, quite apart from anything He did or had to do. He was ' the personal realisation and the power of the gospel, and is ever again experienced as such.' One might be tempted to criticise this from Kierkegaard's point of view, and to urge that it betrays no adequate appreciation of the gulf between Christ and sinful men, and of the dreadful difficulty of bridging it; but it is sufficient to say that it departs so widely not only from the consciousness of primitive Christianity as it is reflected in the epistles, but from the mind of Christ as we have seen cause to interpret it through the gospels, that it is impossible to assent to it.   Christ not only *was* something in the world, He *did* something.   He did something that made an infinite difference, and that puts us under an infinite obligation: He bore our sins.   That secures His place in the gospel and in the adoration of the church.   That is the impulse and the justification of all Christologies.   Harnack's statement, quoted above, is meant to give a religious justification for lightening the ship of the church by casting Christological controversy overboard; but the Atonement always says to us again, Consider how great this Man was!   As long as it holds its place in the preaching of the gospel, and asserts itself in the church, as it does in the New Testament, as the supreme inspiration to praise, so long will Christians find in the Person of their Lord a subject of high and reverent thought.   It is a common idea that Socinianism (or Unitarianism) is specially connected with the denial of the Incarnation.   It began historically with the denial of the Atonement.   It is with the denial of the Atonement that it always begins anew, and it cannot be too clearly pointed out that to begin here is to end, sooner or later, with putting Christ out of the Christian religion altogether.

It is the more necessary to insist on this point of view because there is in some quarters a strong tendency to put the Atonement out of its place, and to concentrate attention on the Incarnation as something which can be appreciated in entire independence of it.   The motives for this are various.   Sometimes they may not unfairly be described as speculative. ' The great aim of the Christian Platonists,' says Mr. Inge, ' was to bring the Incarnation into closest relation with the cosmic process. It need hardly be said that no Christian philosophy can have any value which does not do this.'[1] Those, therefore, whose interest is in the cosmic process, or in articulating all that is known as Christian into the framework of the universe, devote their attention to the Person of Christ, and seek in it the natural consummation, so to speak, of all that has gone before. Without that Person the universe would be without a crown or a head. It is so constituted that only He gives it unity and completeness. That its unity had been broken before He came to earth, and that He completed it by a work of reversal and not of direct evolution—a work which, however truly it may be said to have carried out the original idea of God, is yet in the strictest sense supernatural, a redemption, not a natural consummation—is practically overlooked. With others, again, the motive may be said to be ethical. To put the Atonement at the foundation of Christianity seems to them to narrow it morally in the most disastrous way. It is as though they lost the breadth and variety of interest and motive which appeal to the conscience from the life of Christ in the pages of the evangelists. But there is a misconception here. Those who make the Atonement fundamental do not turn their backs on the gospels. They are convinced, however, that the whole power of the motives which appeal to us from the life of Jesus is not felt until we see it condensed, concentrated, and transcended in the love in which He bore our sins in His own body on the tree. Others displace the Atonement for what may be called a dogmatic reason. It is a fixed point with them that so great a thing as the Incarnation could not be in any proper sense contingent; the presence of the Son of God in the

[1] *Contentio Veritatis*, p. 74.

world cannot be an 'after-thought' or an 'accident'; the whole intent of it cannot be given in such an expression as 'remedial.' The universe must have been constituted from the first with a view to it, and it would have taken place all the same even though there had been no sin and no need for redemption. When it did take place, indeed, it could not be exactly as had been intended; under the conditions of the fall, the Incarnation entailed a career which meant Atonement; it was Incarnation into a sinful race, and the Atonement was made when the Son of God accepted the conditions which sin had determined, and fulfilled man's destiny under them. Perhaps the truth might be put within the four corners of such a formula, but the tendency in those who adopt this point of view is to minimise all that is said in the New Testament about the death of Christ in relation to sin. The specific assertions and definitions of the apostolic writings are evaded. They are interpreted emotionally but not logically, as if the men who say the strong things on this subject in the New Testament had said them without thinking, or would have been afraid of their own thoughts. The most distinguished representative of this tendency in our own country was Bishop Westcott. Not that what has just been said is applicable in its entirety to him; but the assumption that the Incarnation is something which we can estimate apart from the Atonement, something which has a significance and a function of its own, independent of man's redemption from sin, underlies much of his writing, and tends to keep him from doing full justice to apostolic ideas on this subject. The logic of the position becomes apparent in a writer like Archdeacon Wilson, who frankly merges the Atonement in the Incarnation, assures us that in making a distinct problem of the former we have been asking meaningless questions, getting meaningless answers, and repelling men from the gospel. 'Let us say boldly that the Incarnation, that is the life and death of the Christ—for the life and death were equally necessary—is the identification of the human and the divine life. This identification is the atonement. There is no other.'[1]   One can only regret that this short and easy method was not discovered till the close of the nineteenth century; anything less like the terrible problem sin presented to the apostles, and their intense preoccupation with it, it would not be easy to conceive.

There are three broad grounds on which the interpretation of the Atonement as a mere incident, or consequence, or modification of the Incarnation—the Incarnation being regarded as something in itself natural and intelligible on grounds which have no relation to sin—ought to be discounted by the evangelist and the theologian alike.   (1) It shifts the centre of gravity in the New Testament.   The Incarnation may be the thought round which everything gravitates in the Nicene Creed, and in the theology of the ancient Catholic Church which found in that creed its first dogmatic expression; but that only shows how far the first ecclesiastical apprehension of Christianity was from doing justice to New Testament conceptions.   Even in the Gospel and the Epistles of St. John, as has been shown above, the Incarnation cannot be said (without serious qualification) to have the character here claimed for it, and it cannot be asserted with the faintest plausibility for the synoptic gospels or the Epistles of St. Paul. The New Testament knows nothing of an incarnation which can be defined apart from its relation to atonement; it is to put away sin, and to destroy the works of the devil, that even in the evangelist of the Incarnation the Son of God is made manifest.   It is not in His being here, but in His being here as a pro- pitiation for the sins of the world, that the love of God is revealed.   Not Bethlehem, but Calvary, is the focus of

----

[1] *The Gospel of the Atonement,* p. 89.

revelation, and any construction of Christianity which ignores or denies this distorts Christianity by putting it out of focus. (2) A second ground for resisting the tendency to put the Incarnation into the place which properly belongs to the Atonement is that it is concerned under these conditions with metaphysical, rather than with moral problems. Now Scripture has no interest in metaphysics except as metaphysical questions are approached through and raised by moral ones. The Atonement comes to us in the moral world and deals with us there; it is concerned with conscience and the law of God, with sin and grace, with alienation and peace, with death to sin and life to holiness; it has its being and its efficacy in a world where we can find our footing, and be assured that we are dealing with realities. The Incarnation, when it is not defined by relation to these realities—in other words, when it is not conceived as the means to the Atonement, but as part of a speculative theory of the world quite independent of man's actual moral necessities—can never attain to a reality as vivid and profound. It can never become thoroughly credible, just because it is not essentially related to anything in human or Christian experience sufficiently great to justify it. It does not answer moral questions, especially those which bring the sinful man to despair; at best it answers metaphysical questions about the relation of the human to the divine, about the proper way to define these words in relation to each other, whether it be by contrast or by mutual affinity, about the divine as being the truth of the human and the human as being the reality of the divine, and so forth. It does not contain a gospel for lost souls, but a philosophy for speculative minds. Now the New Testament is a gospel for lost souls, or it is nothing; and whatever philosophy it may lead to or justify, we cannot see that philosophy itself in the light in which it demands to be seen, unless we keep the gospel in its New Testament place. If we start in the abstract speculative way there is no getting out of it, or getting any specifically Christian good out of it either; it is only when the Person of Christ is conceived as necessarily related to a work in which we have a life and death moral interest, that it has religious import, and can be a real subject for us. There is in truth only one religious problem in the world—the existence of sin; and one religious solution of it—the Atonement, in which the love of God bears the sin, taking it, in all its terrible reality for us, upon itself. And nothing can be central or fundamental either in Christian preaching or in Christian thinking which is not in direct and immediate relation to this problem and its solution. (3) The third ground on which we should deprecate the obtrusion of the Incarnation at the cost of the Atonement is that in point of fact— whether it is an inevitable result or not need not be inquired —it tends to sentimentality. It is dangerous to bring into religion anything which is not vitally related to morals, and Incarnation not determined by Atonement is open to this charge. The Christmas celebrations in many churches supply all the proof that is needed : they are an appeal to anything and everything in man except that to which the gospel is designed to appeal. The New Testament is just as little sentimental as it is metaphysical : it is ethical, not metaphysical; passionate, not sentimental. And its passionate and ethical character are condensed and guaranteed in that atoning work of Christ which is in every sense of the word its vital centre.

If it is a right conception of the Atonement which enables us to attain to a right conception of the Person of Christ, similarly we may say it is through a right conception of the Atonement that we come to a right conception of the nature or character of God. In the Atonement revelation is complete, and we must have it fully in view in all affirmations we make about God as the ultimate truth and reality. The more imperfect our conceptions of God, the more certainly they tend to produce scepticism and unbelief; and nothing presents greater difficulties to faith than the idea of a God who either gives no heed to the sin and misery of man, or saves sinners, as it were, from a distance, without entering into the responsibility and tragedy of their life and making it His own. To put the same thing in other words, nothing presents greater difficulties to faith than a conception of God falling short of that which the New Testament expresses in the words, God is love. Not that this conception is self-interpreting or self-accrediting, as is often supposed. There is no proposition which is more in need both of explanation and of proof. We may say God is love, and know just as little what love means as what God means. Love is like every word of moral or spiritual import; it has no fixed meaning, like a word denoting a physical object or attribute; it stands, so to speak, upon a sliding scale, and it stands higher or lower as the experience of those who use it enables them to place it. St. John, when he placed it where he did, was only enabled to do so by the experience in which Christ was revealed to him as the propitiation for sins. It is with this in his mind that he says, *Hereby* perceive we love. The word love, especially in such a proposition as God is love, has to fill with its proper meaning before it can be said to have any meaning at all; it is used in a thousand senses which in such a proposition would only be absurd or profane. Now the person who first uttered that sublime sentence felt his words fill with meaning as he contemplated Christ sent by God a propitiation for the whole world. A God who could do that— a God who could bear the sin of the world in order to restore to man the possibility of righteousness and eternal life—such a God is love. Such love, too, is the ultimate truth about God. But apart from this the apostle would not have said that God is love, nor is it quite real or specifically Christian for any one else to say so. There is no adequate way of telling what he means. Until it is demonstrated as it is in the Atonement, love remains an indeterminate sentimental expression, with no clear moral value, and with infinite possibilities of moral misunderstanding; when it fills with meaning through the contemplation of the Atonement, the danger of mere sentimentalism and other moral dangers are provided against, for love in the Atonement is inseparable from law. The universal moral elements in the relations of God and man are unreservedly acknowledged, and it is in the cost at which justice is done to them in the work of redemption that the love of God is revealed and assured. We see then its reality and its scale. We see what it is willing to do, or rather what it has done. We see something of the breadth and length and depth and height which pass knowledge. We believe and know the love which God has in our case, and can say God is love. And it is from the vantage-ground of this assurance that we look out henceforth on all the perplexities of the world and of our own life in it. We are certain that it is in God to take the burden and responsibility of it upon Himself. We are certain that it is in the divine nature not to be indifferent to the tragedy of human life, not to help it from afar off, not to treat as unreal in it the very thing which makes it real to us—the eternal difference of right and wrong—but to bear its sin, and to establish the law in the very act and method of justifying the ungodly. It is a subordinate remark in this connection, but not for that reason an insignificant one, that this final revelation of love in God is at the same time the final revelation of sin : for sin, too, needs to be revealed, and there is a theological doctrine of it as well as an experience antecedent to all doctrines. Love is that which is willing to take the responsibility of sin upon it for the sinner's sake, and which does so; and sin, in the last resort—sin as that which cuts man finally off from God—is that which is proof against the appeal of such love.

There is another great department of Christian science to which the Atonement is of fundamental importance—the department of Christian ethics, the scientific interpretation of the new life. It has undoubtedly been a fault in much systematic theology, that in dealing with the work which Christ finished in His death it has shown no relation, or no adequate and satisfactory relation, between that death and the Christian life which is born of faith in it. There must be such a relation, or there would be no such thing in the world as Christian life or the Christian religion. The only difficulty, indeed, in formulating it is that the connection is so close and immediate that it might be supposed to be impossible to hold apart, even in imagination, the two things which we wish to define by relation to each other. But it may be put thus. The death of Christ, interpreted as the New Testament interprets it, constitutes a great appeal to sinful men. It appeals for faith. To yield to its appeal, to abandon oneself in faith to the love of God which is manifested in it, is to enter into life. It is the only way in which a sinful man can enter into life at all. The new life is constituted in the soul by the response of faith to the appeal of Christ's death, or by Christ's death evoking the response of faith. It does not matter which way we put it. We may say that we have received the Atonement, and that the Atonement regenerates; or that we have been justified by faith, and that justification regenerates; or that we have received an assurance of God's love which is deeper than our sin, and extends to all our life past, present, and to come; and that such an assurance, which is the gift of the Spirit shed abroad in our hearts, regenerates: it is all one. It is the same experience which is described, and truly described, in every case. But both the power and the law of the new life, the initiation of which can be so variously expressed, are to be found in the atoning death of Christ, by which faith is evoked, and there only ; and the Atonement, therefore, is the presupposition of Christian ethics as it is the inspiring and controlling force in Christian life. Nothing can beget in the soul that life of which we speak except the appeal of the Cross, and what the appeal of the Cross does beget is a life which, in its moral quality, corresponds to the death of Christ itself. It is a life, as it has been put already, which has that death in it, and which only lives upon this condition. It is a life to which sin is all that sin was to Christ—law, and holiness, and God, all that law and holiness and God were to Christ as He hung upon the tree ; a life which is complete and self-sufficing, because it is sustained at every moment by the inspiration of the Atonement. This is why St. Paul is not afraid to trust the new life to its own resources, and why he objects equally to supplementing it by legal regulations afterwards, or by what are supposed to be ethical securities beforehand. It does not need them, and is bound to repel them as dishonouring to Christ. To demand moral guarantees from a sinner before you give him the benefit of the Atonement, or to impose legal restrictions on him after he has yielded to its appeal, and received it through faith, is to make the Atonement itself of no effect. St. Paul, taught by his own experience, scorned such devices. The Son of God, made sin for men, so held his eyes and heart, entered into his being with such annihilative, such creative power, that all he was and all he meant by life were due to Him alone. He does not look anywhere but to the Cross for the ideals and motives of the Christian : they are all there. And the more one dwells in the New Testament, and tries to find the point of view from which to reduce it to unity, the more is he convinced that the Atonement is the key to

Christianity as a whole. 'The Son of Man came to give His life a ransom for many.' 'Christ died for the ungodly.' 'He bore our sins in His own body on the tree.' 'He is the propitiation for the whole world.' 'I beheld, and lo, a lamb as it had been slain.' It is in words like these that we discover the open secret of the new creation.

CHAPTER VII

THE ATONEMENT AND THE MODERN MIND

IT will be admitted by most Christians that if the Atonement, quite apart from precise definitions of it, is anything to the mind, it is everything. It is the most profound of all truths, and the most recreative. It determines more than anything else our conceptions of God, of man, of history, and even of nature; it determines them, for we must bring them all in some way into accord with it. It is the inspiration of all thought, the impulse and the law of all action, the key, in the last resort, to all suffering. Whether we call it a fact or a truth, a power or a doctrine, it is that in which the *differentia* of Christianity, its peculiar and exclusive character, is specifically shown; it is the focus of revelation, the point at which we see deepest into the truth of God, and come most completely under its power. For those who recognise it at all it is Christianity in brief; it concentrates in itself, as in a germ of infinite potency, all that the wisdom, power and love of God mean in relation to sinful men.

Accordingly, when we speak of the Atonement and the modern mind, we are really speaking of the modern mind and the Christian religion. The relation between these two magnitudes may vary. The modern mind is no more than a modification of the human mind as it exists in all ages, and the relation of the modern mind to the Atonement is one phase—it may be a specially interesting or a specially well-defined phase—of the perennial relation of the mind of man to the truth of God. There is always an affinity between the two, for God made man in His own image, and the mind can only rest in truth ; but there is always at the same time an antipathy, for man is somehow estranged from God, and resents divine intrusion into his life. This is the situation at all times, and therefore in modern times ; we only need to remark that when the Atonement is in question, the situation, so to speak, becomes acute. All the elements in it define themselves more sharply. If there is sympathy between the mind and the truth, it is a profound sympathy, which will carry the mind far ; if there are lines of approach, through which the truth can find access to the mind, they are lines laid deep in the nature of things and of men, and the access which the truth finds by them is one from which it will not easily be dislodged. On the other hand, if it is antagonism which is roused in the mind by the Atonement, it is an antagonism which feels that everything is at stake. The Atonement is a reality of such a sort that it can make no compromise. The man who fights it knows that he is fighting for his life, and puts all his strength into the battle. To surrender is literally to give up himself, to cease to be the man he is, and to become another man. For the modern mind, therefore, as for the ancient, the attraction and the repulsion of Christianity are concentrated at the same point ; the cross of Christ is man's only glory, or it is his final stumbling-block.

What I wish to do in the following pages is so to present the facts as to mediate, if possible, between the mind of our time and the Atonement—so to exhibit the specific truth of Christianity as to bring out its affinity for what is deepest in the nature of man and in human experience—so to appreciate the modern mind itself, and the influences which have given it its constitution and temper, as to discredit what is false in it, and enlist on the side of the Atonement that which is profound and true. And if any one is disposed to marvel at the ambition or the conceit of such a programme, I would ask him to consider if it is not the programme prescribed to every Christian, or at least to every Christian minister who would do the work of an evangelist. To commend the eternal truth of God, as it is finally revealed in the Atonement, to the mind in which men around us live and move and have their being, is no doubt a difficult and perilous task; but if we approach it in a right spirit, it need not tempt us to any presumption; it cannot tempt us, as long as we feel that it is our duty. *' Who is sufficient for these things? . . . Our sufficiency is of God.'*

The Christian religion is a historical religion, and whatever we say about it must rest upon historical ground. We cannot define it from within, by reference merely to our individual experience. Of course it is equally impossible to define it apart from experience; the point is that such experience itself must be historically derived; it must come through something outside of our individual selves. What is true of the Christian religion as a whole is pre-eminently true of the Atonement in which it is concentrated. The experience which it brings to us, and the truth which we teach on the basis of it, are historically mediated. They rest ultimately on that testimony to Christ which we find in the Scriptures and especially in the New Testament. No one can tell what the Atonement is except on this basis. No one can consciously approach it—no one can be influenced by it to the full extent to which it is capable of influencing human nature—except through this medium. We may hold that just because it is divine, it must be eternally true, omnipresent in its gracious power; but even granting this, it is not known as an abstract or eternal somewhat; it is historically, and not otherwise than historically, revealed. It is achieved by Christ, and the testimony to Christ, on the strength of which we accept it, is in the last resort the testimony of Scripture.

In saying so, I do not mean that the Atonement is merely a problem of exegesis, or that we have simply to accept as authoritative the conclusions of scholars as to the meaning of New Testament texts. The modern mind here is ready with a radical objection. The writers of the New Testament, it argues, were men like ourselves; they had personal limitations and historical limitations; their forms of thought were those of a particular age and upbringing; the doctrines they preached may have had a relative validity, but we cannot so benumb our minds as to accept them without question. The intelligence which has learned to be a law to itself, criticising, rejecting, appropriating, assimilating, cannot deny its nature and suspend its functions when it opens the New Testament. It cannot make itself the slave of men, not even though the men are Peter and Paul and John; no, not even though it were the Son of Man Himself. It resents dictation, not wilfully nor wantonly, but because it must; and it resents it all the more when it claims to be inspired. If, therefore, the Atonement can only be received by those who are prepared from the threshold to acknowledge the inspiration and the consequent authority of Scripture, it can never be received by modern men at all.

This line of remark is familiar inside the Church as well as outside. Often it is expressed in the demand for a historical as opposed to a dogmatic interpretation of the New Testament, a historical interpretation being one to which we can sit freely, because the result to which it leads us is the mind of a time which we have survived and presumably transcended; a dogmatic interpretation, on the other hand, being one which claims to reach an abiding truth,

and therefore to have a present authority. A more popular
and inconsistent expression of the same mood may be found
among those who say petulant things about the rabbinising
of Paul, but profess the utmost devotion to the words of
Jesus. Even in a day of overdone distinctions, one might
point out that interpretations are not properly to be classified
as historical or dogmatic, but as true or false. If they are
false, it does not matter whether they are called dogmatic or
historical; and if they are true, they may quite well be both.
But this by the way. For my own part, I prefer the objection in its most radical form, and indeed find nothing in it
to which any Christian, however sincere or profound his
reverence for the Bible, should hesitate to assent. Once
the mind has come to know itself, there can be no such thing
for it as blank authority. It cannot believe things—the
things by which it has to live—simply on the word of Paul
or John. It is not irreverent, it is simply the recognition of
a fact, if we add that it can just as little believe them simply
on the word of Jesus.[1] This is not the sin of the mind, but
the nature and essence of mind, the being which it owes to
God. If we are to speak of authority at all in this connection, the authority must be conceived as belonging not to
the speaker but to that which he says, not to the witness but
to the truth. Truth, in short, is the only thing which has
authority for the mind, and the only way in which truth finally
evinces its authority is by taking possession of the mind for
itself. It may be that any given truth can only be reached by
testimony—that is, can only come to us by some historical
channel; but if it is a truth of eternal import, if it is
part of a revelation of God the reception of which is

---

[1] Of course this does not touch the fact that the whole 'authority' of the
Christian religion is in Jesus Himself—in His historical presence in the world,
His words and works, His life and death and resurrection. He *is* the truth,
the acceptance of which by man is life eternal.

eternal life, then its authority lies in itself and in its power to win the mind, and not in any witness however trustworthy.

Hence in speaking of the Atonement, whether in preaching or in theologising, it is quite unnecessary to raise any question about the inspiration of Scripture, or to make any claim of 'authority' either for the Apostles or for the Lord. Belief in the inspiration of Scripture is neither the beginning of the Christian life nor the foundation of Christian theology; it is the last conclusion—a conclusion which becomes every day more sure—to which experience of the truth of Scripture leads. When we tell, therefore, what the Atonement is, we are telling it not on the authority of any person or persons whatever, but on the authority of the truth in it by which it has won its place in our minds and hearts. We find this truth in the Christian Scriptures undoubtedly, and therefore we prize them; but the truth does not derive its authority from the Scriptures, or from those who penned them. On the contrary, the Scriptures are prized by the Church because through them the soul is brought into contact with this truth. No doubt this leaves it open to any one who does not see in Scripture what we see, or who is not convinced as we are of its truth, to accuse us here of subjectivity, of having no standard of truth but what appeals to us individually, but I could never feel the charge a serious one. It is like urging that a man does not see at all, or does not see truly, because he only sees with his own eyes. This is the only authentic kind of seeing yet known to mankind. We do not judge at all those who do not see what we do. We do not know what hinders them, or whether they are at all to blame for it; we do not know how soon the hindrance is going to be put out of the way. To-day, as at the beginning, the light shines in the darkness, and the darkness comprehends it not. But that is the situation which calls for evangelists; not a situation in which the evangelist is called to renounce his experience and his vocation.

What, then, is the Atonement, as it is presented to us in the Scriptures, and vindicates for itself in our minds the character of truth, and indeed, as I have said already, the character of the ultimate truth of God?

The simplest expression that can be given to it in words is: Christ died for our sins. Taken by itself, this is too brief to be intelligible; it implies many things which need to be made explicit both about Christ's relation to us and about the relation of sin and death. But the important thing, to begin with, is not to define these relations, but to look through the words to the broad reality which is interpreted in them. What they tell us, and tell us on the basis of an incontrovertible experience, is that the forgiveness of sins is for the Christian mediated through the death of Christ. In one respect, therefore, there is nothing singular in the forgiveness of sins: it is in the same position as every other blessing of which the New Testament speaks. It is the presence of a Mediator, as Westcott says in one of his letters, which makes the Christian religion what it is; and the forgiveness of sins is mediated to us through Christ, just as the knowledge of God as the Father is mediated, or the assurance of a life beyond death. But there is something *specific* about the mediation of forgiveness; the gift and the certainty of it come to us, not simply through Christ, but through the blood of His Cross. The sum of His relation to sin is that He died for it. God forgives, but this is the way in which His forgiveness comes. He forgives freely, but it is at this cost to Himself and to the Son of His love.

This, it seems to me, is the simplest possible statement of what the New Testament means by the Atonement, and probably there are few who would dispute its correctness. But it is possible to argue that there is a deep cleft in the

New Testament itself, and that the teaching of Jesus on the subject of forgiveness is completely at variance with that which we find in the Epistles, and which is implied in this description of the Atonement. Indeed there are many who do so argue. But to follow them would be to forget the place which Jesus has in His own teaching. Even if we grant that the main subject of that teaching is the Kingdom of God, it is as clear as anything can be that the Kingdom depends for its establishment on Jesus, or rather that in Him it is already established in principle ; and that all participation in its blessings depends on some kind of relation to Him. All things have been delivered to Him by the Father, and it is by coming under obligation to Him, and by that alone, that men know the Father. It is by coming under obligation to Him that they know the pardoning love of the Father, as well as everything else that enters into Christian experience and constitutes the blessedness of life in the Kingdom of God. Nor is it open to any one to say that he knows this simply because Christ has told it. We are dealing here with things too great to be simply told. If they are ever to be known in their reality, they must be revealed by God, they must rise upon the mind of man experimentally, in their awful and glorious truth, in ways more wonderful than words. They can be spoken about afterwards, but hardly beforehand. They can be celebrated and preached—that is, declared as the speaker's experience, delivered as his testimony—but not simply told. It was enough if Jesus made His disciples feel, as surely He did make them feel, not only in every word He spoke, but more emphatically still in His whole attitude toward them, that He was Himself the Mediator of the new covenant, and that all the blessings of the relation between God and man which we call Christianity were blessings due to Him. If men knew the Father, it was through Him. If they knew the Father's heart to the lost, it was through Him. Through Him, be it remembered, not merely through the words that He spoke. There was more in Christ than even His own wonderful words expressed, and all that He was and did and suffered, as well as what He said, entered into the convictions He inspired. But He knew this as well as His disciples, and for this very reason it is beside the mark to point to what He said, or rather to what He did not say, in confutation of their experience. For it is their experience—the experience that the forgiveness of sins was mediated to them through His cross—that is expressed in the doctrine of Atonement: He died for our sins.

The objection which is here in view is most frequently pointed by reference to the parable of the prodigal son. There is no Atonement here, we are told, no mediation of forgiveness at all. There is love on the one side and penitence on the other, and it is treason to the pure truth of this teaching to cloud and confuse it with the thoughts of men whose Master was over their heads often, but most of all here. Such a statement of the case is plausible, and judging from the frequency with which it occurs must to some minds be very convincing, but nothing could be more superficial, or more unjust both to Jesus and the apostles. A parable is a comparison, and there is a point of comparison in it on which everything turns. The more perfect the parable is, the more conspicuous and dominating will the point of comparison be. The parable of the prodigal illustrates this. It brings out, through a human parallel, with incomparable force and beauty, the one truth of the freeness of forgiveness. God waits to be gracious. His pardoning love rushes out to welcome the penitent. But no one who speaks of the Atonement ever dreams of questioning this. The Atonement is concerned with a different point—not the freeness of pardon, about which all are agreed, but the cost of it; not the spontaneity of God's love, which no one questions, but the necessity under which it lay to manifest itself in a particular way if God was to be true to Himself, and to win the heart of sinners for the holiness which they had offended. The Atonement is not the denial that God's love is free; it is that specific manifestation or demonstration of God's free love which is demanded by the situation of men. One can hardly help wondering whether those who tell us so confidently that there is no Atonement in the parable of the prodigal have ever noticed that there is no Christ in it either—no elder brother who goes out to seek and to save the lost son, and to give his life a ransom for him. Surely we are not to put the Good Shepherd out of the Christian religion. Yet if we leave Him His place, we cannot make the parable of the prodigal the measure of Christ's mind about the forgiveness of sins. One part of His teaching it certainly contains—one part of the truth about the relation of God the Father to His sinful children; but another part of the truth was present, though not on that occasion rendered in words, in the presence of the Speaker, when 'all the publicans and sinners drew near to Him for to hear Him.' The love of God to the sinful was apprehended in Christ Himself, and not in what He said as something apart from Himself; on the contrary, it was in the identity of the Speaker and the word that the power of the word lay; God's love evinced itself to men as a reality in Him, in His presence in the world, and in His attitude to its sin; it so evinced itself, finally and supremely, in His death. It is not the idiosyncrasy of one apostle, it is the testimony of the Church, a testimony in keeping with the whole claim made by Christ in His teaching and life and death: *in Him* we have our redemption, *through His blood*, even the forgiveness of our trespasses.' And this is what the Atonement means: it means the mediation of forgiveness through Christ, and specifically through

His death.   Forgiveness, in the Christian sense of the term, is only realised as we believe in the Atonement : in other words, as we come to feel the cost at which alone the love of God could assert itself as divine and holy love in the souls of sinful men.   We may say, if we please, that forgiveness is bestowed freely upon repentance ; but we must add, if we would do justice to the Christian position, that repentance in its ultimate character is the fruit of the Atonement.   Repentance is not possible apart from the apprehension of the mercy of God *in Christ*.   It is the experience of the regenerate —*pœnitentiam interpretor regenerationem*, as Calvin says— and it is the Atonement which regenerates.

This, then, in the broadest sense, is the truth which we wish to commend to the modern mind : the truth that there is forgiveness with God, and that this forgiveness comes to us only through Christ, and signally or specifically through His death.   Unless it becomes true to us that *Christ died for our sins*, we cannot appreciate forgiveness at its specifically Christian value.   It cannot be for us that kind of reality, it cannot have for us that kind of inspiration, which it unquestionably is and has in the New Testament.

But what, we must now ask, is the modern mind to which this primary truth of Christianity has to be commended ? Can we diagnose it in any general yet recognisable fashion, so as to find guidance in seeking access to it for the gospel of the Atonement ?   There may seem to be something presumptuous in the very idea, as though any one making the attempt assumed a superiority to the mind of his time, an exemption from its limitations and prejudices, a power to see over it and round about it.   All such presumption is of course disclaimed here ; but even while we disclaim it, the attempt to appreciate the mind of our time is forced upon us.   Whoever has tried to preach the gospel, and to persuade men of truth as truth is in Jesus, and especially of the truth of God's forgiveness as it is in the death of Jesus for sin, knows that there is a state of mind which is somehow inaccessible to this truth, and to which the truth consequently appeals in vain. I do not speak of unambiguous moral antipathy to the ideas of forgiveness and atonement, although antipathy to these ideas in general, as distinct from any given presentation of them, cannot but have a moral character, just as a moral character always attaches to the refusal to acknowledge Christ or to become His debtor; but of something which, though vaguer and less determinate, puts the mind wrong, so to speak, with Christianity from the start. It is clear, for instance, in all that has been said about forgiveness, that certain relations are presupposed as subsisting between God and man, relations which make it possible for man to sin, and possible for God, not indeed to ignore his sin, but in the very act of recognising it as all that it is to forgive it, to liberate man from it, and to restore him to Himself and righteousness. Now if the latent presuppositions of the modern mind are to any extent inconsistent with such relations, there will be something to overcome before the conceptions of forgiveness or atonement can get a hearing. These conceptions have their place in a certain view of the world as a whole, and if the mind is preoccupied with a different view, it will have an instinctive consciousness that it cannot accommodate them, and a disposition therefore to reject them *ab initio*. This is, in point of fact, the difficulty with which we have to deal. And let no one say that it is transparently absurd to suggest that we must get men to accept a true philosophy before we can begin to preach the gospel to them, as though that settled the matter or got over the difficulty. We have to take men as we find them ; we have to preach the gospel to the mind which is around us ; and if that mind is rooted in a view of the world which leaves no room for Christ and His work as Christian experience has realised them, then that view of the world must be appreciated by the evangelist, it must be undermined at its weak places, its inadequacy to interpret all that is present even in the mind which has accepted it —in other words, its inherent inconsistency—must be demonstrated ; the attempt must be made to liberate the mind, so that it may be open to the impression of realities which under the conditions supposed it could only encounter with instinctive antipathy. It is necessary, therefore, at this point to advert to the various influences which have contributed to form the mind of our time, and to give it its instinctive bias in one direction or another. Powerful and legitimate as these influences have been, they have nevertheless been in various ways partial, and because of their very partiality they have, when they absorbed the mind, as new modes of thought are apt to do, prejudiced it against the consideration of other, possibly of deeper and more far-reaching, truths.

First, there is the enormous development of physical science. This has engrossed human intelligence in our own times to an extent which can hardly be over-estimated. Far more mind has been employed in constructing the great fabric of knowledge, which we call science, than in any other pursuit of men. Far more mind has had its characteristic qualities and temper imparted to it by scientific study than by study in any other field. It is of science—which to all intents and purposes means physical science—of science and its methods and results that the modern mind is most confident, and speaks with the most natural and legitimate pride. Now science, even in this restricted sense, covers a great range of subjects ; it may be physics in the narrowest meaning of the word, or chemistry, or biological science. The characteristic of our own age has been the development of the last, and in particular its extension to man. It is impossible to dispute the legitimacy of this extension. Man has his place in nature ; the phenomena of life have one of their signal illustrations in him, and he is as proper a subject of biological study as any other living being. But the intense preoccupation of much of the most vigorous intelligence of our time with the biological study of man is not without effects upon the mind itself, which we need to consider. It tends to produce a habit of mind to which certain assumptions are natural and inevitable, certain other assumptions incredible from the first. This habit of mind is in some ways favourable to the acceptance of the Atonement. For example, the biologist's invincible conviction of the unity of life, and of the certainty and power with which whatever touches it at one point touches it through and through, is in one way entirely favourable. Many of the most telling popular objections to the idea of Atonement rest on an atomic conception of personality—a conception according to which every human being is a closed system, incapable in the last resort of helping or being helped, of injuring or being injured, by another. This conception has been finally discredited by biology, and so far the evangelist must be grateful. The Atonement presupposes the unity of human life and its solidarity ; it presupposes a common and universal responsibility. I believe it presupposes also such a conception of the unity of man and nature as biology proceeds upon ; and in all these respects its physical presuppositions, if we may so express ourselves, are present to the mind of to-day, thanks to biology, as they were not even so lately as a hundred years ago.

But this is not all that we have to consider. The mind has been influenced by the movement of physical and even of biological science, not only in a way which is favourable, but in ways which are prejudicial to the acceptance of the

Atonement. Every physical science seems to have a boundless ambition ; it wants to reduce everything to its own level, to explain everything in the terms and by the categories with which it itself works. The higher has always to fight for its life against the lower. The physicist would like to reduce chemistry to physics ; the chemist has an ambition to simplify biology into chemistry ; the biologist in turn looks with suspicion on anything in man which cannot be interpreted biologically. He would like to give, and is sometimes ready to offer, a biological explanation of self-consciousness, of freedom, of religion, morality, sin. Now a biological explanation, when all is done, is a physical explanation, and a physical explanation of self-consciousness or the moral life is one in which the very essence of the thing to be explained is either ignored or explained away. Man's life is certainly rooted in nature, and therefore a proper subject for biological study ; but unless it somehow transcended nature, and so demanded other than physical categories for its complete interpretation, there could not be any study or any science at all. If there were nothing but matter, as M. Naville has said, there would be no materialism ; and if there were nothing but life, there would be no biology. Now it is in the higher region of human experience, to which all physical categories are unequal, that we encounter those realities to which the Atonement is related, and in relation to which it is real ; and we must insist upon these *higher* realities, in their specific character, against a strong tendency in the scientifically trained modern mind, and still more in the general mind as influenced by it, to reduce them to the merely physical level.

Take, for instance, the consciousness of sin. Evidently the Atonement becomes incredible if the consciousness of sin is extinguished or explained away. There is nothing for the Atonement to do ; there is nothing to relate it to ; it is as unreal as a rock in the sky.   But many minds at the present time, under the influence of current conceptions in biology, do explain it away.   All life is one, they argue.   It rises from the same spring, it runs the same course, it comes to the same end.   The life of man is rooted in nature, and that which beats in my veins is an inheritance from an immeasurable past.   It is absurd to speak of my responsi- bility for it, or of my guilt because it manifests itself in me, as it inevitably does, in such and such forms.   There is no doubt that this mode of thought is widely prevalent, and that it is one of the most serious hindrances to the accept- ance of the gospel, and especially of the Atonement.   How are we to appreciate it ?   We must point out, I think, the consequence to which it leads.   If a man denies that he is responsible for the nature which he has inherited—denies responsibility for it on the ground that it *is* inherited—it is a fair question to ask him for what he *does* accept respon- sibility.   When he has divested himself of the inherited nature, what is left ?   The real meaning of such disowning of responsibility is that a man asserts that his life is a part of the physical phenomena of the universe, and nothing else ; and he forgets, in the very act of making the assertion, that if it were true, it could not be so much as made.   The merely physical is transcended in every such assertion ; and the man who has transcended it, rooted though his life be in nature, and one with the life of the whole and of all the past, must take the responsibility of living that life out on the high level of self-consciousness and morality which his very disclaimer involves.   The sense of sin which wakes spontaneously with the perception that he is not what he ought to have been must not be explained away ; at the level which life has reached in him, this is unscientific as well as immoral ; his sin—for I do not know another word for it—must be realised as all that it is in the moral world if he is ever to be true to himself, not to say if he is ever to welcome the Atonement, and leave his sin behind. We should have no need of words like sin and atonement—we could not have the experiences which they designate—unless we had a higher than merely natural life ; and one of the tendencies of the modern mind which has to be counter-acted by the evangelist is the tendency induced by physical and especially by biological science to explain the realities of personal experience by sub-personal categories. In conscience, in the sense of personal dignity, in the ulti-mate inability of man to deny the self which he is, we have always an appeal against such tendencies, which cannot fail ; but it needs to be made resolutely when conscience is lethargic and the whole bias of the mind is to the other side.

Passing from physical science, the modern mind has perhaps been influenced most by the great idealist movement in philosophy—the movement which in Germany began with Kant and culminated in Hegel. This idealism, just like physical science, gives a certain stamp to the mind ; when it takes possession of intelligence it casts it, so to speak, into a certain mould ; even more than physical science it dominates it so that it becomes incapable of self-criticism, and very difficult to teach. Its importance to the preacher of Christianity is that it assumes certain relations between the human and the divine, relations which foreclose the very questions which the Atonement compels us to raise. To be brief, it teaches the essential unity of God and man. God and man, to speak of them as distinct, are necessary to each other, but man is as necessary to God as God is to man. God is the truth of man, but man is the reality of God. God comes to consciousness of Himself in man, and man in being conscious of himself is at the same time conscious of

God. Though many writers of this school make a copious use of Christian phraseology, it seems to me obvious that it is not in an adequate Christian sense. Sin is not regarded as that which ought not to be, it is that which is to be transcended. It is as inevitable as anything in nature ; and the sense of it, the bad conscience which accompanies it, is no more than the growing pains of the soul. On such a system there is no room for atonement in the sense of the mediation of God's forgiveness through Jesus Christ. We may consistently speak in it of a man being reconciled to himself, or even reconciled to his sins, but not, so far as I can understand, of his being reconciled to God, and still less, reconciled to God through the death of His Son. The penetration of Kant saw from the first all that could be made of atonement on the basis of any such system. What it means to the speculative mind is that the new man bears the sin of the old. When the sinner repents and is converted, the weight of what he has done comes home to him ; the new man in him—the Son of God in him—accepts the responsibility of the old man, and so he has peace with God. Many whose minds are under the influence of this mode of thought do not see clearly to what it leads, and resent criticism of it as if it were a sort of impiety. Their philosophy is to them a surrogate for religion, but they should not be allowed to suppose (if they do suppose) that it is the equivalent of Christianity. There can be no Christianity without Christ ; it is the presence of the Mediator which makes Christianity what it is. But a unique Christ, without whom our religion disappears, is frankly disavowed by the more candid and outspoken of our idealist philosophers. Christ, they tell us, was certainly a man who had an early and a magnificently strong faith in the unity of the human and the divine ; but it was faith in a fact which enters into the constitution of every human consciousness, and it is absurd to suppose that the recognition of the fact, or the realisation of it, is essentially dependent on Him. He was not sinless—which is an expression without meaning, when we think of a human being which has to rise by conflict and self-suppression out of nature into the world of self-consciousness and right and wrong ; He was not in any sense unique or exceptional ; He was only what we all are in our degree ; at best, He was only one among many great men who have contributed in their place and time to the spiritual elevation of the race. Such, I say, is the issue of this mode of thought as it is frankly avowed by some of its representative men ; but the peculiarity of it, when it is obscurely fermenting as a leaven in the mind, is that it appeals to men as having special affinities to Christianity. In our own country it is widely prevalent among those who have had a university education, and indeed in a much wider circle, and it is a serious question how we are to address our gospel to those who confront it in such a mental mood.

I have no wish to be unsympathetic, but I must frankly express my conviction that this philosophy only lives by ignoring the greatest reality of the spiritual world. There is something in that world—something with which we can come into intelligible and vital relations—something which can evince to our minds its truth and reality, for which this philosophy can make no room : Christ's consciousness of Himself. It is a theory of the universe which (on principle) cannot allow Christ to be anything else than an additional unit in the world's population ; but if this were the truth about Him, no language could be strong enough to express the self-delusion in which He lived and died. That He was thus self-deluded is a hypothesis I do not feel called to discuss. One may be accused of subjectivity again, of course, though a subjective opinion which has the consent of the Christian centuries behind it need not tremble at hard

names; but I venture to say that there is no reality in the
world which more inevitably and uncompromisingly takes
hold of the mind as a reality than our Lord's consciousness
of Himself as it is attested to us in the Gospels. But when
we have taken this reality for all that it is worth, the
idealism just described is shaken to the foundation. What
seemed to us so profound a truth—the essential unity of the
human and the divine—may come to seem a formal and
delusive platitude; in what we once regarded as the formula
of the perfect religion—the divinity of man and the
humanity of God—we may find quite as truly the formula
of the first, not to say the final, sin. To see Christ not in
the light of this speculative theorem, but in the light of His
own consciousness of Himself, is to realise not only our kin-
ship to God, but our remoteness from Him; it is to realise
our incapacity for self-realisation when we are left to ourselves; it is to realise the need of the Mediator if we would
come to the Father; it is to realise, in principle, the need of
the Atonement, the need, and eventually the fact. When
the modern mind therefore presents itself to us in this mood
of philosophical competence, judging Christ from the point
of view of the whole, and showing Him His place, we can
only insist that the place is unequal to His greatness, and
that His greatness cannot be explained away. The mind
which is closed to the fact of His unique claims, and the
unique relation to God on which they rest, is closed inevitably to the mediation of God's forgiveness through His death.

There is one other modification of mind, characteristic of
modern times, of which we have yet to take account—I mean
that which is produced by devotion to historical study.
History is, as much as science, one of the achievements of
our age; and the historical temper is as characteristic of the
men we meet as the philosophical or the scientific. The
historical temper, too, is just as apt as these others, perhaps

unconsciously, perhaps quite consciously, but under the engaging plea of modesty, to pronounce absolute sentences which strike at the life of the Christian religion, and especially, therefore, at the idea of the Atonement. Sometimes this is done broadly, so that every one sees what it means. If we are told, for example, that everything historical is relative, that it belongs of necessity to a time, and is conditioned in ways so intricate that no knowledge can ever completely trace them; if we are told, further, that for this very reason nothing historical can have absolute significance, or can condition the eternal life of man, it is obvious that the Christian religion is being cut at the root. It is no use speaking about the Atonement—about the mediation of God's forgiveness to the soul through a historical person and work—if this is true. The only thing to be done is to raise the question whether it *is* true. It is no more for historical than for physical science to exalt itself into a theory of the universe, or to lay down the law with speculative absoluteness as to the significance and value which shall attach to facts. When we face the fact with which we are here concerned—the fact of Christ's consciousness of Himself and His vocation, to which reference has already been made—are we not forced to the conclusion that here a new spiritual magnitude has appeared in history, the very *differentia* of which is that it *has* eternal significance, and that it is eternal life to know it? If we are to preach the Atonement, we cannot allow either history or philosophy to proceed on assumptions which ignore or degrade the fact of Christ. Only a person in whom the eternal has become historical can be the bearer of the Atonement, and it must be our first concern to show, against all assumptions whether made in the name of history or of philosophy, that in point of fact there is such a person here.

This consideration requires to be kept in view even when

we are dealing with the modern mind inside the Church. Nothing is commoner than to hear those who dissent from any given construction of the Atonement plead for a historical as opposed to a dogmatic interpretation of Christ. It is not always clear what is meant by this distinction, nor is it clear that those who use it are always conscious of what it would lead to if it were made absolute. Sometimes a dogmatic interpretation of the New Testament means an interpretation vitiated by dogmatic prejudice, an interpretation in which the meaning of the writers is missed because the mind is blinded by prepossessions of its own : in this sense a dogmatic interpretation is a thing which no one would defend. Sometimes, however, a dogmatic interpretation is one which reveals or discovers in the New Testament truths of eternal and divine significance, and to discredit such interpretation in the name of the historical is another matter. The distinction in this case, as has been already pointed out, is not absolute. It is analogous to the distinction between fact and theory, or between thing and meaning, or between efficient cause and final cause. None of these distinctions is absolute, and no intelligent mind would urge either side in them to the disparagement of the other. If we are to apprehend the whole reality presented to us, we must apprehend the theory as well as the fact, the meaning as well as the thing, the final as well as the efficient cause. In the subject with which we are dealing, this truth is frequently ignored. It is assumed, for example, that because Christ was put to death by His enemies, or because He died in the faithful discharge of His calling, therefore He did not die, in the sense of the Atonement, for our sins : the historical causes which brought about His death are supposed to preclude that interpretation of it according to which it mediates to us the divine forgiveness. But there is no incompatibility between the two things. To set aside

an interpretation of Christ's death as dogmatic, on the
ground that there is another which is historical, is like setting aside the idea that a watch is made to measure time
because you know it was made by a watchmaker.   It was
both made by a watchmaker and made to measure time.
Similarly it may be quite true both that Christ was crucified
and slain by wicked men, and that He died for our sins.
But without entering into the questions which this raises as
to the relation between the wisdom of God and the course
of human history, it is enough to be conscious of the prejudice which the historical temper is apt to generate
against the recognition of the eternal in time.   Surely it is
a significant fact that the New Testament contains a whole
series of books—the Johannine books—which have as their
very burden the eternal significance of the historical : eternal
life in Jesus Christ, come in flesh, the propitiation for the
whole world.   Surely also it is a significant fact of a different
and even an ominous kind that we have at present in the
Church a whole school of critics which is so far from appreciating the truth in this that it is hardly an exaggeration to
say that it has devoted itself to a paltry and peddling
criticism of these books in which the impression of the
eternal is lost.   But whether we are to be indebted to John's
eyes, or to none but our own, if the eternal is not to be seen
in Jesus, He can have no place in our religion ; if the historical has no dogmatic content, it cannot be essential to
eternal life.   Hence if we believe and know that we have
eternal life in Jesus, we must assert the truth which is
implied in this against any conception of history which
denies it.   Nor is it really difficult to do so.   With the experience of nineteen centuries behind us, we have only to
confront this particular historical reality, Jesus Christ, without prejudice ; in evangelising, we have only to confront
others with Him ; and we shall find it still possible to see

God in Him, the Holy Father who through the Passion of His Son ministers to sinners the forgiveness of their sins.

In what has been said thus far by way of explaining the modern mind, emphasis may seem to have fallen mainly on those characteristics which make it less accessible than it might be to Christian truth, and especially to the Atonement. I have tried to point out the assailable side of its prepossessions, and to indicate the fundamental truths which must be asserted if our intellectual world is to be one in which the gospel may find room. But the modern mind has other characteristics. Some of these may have been exhibited hitherto mainly in criticising current representations of the Atonement; but in themselves they are entirely legitimate, and the claims they put forward are such as we cannot disown. Before proceeding to a further statement of the Atonement, I shall briefly refer to one or two of them: a doctrine of Atonement which did not satisfy them would undoubtedly stand condemned.

(1) The modern mind requires that everything shall be based on experience. Nothing is true or real to it which cannot be experimentally verified. This we shall all concede. But there is an inference sometimes drawn from it at which we may look with caution. It is the inference that, because everything must be based on experience, no appeal to Scripture has any authority. I have already explained in what sense it is possible to speak of the authority of Scripture, and here it is only necessary to make the simple remark that there is no proper contrast between Scripture and experience. Scripture, so far as it concerns us here, is a record of experience or an interpretation of it. It was the Church's experience that it had its redemption in Christ; it was the interpretation of that experience that Christ died for our sins. Yet in emphasising experience the modern mind is right, and Scripture would lose its

authority if the experience it describes were not perpetually verified anew.

(2) The modern mind desires to have everything in religion ethically construed. As a general principle this must command our unreserved assent. Anything which violates ethical standards, anything which is immoral or less than moral, must be excluded from religion. It may be, indeed, that ethical has sometimes been too narrowly defined. Ideas have been objected to as unethical which are really at variance not with a true perception of the constitution of humanity, and of the laws which regulate moral life, but with an atomic theory of personality under which moral life would be impossible. Persons are not atoms ; in a sense they interpenetrate, though individuality has been called the true impenetrability. The world has been so constituted that we do not stand absolutely outside of each other ; we can do things for each other. We can bear each other's burdens, and it is not unethical to say so, but the reverse. And again, it need not be unethical, though it transcends the ordinary sphere and range of ethical action, if we say that God in Christ is able to do for us what we cannot do for one another. With reference to the Atonement, the demand for ethical treatment is usually expressed in two ways. (a) There is the demand for analogies to it in human life. The demand is justifiable in so far as God has made man in His own image ; but, as has been suggested above, it has a limit, in so far as God is God and not man, and must have relations to the human race which its members do not and cannot have to each other. (b) There is the demand that the Atonement shall be exhibited in vital relation to a new life in which sin is overcome. This demand also is entirely legitimate, and it touches a weak point in the traditional Protestant doctrine. Dr. Chalmers tells us that he was brought up—such was

the effect of the current orthodoxy upon him—in a certain distrust of good works. Some were certainly wanted, but not as being themselves salvation; only, as he puts it, as tokens of justification. It was a distinct stage in his religious progress when he realised that true justification sanctifies, and that the soul can and ought to abandon itself spontaneously and joyfully to do the good that it delights in. The modern mind assumes what Dr. Chalmers painfully discovered. An atonement that does not regenerate, it truly holds, is not an atonement in which men can be asked to believe. Such then, in its prejudices good and bad, is the mind to which the great truth of the Christian religion has to be presented.

CHAPTER VIII

SIN AND THE DIVINE REACTION AGAINST IT

WE have now seen in a general way what is meant by the Atonement, and what are the characteristics of the mind to which the Atonement has to make its appeal. In that mind there is, as I believe, much which falls in with the Atonement, and prepares a welcome for it; but much also which creates prejudice against it, and makes it as possible still as in the first century to speak of the offence of the cross. No doubt the Atonement has sometimes been presented in forms which provoke antagonism, which challenge by an ostentation of unreason, or by a defiance of morality, the reason and conscience of man; but this alone does not explain the resentment which it often encounters. There is such a thing to be found in the world as the man who will have nothing to do with Christ on any terms, and who will least of all have anything to do with Him when Christ presents Himself in the character which makes man His debtor for ever. All men, as St. Paul says, have not faith: it is a melancholy fact, whether we can make anything of it or not. Discounting, however, this irrational or inexplicable opposition, which is not expressed in the mind but in the will, how are we to present the Atonement so that it shall excite the least prejudice, and find the most unimpeded access to the mind of our own generation? This is the question to which we have now to address ourselves.

To conceive the Atonement, that is, the fact that forgiveness is mediated to us through Christ, and specifically through His death, as clearly and truly as possible, it is necessary for us to realise the situation to which it is related. We cannot think of it except as related to a given situation. It is determined or conditioned by certain relations subsisting between God and man, as these relations have been affected by sin. What we must do, therefore, in the first instance, is to make clear to ourselves what these relations are, and how sin affects them.

To begin with, they are personal relations; they are relations the truth of which cannot be expressed except by the use of personal pronouns. We need not ask whether the personality of God can be proved antecedent to religion, or as a basis for a religion yet to be established; in the only sense in which we can be concerned with it, religion is an experience of the personality of God, and of our own personality in relation to it. 'O Lord, *Thou* hast searched *me* and known *me*.' '*I* am continually with *Thee*.' No human experience can be more vital or more normal than that which is expressed in these words, and no argument, be it ever so subtle or so baffling, can weigh a feather's-weight against such experience. The same conception of the relations of God and man is expressed again as unmistakably in every word of Jesus about the Father and the Son and the nature of their communion with each other. It is only in such personal relations that the kind of situation can emerge, and the kind of experience be had, with which the Atonement deals; and antecedent to such experience, or in independence of it, the Atonement must remain an incredible because an unrealisable thing.

But to say that the relations of God and man are personal is not enough. They are not only personal, but universal. *Personal* is habitually used in a certain contrast with *legal*, and it is very easy to lapse into the idea that personal relations, because distinct from legal ones, are independent of law; but to say the least of it, that is an ambiguous and misleading way of describing the facts. The relations of God and man are not lawless, they are not capricious, incalculable, incapable of moral meaning; they are personal, but determined by something of universal import; in other words, they are not merely personal but ethical. That is ethical which is at once personal and universal. Perhaps the simplest way to make this evident is to notice that the relations of man to God are the relations to God not of atoms, or of self-contained individuals, each of which is a world in itself, but of individuals which are essentially related to each other, and bound up in the unity of a race. The relations of God to man therefore are not capricious though they are personal: they are reflected or expressed in a moral constitution to which all personal beings are equally bound, a moral constitution of eternal and universal validity, which neither God nor man can ultimately treat as anything else than what it is.

This is a point at which some prejudice has been raised against the Atonement by theologians, and more, perhaps, by persons protesting against what they supposed theologians to mean. If one may be excused a personal reference, few things have astonished me more than to be charged with teaching a 'forensic' or 'legal' or 'judicial' doctrine of Atonement, resting, as such a doctrine must do, on a 'forensic' or 'legal' or 'judicial' conception of man's relation to God. It is all the more astonishing when the charge is combined with what one can only decline as in the circumstances totally unmerited compliments to the clearness with which he has expressed himself. There is nothing which I should wish to reprobate more wholeheartedly than the conception which is expressed by these words. To say that the relations of God and man are forensic is to say that they are regulated by statute—that sin is a breach of statute—that the sinner is a criminal— and that God adjudicates on him by interpreting the statute in its application to his case. Everybody knows that this is a travesty of the truth, and it is surprising that any one should be charged with teaching it, or that any one should applaud himself, as though he were in the foremost files of time, for not believing it. It is superfluously apparent that the relations of God and man are not those of a magistrate on the bench pronouncing according to the act on the criminal at the bar. To say this, however, does not make these relations more intelligible. In particular, to say that they are personal, as opposed to forensic, does not make them more intelligible. If they are to be rational, if they are to be moral, if they are to be relations in which an ethical life can be lived, and ethical responsibilities realised, they must be not only personal, but universal; they must be relations that in some sense are determined by law. Even to say that they are the relations, not of judge and criminal, but of Father and child, does not get us past this point. The relations of father and child are undoubtedly more adequate to the truth than those of judge and criminal; they are more adequate, but so far as our experience of them goes, they are not equal to it. If the sinner is not a criminal before his judge, neither is he a naughty child before a parent whose own weakness or affinity to evil introduces an incalculable element into his dealing with his child's fault. I should not think of saying that it is the desire to escape from the inexorableness of law to a God capable of indulgent human tenderness that inspires the violent protests so often heard against 'forensic' and 'legal' ideas: but that is the impression which one

sometimes involuntarily receives from them.   It ought to
be apparent to every one that even the relation of parent
and child, if it is to be a moral relation, must be determined
in a way which has universal and final validity.   It must be
a relation in which—ethically speaking—some things are
for ever obligatory, and some things for ever impossible ; in
other words, it must be a relation determined by law, and
law which cannot deny itself.   But law in this sense is
not 'legal.'   It is not 'judicial,' or 'forensic,' or 'statutory.'
None the less it is real and vital, and the whole moral value
of the relation depends upon it.   When a man says—as
some one has said—'There are many to whom the conception of forgiveness resting on a judicial transaction does
not appeal at all,' I entirely agree with him ; it does not
appeal at all to me.   But what would be the value of a
forgiveness which did not recognise in its eternal truth and
worth that universal law in which the relations of God and
man are constituted ?   Without the recognition of that
law—that moral order or constitution in which we have
our life in relation to God and each other—righteousness
and sin, atonement and forgiveness, would all alike be words
without meaning.

In connection with this, reference may be made to an
important point in the interpretation of the New Testament.   The responsibility for what is called the forensic
conception of the Atonement is often traced to St. Paul,
and the greatest of all the ministers of grace is not infre-
quently spoken of as though he had deliberately laid the
most insuperable of stumbling-blocks in the way to the gospel.
Most people, happily, are conscious that they do not look
well talking down to St. Paul, and occasionally one can detect
a note of misgiving in the brave words in which his doctrine
is renounced, a note of misgiving which suggests that the
charitable course is to hear such protests in silence, and to

let those who utter them think over the matter again. But there is what claims to be a scientific way of expressing dissent from the apostle, a way which, equally with the petulant one, rests, I am convinced, on misapprehension of his teaching. This it would not be fair to ignore. It interprets what the apostle says about law solely by reference to the great question at issue between the Jewish and the Christian religions, making the word law mean the statutory system under which the Jews lived, and nothing else. No one will deny that Paul does use the word in this sense; the law often means for him specifically the law of Moses. The law of Moses, however, never means for him anything less than the law of God; it is one specific form in which the universal relations subsisting between God and man, and making religion and morality possible, have found historical expression. But Paul's mind does not rest in this one historical expression. He generalises it. He has the conception of a universal law, to which he can appeal in Gentile as well as in Jew—a law in the presence of which sin is revealed, and by the reaction of which sin is judged—a law which God could not deny without denying Himself, and to which justice is done (in other words, which is maintained in its integrity), even when God justifies the ungodly. But when law is thus universalised, it ceases to be legal; it is not a statute, but the moral constitution of the world. Paul preached the same gospel to the Gentiles as he did to the Jews; he preached in it the same relation of the Atonement and of Christ's death to divine law. But he did not do this by extending to all mankind a Pharisaic, legal, forensic relation to God: he did it by rising above such conceptions, even though as a Pharisee he may have had to start from them, to the conception of a relation of all men to God expressing itself in a moral constitution—or, as he would have said, but in an entirely unforensic sense, in a law—of divine and unchanging validity. The maintenance of this law, or of this moral constitution, in its inviolable integrity was the signature of the forgiveness Paul preached. The Atonement meant to him that forgiveness was mediated through One in whose life and death the most signal homage was paid to this law : the very glory of the Atonement was that it manifested the righteousness of God ; it demonstrated God's consistency with His own character, which would have been violated alike by indifference to sinners and by indifference to that universal moral order—that law of God—in which alone eternal life is possible.

Hence it is a mistake to say—though this also has been said—that ' Paul's problem was not that of the possibility of forgiveness ; it was the Jewish law, the Old Testament dispensation : how to justify his breach with it, how to demonstrate that the old order had been annulled and a new order inaugurated.' There is a false contrast in all such propositions. Paul's problem was that of the Jewish law, and it was also that of the possibility of forgiveness ; it was that of the Jewish law, and it was also that of a revelation of grace, in which God should justify the ungodly, Jew or Gentile, and yet maintain inviolate those universal moral relations between Himself and man for which law is the compendious expression. It does not matter whether we suppose him to start from the concrete instance of the Jewish law, and to generalise on the basis of it ; or to start from the universal conception of law, and to recognise in existing Jewish institutions the most available and definite illustration of it : in either case, the only Paul whose mind is known to us has completely transcended the forensic point of view. The same false contrast is repeated when we are told that, ' That doctrine (Paul's "juristic doctrine") had its origin, not so much in his religious experience, as in apologetic necessities.' The only apologetic necessities which give rise to fundamental doctrines are those created by religious experience. The apologetic of any religious experience is just the definition of it as real in relation to other acknowledged realities. Paul had undoubtedly an apologetic of forgiveness — namely, his doctrine of atonement. But the acknowledged reality in relation to which he defined forgiveness—the reality with which, by means of his doctrine of atonement, he showed forgiveness to be consistent—was not the law of the Jews (though that was included in it, or might be pointed to in illustration of it): it was the law of God, the universal and inviolable order in which alone eternal life is possible, and in which all men, and not the Jews only, live and move and have their being. It was the perception of this which made Paul an apostle to the Gentiles, and it is this very thing itself which some would degrade into an awkward, unintelligent, and outworn rag of Pharisaic apologetic, which is the very heart and soul of Paul's Gentile gospel. Paul himself was perfectly conscious of this; he could not have preached to the Gentiles at all unless he had been. But there is nothing in it which can be characterised as 'legal,' 'judicial,' or 'forensic'; and of this also, I have no doubt, the apostle was well aware. Of course he occupied a certain historical position, had certain historical questions to answer, was subject to historical limitations of different kinds; but I have not the courage to treat him, nor do his words entitle any one to do so, as a man who in the region of ideas could not put two and two together.

But to return to the point from which this digression on St. Paul started. We have seen that the relations of God and man are personal, and also that they are universal, that is, there is a law of them, or, if we like to say so, a law in them, on the maintenance of which their whole ethical value depends.   The next point to be noticed is that these relations are deranged or disordered by sin.   Sin is, in fact, nothing else than this derangement or disturbance: it is that in which wrong is done to the moral constitution under which we live.   And let no one say that in such an expression we are turning our back on the personal world, and lapsing, or incurring the risk of lapsing, into mere legalism again.   It cannot be too often repeated that if the universal element, or law, be eliminated from personal relations, there is nothing intelligible left: no reason, no morality, no religion, no sin or righteousness or forgiveness, nothing to appeal to mind or conscience.   In the widest sense of the word, sin, as a disturbance of the personal relations between God and man, is a violence done to the constitution under which God and man form one moral community, share, as we may reverently express it, one life, have in view the same moral ends.

It is no more necessary in connection with the Atonement than in any other connection that we should have a doctrine of the origin of sin.   We do not know its origin, we only know that it is here.   We cannot observe the genesis of the bad conscience any more than we can observe the genesis of consciousness in general.   We see that consciousness does stand in relief against the background of natural life ; but though we believe that, as it exists in us, it has emerged from that background, we cannot see it emerge; it is an ultimate fact, and is assumed in all that we can ever regard as its physical antecedents and presuppositions.   In the same way, the moral consciousness is an ultimate fact, and irreducible.   The physical theory of evolution must not be allowed to mislead us here, and in particular it must not be allowed to discredit the conception of moral responsibility for sin which is embodied in the story of the Fall.   Each of us individually has risen into moral life from a mode of being which was purely natural; in other words, each of us, individually, has been a subject of evolution; but each of us also has fallen—fallen, presumably, in ways determined by his natural constitution, yet certainly, as conscience assures us, in ways for which we are morally answerable, and to which, in the moral constitution of the world, consequences attach which we must recognise as our due. They are not only results of our action, but results which that action has merited, and there is no moral hope for us unless we accept them as such. Now what is true of any, or rather of all, of us, without compromise of the moral consciousness, may be true of the race, or of the first man, if there was a first man. Evolution and a Fall cannot be inconsistent, for both enter into every moral experience of which we know anything; and no opinion we hold about the origin of sin can make it anything else than it is in conscience, or give its results any character other than that which they have to conscience. Of course when one tries to interpret sin outside of conscience, as though it were purely physical, and did not have its being in personality, consciousness, and will, it disappears; and the laborious sophistries of such interpretations must be left to themselves. The point for us is that no matter how sin originated, in the moral consciousness in which it has its being it is recognised as a derangement of the vital relations of man, a violation of that universal order outside of which he has no true good.

In what way, now, let us ask, does the reality of sin come home to the sinner? How does he recognise it as what it is? What is the reaction against the sinner, in the moral order under which he lives, which reveals to him the meaning of his sinful act or state?

In the first place, there is that instantaneous but abiding reaction which is called the bad conscience—the sense of guilt, of being answerable to God for sin. The sin may be an act which is committed in a moment, but in this aspect of it, at least, it does not fade into the past. An animal may have a past, for anything we can tell, and naturalistic interpreters of sin may believe that sin dies a natural death with time, and need not trouble us permanently; but this is not the voice of conscience, in which alone sin exists, and which alone can tell us the truth about it. The truth is that the spiritual being has no past. Just as he is continually with God, his sin is continually with him. He cannot escape it by not thinking. When he keeps silence, as the Psalmist says—and that is always his first resource, as though, if he were to say nothing about it, God might say nothing about it, and the whole thing blow over—it devours him like a fever within : his bones wax old with his moaning all day long. This sense of being wrong with God, under His displeasure, excluded from His fellowship, afraid to meet Him yet bound to meet Him, is the sense of guilt. Conscience confesses in it its liability to God, a liability which in the very nature of the case it can do nothing to meet, and which therefore is nearly akin to despair.

But the bad conscience, real as it is, may be too abstractly interpreted. Man is not a pure spirit, but a spiritual being whose roots strike to the very depths of nature, and who is connected by the most intimate and vital relations not only with his fellow-creatures of the same species, but with the whole system of nature in which he lives. The moral constitution in which he has his being comprehends, if we may say so, nature in itself : the God who has established the moral order in which man lives, has established the natural order also as part of the same whole with it. In some profound way the two are one. We distinguish in man, legitimately enough, between the spiritual and the physical ; but man is one, and the universe in which he lives is one, and in man's relation to God the distinction of physical and spiritual must ultimately disappear. The sin which introduces disorder into man's relations to God produces reactions affecting man as a whole—not reactions that, as we sometimes say, are purely spiritual, but reactions as broad as man's being and as the whole divinely constituted environment in which it lives. I am well aware of the difficulty of giving expression to this truth, and of the hopelessness of trying to give expression to it by means of those very distinctions which it is its nature to transcend. The distinctions are easy and obvious; what we have to learn is that they are not final. It seems so conclusive to say, as some one has done in criticising the idea of atonement, that spiritual transgressing brings spiritual penalty, and physical brings physical; it seems so conclusive, and it is in truth so completely beside the mark. We cannot divide either man or the universe in this fashion into two parts which move on different planes and have no vital relations ; we cannot, to apply this truth to the subject before us, limit the divine reaction against sin, or the experiences through which, in any case whatever, sin is brought home to man as what it is, to the purely spiritual sphere. Every sin is a sin of the indivisible human being, and the divine reaction against it expresses itself to conscience through the indivisible frame of that world, at once natural and spiritual, in which man lives. We cannot distribute evils into the two classes of physical and moral, and subsequently investigate the relation between them : if we could, it would be of no service here. What we have to understand is that when a man sins he does something in which his whole being participates, and that the reaction of God against his sin is a reaction in which he is conscious, or might be conscious, that the whole system of things is in arms against him.

There are those, no doubt, to whom this will seem fantastic, but it is a truth, I am convinced, which is presupposed in the Christian doctrine of Atonement, as the mediation of forgiveness through the suffering and death of Christ: and it is a truth also, if I am not much mistaken, to which all the highest poetry, which is also the deepest vision of the human mind, bears witness. We may distinguish natural law and moral law as sharply as we please, and it is as necessary sometimes as it is easy to make these sharp and absolute distinctions; but there is a unity in experience which makes itself felt deeper than all the antitheses of logic, and in that unity nature and spirit are no more defined by contrast with each other: on the contrary, they interpenetrate and support each other: they are aspects of the same whole. When we read in the prophet Amos, ' Lo, He that formeth the mountains, and createth the wind, and declareth unto man what is his thought, that maketh the morning darkness and treadeth upon the high places of the earth, the Lord, the God of hosts, is His name,' this is the truth which is expressed. The power which reveals itself in conscience—telling us all things that ever we did, declaring unto us what is our thought—is the same which reveals itself in nature, establishing the everlasting hills, creating the winds which sweep over them, turning the shadow of death into the morning and making the day dark with night, calling for the waters of the sea, and pouring them out on the face of the earth. Conscience speaks in a still small voice, but it is no impotent voice; it can summon the thunder to give it resonance; the power which we sometimes speak of as if it were purely spiritual is a power which clothes itself spontaneously and of right in all the majesty and omnipotence of nature. It is the same truth, again, in another aspect of it, which is expressed in Wordsworth's sublime lines to Duty:

' Thou dost preserve the Stars from wrong,
And the most ancient Heavens through Thee are fresh and strong.'

When the mind sees deepest, it is conscious that it needs more than physical astronomy, more than spectrum analysis, to tell us everything even about the stars.   There is a moral constitution, it assures us, even of the physical world ; and though it is impossible for us to work it out in detail, the assumption of it is the only assumption on which we can understand the life of a being related as man is related both to the natural and the spiritual.   I do not pretend to prove that there is articulate or conscious reflection on this in either the Old Testament or the New ; I take it for granted, as self-evident, that this sense of the ultimate unity of the natural and the spiritual—which is, indeed, but one form of belief in God—pervades the Bible from beginning to end. It knows nothing of our abstract and absolute distinctions ; to come to the matter in hand, it knows nothing of a sin which has merely spiritual penalties.   Sin is the act or the state of man, and the reaction against it is the reaction of the whole order, at once natural and spiritual, in which man lives.

Now the great difficulty which the modern mind has with the Atonement, or with the representation of it in the New Testament, is that it assumes some kind of connection between sin and death.   Forgiveness is mediated through Christ, but specifically through His death.   He died for our sins ; if we can be put right with God apart from this, then, St. Paul tells us, He died for nothing.   One is almost ashamed to repeat that this is not Paulinism, but the Christianity of the whole Apostolic Church.   What St. Paul made the basis of his preaching, that Christ died for our sins, according to the Scriptures, he had on his own showing received as the common Christian tradition.   But is there anything in it ?   Can we receive it simply on the authority of the primitive Church ?   Can we realise any such connection between death and sin as makes it a truth to us, an intelligible, impressive, overpowering thought, that Christ died for our sins?

I venture to say that a great part of the difficulty which is felt at this point is due to the false abstraction just referred to. Sin is put into one world—the moral; death is put into another world—the natural; and there is no connection between them. This is very convincing if we find it possible to believe that we live in two unconnected worlds. But if we find it impossible to believe this—and surely the impossibility is patent—its plausibility is gone. It is a shining example of this false abstraction when we are told, as though it were a conclusive objection to all that the New Testament has to say about the relation of sin and death, that 'the specific penalty of sin is not a fact of the natural life, but of the moral life.' What right has any one, in speaking of the ultimate realities in human life, of those experiences in which man becomes conscious of all that is involved in his relations to God and their disturbance by sin, to split that human life into 'natural' and 'moral,' and fix an impassable gulf between? The distinction is legitimate, as has already been remarked, within limits, but it is not final; and what the New Testament teaches, or rather assumes, about the relation of sin and death, is one of the ways in which we are made sensible that it is not final. Sin and death do not belong to unrelated worlds. As far as man is concerned, the two worlds, to use an inadequate figure, intersect; and at one point in the line of their inter-section sin and death meet and interpenetrate. In the indivisible experience of man he is conscious that they are parts or aspects of the same thing.

That this is what Scripture means when it assumes the connection of death and sin is not to be refuted by pointing either to the third chapter of Genesis or to the fifth of Romans. It does not, for example, do justice either to

Genesis or to St. Paul to say, as has been said, that according to their representation, ' Death—not spiritual, but
natural death—is the direct consequence of sin and its
specific penalty.' In such a dictum, the distinctions again
mislead. To read the third chapter of Genesis in this sense
would mean that what we had to find in it was a mythological explanation of the origin of physical death. But
does any one believe that any Bible writer was ever curious
about this question ? or does any one believe that a mythological solution of the problem, how death originated—a
solution which *ex hypothesi* has not a particle of truth or
even of meaning in it—could have furnished the presupposition for the fundamental doctrine of the Christian religion,
that Christ died for our sins, and that in Him we have our
forgiveness through His blood ? A truth which has appealed
so powerfully to man cannot be sustained on a falsehood.
That the third chapter of Genesis is mythological in form,
no one who knows what mythology is will deny ; but even
mythology is not made out of nothing, and in this chapter
every atom is ' stuff o' the conscience.' What we see in it is
conscience, projecting as it were in a picture on a screen its
own invincible, dear-bought, despairing conviction that sin
and death are indissolubly united—that from death the
sinful race can never get away—that it is part of the indivisible reality of sin that the shadow of death darkens the
path of the sinner, and at last swallows him up. It is this
also which is in the mind of St. Paul when he says that by
one man sin entered into the world and death by sin. It is
not the origin of death he is interested in, nor the origin of
sin either, but the fact that sin and death hang together.
And just because sin is sin, this is not a fact of natural history,
or a fact which natural history can discredit. Scripture has
no interest in natural history, nor does such an interest help us
to understand it. It is no doubt perfectly true that to the

biologist death is part of the indispensable machinery of
nature ; it is a piece of the mechanism without which the
movement of the whole would be arrested ; to put it so,
death to the biologist is part of the same whole as life, or
life and death are for him aspects of one thing.   One can
admit this frankly without compromising, because without
touching, the other and deeper truth which is so interesting
and indeed so vital alike in the opening pages of revelation
and in its consummation in the Atonement.   The biologist,
when he deals with man, and with his life and death,
deliberately deals with them in abstraction, as merely
physical phenomena ; to him man is a piece of nature, and he
is nothing more.   But the Biblical writers deal with man in
the integrity of his being, and in his relations to God ; they
transcend the distinction of natural and moral, because for
God it is not final : they are sensible of the unity in things
which the everyday mind, for practical purposes, finds it
convenient to keep apart.   It is one great instance of this
that they are sensible of the unity of sin and death.   We
may call sin a spiritual thing, but the man who has never
felt the shadow of death fall upon it does not know what
that spiritual thing is : and we may call death a natural
thing, but the man who has not felt its natural pathos deepen
into tragedy as he faced it with the sense of sin upon him
does not know what that natural thing is.   We are here, in
short, at the vanishing point of this distinction—God is
present, and nature and spirit interpenetrate in His presence.
We hear much in other connections of the sacramental
principle, and its importance for the religious interpretation
of nature.   It is a sombre illustration of this principle if we
say that death is a kind of sacrament of sin.   It is in death,
ultimately, that the whole meaning of sin comes home to the
sinner ; he has not sounded it to its depths till he has discovered that this comes into it at last.   And we must not

suppose that when Paul read the third chapter of Genesis he read it as a mythological explanation of the origin of physical death, and accepted it as such on the authority of inspiration. With all his reverence for the Old Testament, Paul accepted nothing from it that did not speak to his conscience, and waken echoes there; and what so spoke to him from the third chapter of Genesis was not a mythical story of how death invaded Paradise, but the profound experience of the human race expressed in the story, an experience in which sin and death interpenetrate, interpret, and in a sense constitute each other. To us they are what they are only in relation to each other, and when we deny the relation we see the reality of neither. This is the truth, as I apprehend it, of all we are taught either in the Old Testament or in the New about the relation of sin and death. It is part of the greater truth that what we call the physical and spiritual worlds are ultimately one, being constituted with a view to each other; and most of the objections which are raised against it are special cases of the objections which are raised against the recognition of this ultimate unity. So far as they are such, it is not necessary to discuss them further; and so far as the ultimate unity of the natural and the spiritual is a truth rather to be experienced than demonstrated, it is not probable that much can be done by argument to gain acceptance for the idea that sin and death have essential relations to each other. But there are particular objections to this idea to which it may be worth while to refer.

There is, to begin with, the undoubted fact that many people live and die without, consciously at least, recognising this relation. The thought of death may have had a very small place in their lives, and when death itself comes it may, for various reasons, be a very insignificant experience to them. It may come in a moment, suddenly, and give no time for feeling; or it may come as the last step in a natural process

of decay, and arrest life almost unconsciously; or it may
come through a weakness in which the mind wanders to
familiar scenes of the past, living these over again, and in a
manner escaping by so doing the awful experience of death
itself; or it may come in childhood before the moral
consciousness is fully awakened, and moral reflection and
experience possible.   This last case, properly speaking, does
not concern us; we do not know how to define sin in relation
to those in whom the moral consciousness is as yet unde-
veloped: we only know that somehow or other they are
involved in the moral as well as in the natural unity of the
race.   But leaving them out of account, is there any real
difficulty in the others? any real objection to the Biblical
idea that sin and death in humanity are essentially related?
I do not think there is.   To say that many people are
unconscious of the connection is only another way of saying
that many people fail to realise in full and tragic reality
what is meant by death and sin.   They think very little
about either.   The third chapter of Genesis could never have
been written out of their conscience.   Sin is not for them
all one with despair: they are not, through fear of death,
all their lifetime subject to bondage.   Scripture, of course,
has no difficulty in admitting this; it depicts, on the amplest
scale, and in the most vivid colours, the very kind of life and
death which are here supposed.   But it does not consider
that such a life and death are *ipso facto* a refutation of the
truth it teaches about the essential relations of death and sin.
On the contrary, it considers them a striking demonstration
of that moral dulness and insensibility in man which must
be overcome if he is ever to see and feel his sin as what it is
to God, or welcome the Atonement as that in which God's
forgiveness of sin is mediated through the tremendous
experience of death.   I know there are those who will call
this arrogant, or even insolent, as though I were passing a

moral sentence on all who do not accept a theorem of mine ;
but I hope I do not need here to disclaim any such unchristian
temper.   Only, it is necessary to insist that the connection
of sin and death in Scripture is neither a fantastic piece of
mythology, explaining, as mythology does, the origin of a
physical law, nor, on the other hand, a piece of supernaturally
revealed history, to be accepted on the authority of Him
who has revealed it ; in such revelations no one believes any
longer ; it is a profound conviction and experience of the
human conscience, and all that is of interest is to show that
such a conviction and experience can never be set aside by
the protest of those who aver that they know nothing about
it.   One must insist on this, however it may expose him to
the charge of judging.   Can we utter any truth at all, in
which conscience is concerned, and which is not universally
acknowledged, without seeming to judge ?

Sometimes, apart from the general denial of any connection between death and sin, it is pointed out that death has
another and a totally different character.   Death in any
given case may be so far from coming as a judgment of God,
that it actually comes as a gracious gift from Him ; it may
even be an answer to prayer, a merciful deliverance from pain,
an event welcomed by suffering human nature, and by all
who sympathise with it.   This is quite true, but again, one
must point out, rests on the false abstraction so often referred
to.   Man is regarded in all this simply in the character of a
sufferer, and death as that which brings suffering to an end ;
but that is not all the truth about man, nor all the truth
about death.   Physical pain may be so terrible that consciousness is absorbed and exhausted in it, sometimes even
extinguished, but it is not to such abnormal conditions we
should appeal to discover the deepest truths in the moral
consciousness of man.   If the waves of pain subsided, and the
whole nature collected its forces again, and conscience was

once more audible, death too would be seen in a different light.   It might not indeed be apprehended at once, as Scripture apprehends it, but it would not be regarded simply as a welcome relief from pain.   It would become possible to see in it something through which God spoke to the conscience, and eventually to realise its intimate relation to sin.

The objections we have just considered are not very serious, because they practically mean that death has no moral character at all; they reduce it to a natural phenomenon, and do not bring it into any relation to the conscience.   It is a more respectable, and perhaps a more formidable objection, when death is brought into the moral world, and when the plea is put forward that so far from being God's judgment upon sin, it may be itself a high moral achievement.   A man may die greatly; his death may be a triumph; nothing in his life may become him like the leaving it.   Is not this inconsistent with the idea that there is any peculiar connection between death and sin?   From the Biblical point of view the answer must again be in the negative.   There is no such triumph over death as makes death itself a noble ethical achievement, which is not at the same time a triumph over sin.   Man vanquishes the one only as in the grace of God he is able to vanquish the other.   The doom that is in death passes away only as the sin to which it is related is transcended.   But there is more than this to be said.   Death cannot be so completely an action that it ceases to be a passion; it cannot be so completely achieved that it ceases to be accepted or endured.   And in this last aspect of it the original character which it bore in relation to sin still makes itself felt.   Transfigure it, as it may be transfigured, by courage, by devotion, by voluntary abandonment of life for a higher good, and it remains nevertheless the last enemy.   There is something in it monstrous and alien to the spirit, something which baffles the moral intelligence, till the truth dawns upon us that for all our race sin and death are aspects of one thing. If we separate them, we understand neither ; nor do we understand the solemn greatness of martyrdom itself if we regard it as a triumph only, and eliminate from the death which martyrs die all sense of the universal relation in humanity of death and sin. No one knew the spirit of the martyr more thoroughly than St. Paul. No one could speak more confidently and triumphantly of death than he. No one knew better how to turn the passion into action, the endurance into a great spiritual achievement. But also, no one knew better than he, in consistency with all this, that sin and death are needed for the interpretation of each other, and that fundamentally, in the experience of the race, they constitute one whole. Even when he cried, ' O death, where is thy sting ? ' he was conscious that ' the sting of death is sin.' Each, so to speak, had its reality in the other. No one could vanquish death who had not vanquished sin. No one could know what sin meant without tasting death. These were not mythological fancies in St. Paul's mind, but the conviction in which the Christian conscience experimentally lived, and moved, and had its being. And these convictions, I repeat, furnish the point of view from which we must appreciate the Atonement, *i.e.* the truth that forgiveness, as Christianity preaches it, is specifically mediated through Christ's death.

CHAPTER IX

CHRIST AND MAN IN THE ATONEMENT

Our conception of the relations subsisting between God and man, of the manner in which these relations are affected by sin, and particularly of the Scripture doctrine of the connection between sin and death, must determine, to a great extent, our attitude to the Atonement. The Atonement, as the New Testament presents it, assumes the connection of sin and death. Apart from some sense and recognition of such connection, the mediation of forgiveness through the death of Christ can only appear an arbitrary, irrational, unacceptable idea. But leaving the Atonement meanwhile out of sight, and looking only at the situation created by sin, the question inevitably arises, What can be done with it? Is it possible to remedy or to reverse it? It is an abnormal and unnatural situation; can it be annulled, and the relations of God and man put upon an ideal footing? Can God forgive sin and restore the soul? Can we claim that He shall? And if it is possible for Him to do so, can we tell how or on what conditions it is possible?

When the human mind is left to itself, there are only two answers which it can give to these questions. Perhaps they are not specially characteristic of the modern mind, but the modern mind in various moods has given passionate expression to both of them. The first says roundly that

forgiveness is impossible. Sin is, and it abides. The
sinner can never escape from the past. His future is
mortgaged to it, and it cannot be redeemed. He can
never get back the years which the locust has eaten. His
leprous flesh can never come again like the flesh of a little
child. Whatsoever a man soweth, that shall he also reap,
and reap for ever and ever. It is not eternal punishment
which is incredible ; nothing else has credibility. Let
there be no illusion about this : forgiveness is a violation,
a reversal, of law, and no such thing is conceivable in a
world in which law reigns.

The answer to this is, that sin and its consequences are
here conceived as though they belonged to a purely physical
world, whereas, if the world were only physical, there could
be no such thing as sin. As soon as we realise that sin
belongs to a world in which freedom is real—a world in
which reality means the personal relations subsisting
between man and God, and the experiences realised in
these relations—the question assumes a different aspect.
It is not one of logic or of physical law, but of personality,
of character, of freedom. There is at least a possibility
that the sinner's relation to his sin and God's relation to
the sinner should change, and that out of these changed
relations a regenerative power should spring, making the
sinner, after all, a new creature. The question, of course,
is not decided in this sense, but it is not foreclosed.

At the opposite extreme from those who pronounce
forgiveness impossible stand those who give the second
answer to the great question, and calmly assure us that
forgiveness may be taken for granted. They emphasise
what the others overlooked—the personal character of the
relations of God and man. God is a loving Father ; man
is His weak and unhappy child ; and of course God forgives.
As Heine put it, *c'est son métier*, it is what He is for. But

the conscience which is really burdened by sin does not easily find satisfaction in this cheap pardon. There is something in conscience which will not allow it to believe that God can simply condone sin : to take forgiveness for granted, when you realise what you are doing, seems to a live conscience impious and profane. In reality, the tendency to take forgiveness for granted is the tendency of those who, while they properly emphasise the personal character of the relations of God and man, overlook their universal character—that is, exclude from them that element of law without which personal relations cease to be ethical. But a forgiveness which ignores this stands in no relation to the needs of the soul or the character of God.

What the Christian religion holds to be the truth about forgiveness—a truth embodied in the Atonement—is something quite distinct from both the propositions which have just been considered. The New Testament does not teach, with the naturalistic or the legal mind, that forgiveness is impossible ; neither does it teach, with the sentimental or lawless mind, that it may be taken for granted. It teaches that forgiveness is mediated to sinners through Christ, and specifically through His death : in other words, that it is possible for God to forgive, but possible for God only through a supreme revelation of His love, made at infinite cost, and doing justice to the uttermost to those inviolable relations in which alone, as I have already said, man can participate in eternal life, the life of God Himself—doing justice to them as relations in which there is an inexorable divine reaction against sin, finally expressing itself in death. It is possible on these terms, and it becomes actual as sinful men open their hearts in penitence and faith to this marvellous revelation, and abandon their sinful life unreservedly to the love of God in Christ who died for them.

From this point of view it seems to me possible to present in a convincing and persuasive light some of the truths involved in the Atonement to which the modern mind is supposed to be specially averse.

Thus it becomes credible—we say so not *à priori*, but after experience—that there is a *divine necessity* for it ; in other words, there is no forgiveness possible to God without it : if He forgives at all, it must be in this way and in no other. To say so beforehand would be inconceivably presumptuous, but it is quite another thing to say so after the event. What it really means is that in the very act of forgiving sin—or, to use the daring word of St. Paul, in the very act of justifying the ungodly—God must act in consistency with His whole character. He must demonstrate Himself to be what He is in relation to sin, a God with whom evil cannot dwell, a God who maintains inviolate the moral constitution of the world, taking sin as all that it is in the very process through which He mediates His forgiveness to men.

It is the recognition of this divine necessity—not to forgive, but to forgive in a way which shows that God is irreconcilable to evil, and can never treat it as other or less than it is—it is the recognition of this divine necessity, or the failure to recognise it, which ultimately divides interpreters of Christianity into evangelical and non-evangelical, those who are true to the New Testament and those who cannot digest it.

No doubt the forms in which this truth is expressed are not always adequate to the idea they are meant to convey, and if we are only acquainted with them at second hand they will probably appear even less adequate than they are. When Athanasius, *e.g.*, speaks of God's *truth* in this connection, and then reduces God's truth to the idea that God must keep His word—the word which made death the penalty of sin—we may feel that the form only too easily loses contact with the substance. Yet Athanasius is dealing with the essential fact of the case, that God must be true to Himself, and to the moral order in which men live, in all His dealings with sin for man's deliverance from it ; and that He has been thus true to Himself in sending His son to live our life and to die our death for our salvation. Or again, when Anselm in the *Cur Deus Homo* speaks of the satisfaction which is rendered to God for the infringement of His honour by sin—a satisfaction apart from which there can be no forgiveness—we may feel again, and even more strongly, that the form of the thought is inadequate to the substance. But what Anselm means is that sin makes a real difference to God, and that even in forgiving God treats that difference *as* real, and cannot do otherwise. He cannot ignore it, or regard it as other or less than it is ; if He did so, He would not be more gracious than He is in the Atonement, He would cease to be God. It is Anselm's profound grasp of this truth which, in spite of all its inadequacy in form, and of all the criticism to which its inadequacy has exposed it, makes the *Cur Deus Homo* the truest and greatest book on the Atonement that has ever been written. It is the same truth of a divine necessity for the Atonement which is emphasised by St. Paul in the third chapter of Romans, where he speaks of Christ's death as a demonstration of God's righteousness. Christ's death, we may paraphrase his meaning, is an act in which (so far as it is ordered in God's providence) God does justice to Himself. He does justice to His character as a gracious God, undoubtedly, who is moved with compassion for sinners : if He did not act in a way which displayed His compassion for sinners, He would *not* do justice to Himself; there would be no ἔνδειξις of His δικαιοσύνη : it would be in abeyance : He would do Himself an injustice, or be untrue to Himself. It is with this in view that we can appreciate the arguments of writers like Diestel and Ritschl, that God's righteousness is synonymous with His grace. Such arguments are true to this extent, that God's righteousness includes His grace. He could not demonstrate it, He could not be true to Himself, if His grace remained hidden. We must not, however, conceive of this as if it constituted on our side a claim upon grace or upon forgiveness : such a claim would be a contradiction in terms. All that God does in Christ He does in free love, moved with compassion for the misery and doom of men. But though God's righteousness as demonstrated in Christ's death—in other words, His action in consistency with His character—includes, and, if we choose to interpret the term properly, even necessitates, the revelation of His grace, it is not this only—I do not believe it is this primarily—which St. Paul has here in mind. God, no doubt, would not do justice to Himself if He did not show His compassion for sinners ; but, on the other hand—and here is what the apostle is emphasising—He would not do justice to Himself if He displayed His compassion for sinners in a way which made light of sin, which ignored its tragic reality, or took it for less than it is. In this case He would again be doing Himself injustice ; there would be no demonstration that He was true to Himself as the author and guardian of the moral constitution under which men live ; as Anselm put it, He would have ceased to be God. The apostle combines the two sides. In Christ set forth a propitiation in His blood—in other words, in the Atonement in which the sinless Son of God enters into the bitter realisation of all that sin means for man, yet loves man under and through it all with an everlasting love—there is an ἔνδειξις of God's righteousness, a demonstration of His self-consistency, in virtue of which we can see how He is at the same time just

Himself and the justifier of him who believes on Jesus, a God who is irreconcilable to sin, yet devises means that His banished be not expelled from Him. We may say reverently that this was the only way in which God could forgive. He cannot deny Himself, means at the same time He cannot deny His grace to the sinful, and He cannot deny the moral order in which alone He can live in fellowship with men ; and we see the inviolableness of both asserted in the death of Jesus. Nothing else in the world demonstrates how real is God's love to the sinful, and how real the sin of the world is to God. And the love which comes to us through such an expression, bearing sin in all its reality, yet loving us through and beyond it, is the only love which at once forgives and regenerates the soul.

It becomes credible also that there is a *human necessity* for the Atonement : in other words, that apart from it the conditions of being forgiven could no more be fulfilled by man than forgiveness could be bestowed by God.

There are different tendencies in the modern mind with regard to this point. On the one hand, there are those who frankly admit the truth here asserted. Yes, they say, the Atonement is necessary for us. If we are to be saved from our sins, if our hearts are to be touched and won by the love of God, if we are to be emancipated from distrust and re-conciled to the Father whose love we have injured, there must be a demonstration of that love so wonderful and over-powering that all pride, alienation and fear shall be overcome by it ; and this is what we have in the death of Christ. It is a demonstration of love powerful enough to evoke peni-tence and faith in man, and it is through penitence and faith alone that man is separated from his sins and reconciled to God. A demonstration of love, too, must be given in act; it is not enough to be told that God loves : the reality of love lies in another region than that of words. In Christ on His cross the very thing itself is present, beyond all hope of telling wonderful, and without its irresistible appeal our hearts could never have been melted to penitence, and won for God. On the other hand, there are those who reject the Atonement on the very ground that for pardon and reconciliation nothing is required but repentance, the assumption being that repentance is something which man can and must produce out of his own resources.

On these divergent tendencies in the modern mind I should wish to make the following remarks.

First, the idea that man can repent as he ought, and whenever he will, without coming under any obligation to God for his repentance, but rather (it might almost be imagined) putting God under obligation by it, is one to which experience lends no support. Repentance is an adequate sense not of our folly, nor of our misery, but of our sin : as the New Testament puts it, it is repentance *toward God*. It is the consciousness of what our sin is to Him : of the wrong it does to His holiness, of the wound which it inflicts on His love. Now such a consciousness it is not in the power of the sinner to produce at will. The more deeply he has sinned, the more (so to speak) repentance is needed, the less is it in his power. It is the very nature of sin to darken the mind and harden the heart, to take away the knowledge of God alike in His holiness and in His love. Hence it is only through a revelation of God, and especially of what God is in relation to sin, that repentance can be evoked in the soul. Of all terms in the vocabulary of religion, repentance is probably the one which is most frequently misused. It is habitually applied to experiences which are not even remotely akin to true penitence. The self-centred regret which a man feels when his sin has found him out—the wish, compounded of pride, shame, and anger at his own inconceivable folly, that he had not done it : these are spoken of as repentance.

But they are not repentance at all. They have no relation
to God. They constitute no fitness for a new relation to
Him. They are no opening of the heart in the direction of
His reconciling love. It is the simple truth that that sorrow
of heart, that healing and sanctifying pain in which sin is
really put away, is not ours in independence of God ; it is a
saving grace which is begotten in the soul under that impression of sin which it owes to the revelation of God in
Christ. A man can no more repent than he can do anything
else without a motive, and the motive which makes evangelic
repentance possible does not enter into any man's world till he
sees God as God makes Himself known in the death of Christ.
All true penitents are children of the Cross. Their penitence
is not their own creation : it is the reaction towards God
produced in their souls by this demonstration of what sin is
to Him, and of what His love does to reach and win the
sinful.

The other remark I wish to make refers to those who admit
the death of Christ to be necessary *for us*—necessary, in the
way I have just described, to evoke penitence and trust in
God—but who on this very ground deny it to be *divinely*
necessary. It had to be, because the hard hearts of men could
not be touched by anything less moving : but that is all.
This, I feel sure, is another instance of those false abstractions to which reference has already been made. There is no
incompatibility between a *divine* necessity and a necessity
for us. It may very well be the case that nothing less than
the death of Christ could win the trust of sinful men for
God, and at the same time that nothing else than the death
of Christ could fully reveal the character of God in relation
at once to sinners and to sin. For my own part I am per-
suaded, not only that there is no incompatibility between
the two things, but that they are essentially related, and that
only the acknowledgment of the divine necessity in Christ's

death enables us to conceive in any rational way the power which it exercises over sinners in inducing repentance and faith. It would not evoke a reaction Godward unless God were really present in it, that is, unless it were a real revelation of His being and will: but in a real revelation of God's being and will there can be nothing arbitrary, nothing which is determined only from without, nothing, in other words, that is not divinely necessary. The demonstration of what God is, which is made in the death of Christ, is no doubt a demonstration singularly suited to call forth penitence and faith in man, but the necessity of it does not lie simply in the desire to call forth penitence and faith. It lies in the divine nature itself. God could not do justice to Himself, in relation to man and sin, in any way less awful than this ; and it is the fact that He does not shrink even from this— that in the Person of His Son He enters, if we may say so, into the whole responsibility of the situation created by sin —which constitutes the death of Jesus a demonstration of divine love, compelling penitence and faith. Nothing less would have been sufficient to touch sinful hearts to their depths—in that sense the Atonement is humanly necessary ; but neither would anything else be a sufficient revelation of what God is in relation to sin and to sinful men—in that sense it is divinely necessary. And the divine necessity is the fundamental one. The power exercised over us by the revelation of God at the Cross is dependent on the fact that the revelation is true—in other words, that it exhibits the real relation of God to sinners and to sin. It is not by calculating what will win us, but by acting in consistency with Himself, that God irresistibly appeals to men. We dare not say that He must be gracious, as though grace could cease to be free : but we may say that He must be Himself, and that it is because He is what we see Him to be in the death of Christ, understood as the New Testament under-

stands it, that sinners are moved to repentance and to trust
in Him. That which the eternal being of God made necessary to Him in the presence of sin is the very thing which is
necessary also to win the hearts of sinners. Nothing but
what is divinely necessary could have met the necessities of
sinful men.

When we admit this twofold necessity for the Atonement,
we can tell ourselves more clearly how we are to conceive
Christ in it, in relation to God on the one hand and to man
on the other. The Atonement is God's work. It is God
who makes the Atonement in Christ. It is God who
mediates His forgiveness of sins to us in this way. This is
one aspect of the matter, and probably the one about which
there is least dispute among Christians. But there is another
aspect of it. The Mediator between God and man is Himself
man, Christ Jesus. What is the relation of the man Christ
Jesus to those for whom the Atonement is made? What is
the proper term to designate, in this atoning work, what He
is in relation to them? The doctrine of Atonement current
in the Church in the generation preceding our own answered
frankly that in His atoning work Christ is our substitute.
He comes in our nature, and He comes into our place. He
enters into all the responsibilities that sin has created for us,
and He does justice to them in His death. He does not
deny any of them: He does not take sin as anything less or
else than it is to God; in perfect sinlessness He consents
even to die, to submit to that awful experience in which the
final reaction of God's holiness against sin is expressed.
Death was not *His* due: it was something alien to One who
did nothing amiss; but it was our due, and because it was
ours He made it His. It was thus that He made Atonement.
He bore *our* sins. He took to Himself all that they meant,
all in which they had involved the world. He died for them,
and in so doing acknowledged the sanctity of that order in

which sin and death are indissolubly united. In other words, He did what the human race could not do for itself, yet what had to be done if sinners were to be saved : for how could men be saved if there were not made in humanity an acknowledgment of all that sin is to God, and of the justice of all that is entailed by sin under God's constitution of the world ? Such an acknowledgment, as we have just seen, is divinely necessary, and necessary, too, for man, if sin is to be forgiven.

This was the basis of fact on which the substitutionary character of Christ's sufferings and death in the Atonement was asserted. It may be admitted at once that when the term substitute is interpreted without reference to this basis of fact it lends itself very easily to misconstruction. It falls in with, if it does not suggest, the idea of a transference of merit and demerit, the sin of the world being carried over to Christ's account, and the merit of Christ to the world's account, as if the reconciliation of God and man, or the forgiveness of sins and the regeneration of souls, could be explained without the use of higher categories than are employed in book-keeping. It is surely not necessary at this time of day to disclaim an interpretation of personal relations which makes use only of sub-personal categories. Merit and demerit cannot be mechanically transferred like sums in an account. The credit, so to speak, of one person in the moral sphere cannot become that of another, apart from moral conditions. It is the same truth, in other words, if we say that the figure of paying a debt is not in every respect adequate to describe what Christ does in making the Atonement. The figure, I believe, covers the truth ; if it did not, we should not have the kind of language which frequently occurs in Scripture ; but it is misread into falsehood and immorality whenever it is pressed as if it were exactly equivalent to the truth. But granting these drawbacks which attach to the word, is there not something in the work of Christ, as mediating the forgiveness of sins, which no other word can express ? No matter on what subsequent conditions its virtue for us depends, what Christ did had to be done, or we should never have had forgiveness ; we should never have known God, and His nature and will in relation to sin ; we should never have had the motive which alone could beget real repentance ; we should never have had the spirit which welcomes pardon and is capable of receiving it. We could not procure these things for ourselves, we could not produce them out of our own resources : but He by entering into our nature and lot, by taking on Him our responsibilities and dying our death, has so revealed God to us as to put them within our reach. We owe them to Him ; in particular, and in the last resort, we owe them to the fact that He bore our sins in His own body to the tree. If we are not to say that the Atonement, as a work carried through in the sufferings and death of Christ, sufferings and death determined by our sin, is vicarious or substitutionary, what are we to call it ?

The only answer which has been given to this question, by those who continue to speak of Atonement at all, is that we must conceive Christ not as the substitute but as the representative of sinners. I venture to think that, with some advantages, the drawbacks of this word are quite as serious as those which attach to substitute. It makes it less easy, indeed, to think of the work of Christ as a finished work which benefits the sinner *ipso facto*, and apart from any relation between him and the Saviour : but of what sort is the relation which it does suggest ? A representative, in all ordinary circumstances, is provided or appointed by those whom he represents, and it is practically impossible to divest the term of the associations which this involves, misleading as they are in the present instance. The case for representative as opposed to substitute was put forward with great earnestness in an able review of *The Death of Christ*. The reviewer was far from saying that a writer who finds a substitutionary doctrine throughout the New Testament is altogether wrong. He was willing to admit that 'if we look at the matter from what may be called an external point of view, no doubt we may speak of the death of Christ as in a certain sense substitutionary.' What this 'certain sense' is he does not define. But no one, he held, can do justice to Paul who fails to recognise that the death of Christ was a racial act; and 'if we place ourselves at Paul's point of view, we shall see that to the eye of God the death of Christ presents itself less as an act which Christ does for the race than as an act which the race does in Christ.' In plain English, Paul teaches less that Christ died for the ungodly, than that the ungodly in Christ died for themselves. This brings out the logic of what representative means when representative is opposed to substitute. The representative is ours, we are in Him, and we are supposed to get over all the moral difficulties raised by the idea of substitution just because He is ours, and because we are one with Him. But the fundamental fact of the situation is that, to begin with, Christ is *not* ours, and we are *not* one with Him. In the apostle's view, and in point of fact, we are 'without Christ' (χωρὶς Χριστοῦ). It is not we who have put Him there. It is not to us that His presence and His work in the world are due. If we had produced Him and put Him forward, we might call Him our representative in the sense suggested by the sentences just quoted; we might say it is not so much He who dies for us, as we who die in Him; but a representative not produced by us, but given to us—not chosen by us, but the elect of God—is not a representative at all in the first instance, but a substitute. He stands in our stead, facing all our responsibilities for us as God would have them faced; and it is what He does

for us, and not the effect which this produces in us, still less
the fantastic abstraction of a 'racial act,' which is the
Atonement in the sense of the New Testament.   To speak
of Christ as our representative, in the sense that His death
is to God less an act which He does for the race than an
act which the race does in Him, is in principle to deny
the grace of the gospel, and to rob it of its motive
power.

To do justice to the truth here, both on its religious and
its ethical side, it is necessary to put in their proper relation
to one another the aspects of reality which the terms substitute and representative respectively suggest.   The first is
fundamental.   Christ is God's gift to humanity.   He stands
in the midst of us, the pledge of God's love, accepting our
responsibilities as God would have them accepted, offering
to God, under the pressure of the world's sin and all its
consequences, that perfect recognition of God's holiness in so
visiting sin which men should have offered but could not;
and in so doing He makes Atonement for us.   In so doing,
also, He is our substitute, not yet our representative.   But
the Atonement thus made is not a spectacle, it is a motive.
It is not a transaction in business, or in book-keeping, which
is complete in itself; in view of the relations of God and
man it belongs to its very nature to be a moral appeal.   It
is a divine challenge to men, which is designed to win their
hearts.   And when men are won—when that which Christ
in His love has done for them comes home to their souls—
when they are constrained by His infinite grace to the self-
surrender of faith, then we may say He becomes their representative.   They begin to feel that what He has done for
them must not remain outside of them, but be reproduced
somehow in their own life.   The mind of Christ in relation
to God and sin, as He bore their sins in His own body to
the tree, must become their mind; this and nothing else is

the Christian salvation. The power to work this change in them is found in the death of Christ itself; the more its meaning is realised as something there, in the world, outside of us, the more completely does it take effect within us. In proportion as we see and feel that out of pure love to us He stands in our place—our substitute—bearing our burden—in that same proportion are we drawn into the relation to Him that makes Him our representative. But we should be careful here not to lose ourselves in soaring words. The New Testament has much to say about union with Christ, but I could almost be thankful that it has no such expression as mystical union. The only union it knows is a moral one—a union due to the moral power of Christ's death, operating morally as a constraining motive on the human will, and begetting in believers the mind of Christ in relation to sin; but this moral union remains the problem and the task, as well as the reality and the truth, of the Christian life. Even when we think of Christ as our representative, and have the courage to say we died with Him, we have still to *reckon* ourselves to be dead to sin, and to *put to death* our members which are upon the earth; and to go past this, and speak of a mystical union with Christ in which we are lifted above the region of reflection and motive, of gratitude and moral responsibility, into some kind of metaphysical identity with the Lord, does not promote intelligibility, to say the least. If the Atonement were not, to begin with, outside of us—if it were not in that sense objective, a finished work in which God in Christ makes a final revelation of Himself in relation to sinners and sin—in other words, if Christ could not be conceived in it as our substitute, given by God to do in our place what we could not do for ourselves, there would be no way of recognising or preaching or receiving it as a motive; while, on the other hand, if it did not operate as a motive, if it did not appeal to sinful men in such a way as to draw them into a moral fellowship with Christ—in other words, if Christ did not under it become representative of us, our surety to God that we should yet be even as He in relation to God and to sin, we could only say that it had all been vain. Union with Christ, in short, is not a presupposition of Christ's work, which enables us to escape all the moral problems raised by the idea of a substitutionary Atonement ; it is not a presupposition of Christ's work, it is its fruit. To see that it is its fruit is to have the final answer to the objection that substitution is immoral. If substitution, in the sense in which we must assert it of Christ, is the greatest moral force in the world—if the truth which it covers, when it enters into the mind of man, enters with divine power to assimilate him to the Saviour, uniting him to the Lord in a death to sin and a life to God—obviously, to call it immoral is an abuse of language. The love which can literally go out of itself and make the burden of others its own is the radical principle of all the genuine and victorious morality in the world. And to say that love cannot do any such thing, that the whole formula of morality is, every man shall bear his own burden, is to deny the plainest facts of the moral life.

Yet this is a point at which difficulty is felt by many in trying to grasp the Atonement. On the one hand, there do seem to be analogies to it, and points of attachment for it, in experience. No sin that has become real to conscience is ever outlived and overcome without expiation. There are consequences involved in it that go far beyond our perception at the moment, but they work themselves inexorably out, and our sin ceases to be a burden on conscience, and a fetter on will, only as we 'accept the punishment of our iniquity,' and become conscious of the holy love of God behind it. But the consequences of sin are never limited to the sinner. They spread beyond him in the organism of humanity, and when they strike visibly upon the innocent, the sense of guilt is deepened. We see that we have done we know not what, something deeply and mysteriously bad beyond all our reckoning, something that only a power and goodness transcending our own avail to check. It is one of the startling truths of the moral life that such consequences of sin, striking visibly upon the innocent, have in certain circumstances a peculiar power to redeem the sinful. When they are accepted, as they sometimes are accepted, without repining or complaint—when they are borne, as they sometimes are borne, freely and lovingly by the innocent, because to the innocent the guilty are dear—then something is appealed to in the guilty which is deeper than guilt, something may be touched which is deeper than sin, a new hope and faith may be born in them, to take hold of love so wonderful, and by attaching themselves to it to transcend the evil past. The suffering of such love (they are dimly aware), or rather the power of such love persisting through all the suffering brought on it by sin, opens the gate of righteousness to the sinful in spite of all that has been; sin is outweighed by it, it is annulled, exhausted, transcended in it. The great Atonement of Christ is somehow in line with this, and we do not need to shrink from the analogy. 'If there were no witness,' as Dr. Robertson Nicoll puts it, 'in the world's deeper literature'—if there were no witness, that is, in the universal experience of man—'to the fact of an Atonement, the Atonement would be useless, since the formula expressing it would be unintelligible.' It is the analogy of such experiences which makes the Atonement credible, yet it must always in some way transcend them. There is something in it which is ultimately incomparable. When we speak of others as innocent, the term is used only in a relative sense; there is no human conscience pure to God. When we speak of the sin of others coming in its consequences on the innocent, we speak of something in which the innocent are purely passive; if there is moral response on their part, the situation is not due to moral initiative of theirs. But with Christ it is different. He knew *no* sin, and He entered *freely*, deliberately, and as the very work of His calling, into all that sin meant for God and brought on man. Something that I experience in a particular relation, in which another has borne my sin and loved me through it, may help to open my eyes to the meaning of Christ's love; but when they are opened, what I see is the propitiation for the whole world. There is no guilt of the human race, there is no consequence in which sin has involved it, to which the holiness and love made manifest in Christ are unequal. He reveals to all sinful men the whole relation of God to them and to their sins—a sanctity which is inexorable to sin, and cannot take it as other than it is in all its consequences, and a love which through all these consequences and under the weight of them all, will not let the sinful go. It is in this revelation of the character of God and of His relation to the sin of the world that the forgiveness of sins is revealed. It is not intimated in the air; it is preached, as St. Paul says, ' in this man '; it is mediated to the world through Him and specifically through His death, because it is through Him, and specifically through His death, that we get the knowledge of God's character which evokes penitence and faith, and brings the assurance of His pardon to the heart.

From this point of view we may see how to answer the question that is sometimes asked about the relation of Christ's life to His death, or about the relation of both to the Atonement. If we say that what we have in the Atonement is an assurance of God's character, does it not follow at once that Christ's teaching and His life contribute to it as directly as His death? Is it not a signal illustration of the false abstractions which we have so often had cause to censure, when the death of Christ is taken as if it had an existence or a significance apart from His life, or could be identified with the Atonement in a way in which His life could not? I do not think this is so clear. Of course it is Christ Himself who is the Atonement or propitiation— He Himself, as St. John puts it, and not anything, not even His death, into which He does not enter. But it is He Himself, as making to us the revelation of God in relation to sin and to sinners; and apart from death, as that in which the conscience of the race sees the final reaction of God against evil, this revelation is not fully made. If Christ had done less than die for us, therefore—if He had separated Himself from us, or declined to be one with us, in the solemn experience in which the darkness of sin is sounded and all its bitterness tasted,—there would have been no Atonement. It is impossible to say this of any particular incident in His life, and in so far the unique emphasis laid on His death in the New Testament is justified. But I should go further than this, and say that even Christ's life, taken as it stands in the Gospels, only enters into the Atonement, and has reconciling power, because it is pervaded from beginning to end by the consciousness of His death. Instead of depriving His death of the peculiar significance Scripture assigns to it, and making it no more than the termination, or at least the consummation, of His life, I should rather argue that the Scriptural emphasis is right, and that His life attains its true interpretation only as we find in it everywhere the power and purpose of His death. There is nothing artificial or unnatural in this. There are plenty of people who never have death out of their minds an hour at a time. They are not cowards, nor mad, nor even sombre: they may have purposes and hopes and gaieties as well as others; but they see life steadily and see it whole, and of all their thoughts the one which has most determining and omnipresent power is the thought of the inevitable end. There is death in all their life. It was not, certainly, as the inevitable end, the inevitable 'debt of nature,' that death was present to the mind of Christ; but if we can trust the Evangelists at all, from the hour of His baptism it was present to His mind as something involved in His vocation ; and it was a presence so tremendous that it absorbed everything into itself. 'I have a baptism to be baptized with, and how am I straitened till it be accomplished.' Instead of saying that Christ's life as well as His death contributed to the Atonement—that His active obedience (to use the theological formula) as well as His passive obedience was essential to His propitiation—we should rather say that His life is part of His death : a deliberate and conscious descent, ever deeper and deeper, into the dark valley where at the last hour the last reality of sin was to be met and borne. And if the objection is made that after all this only means that death is the most vital point of life, its intensest focus, I should not wish to make any reply. Our Lord's Passion *is* His sublimest action—an action so potent that all His other actions are sublated in it, and we know everything when we know that He *died* for our sins.

The desire to bring the life of Christ as well as His death into the Atonement has probably part of its motive in the feeling that when the death is separated from the life it loses moral character: it is reduced to a merely physical incident, which cannot carry such vast significance as the Atonement. Such a feeling certainly exists, and finds expression in many forms. How often, for example, we hear it said that it is not the death which atones, but the spirit in which the Saviour died—not His sufferings which expiate sin, but the innocence, the meekness, the love to man and obedience to God in which they were borne. The Atonement, in short, was a moral achievement, to which physical suffering and death are essentially irrelevant. This is our old enemy, the false abstraction, once more, and that in the most aggressive form. The contrast of physical and moral is made absolute at the very point at which it ceases to exist. As against such absolute distinctions we must hold that if Christ had not really died for us, there would have been no Atonement at all, and on the other hand that what are called His physical sufferings and death have no existence simply as physical: they are essential elements in the moral achievement of the Passion. It leads to no truth to say that it is not His death, but the spirit in which He died, that atones for sin: the spirit in which He died has its being in His death, and in nothing else in the world.

It seems to me that what is really wanted here, both by those who seek to co-ordinate Christ's life with His death in the Atonement, and by those who distinguish between His death and the spirit in which He died, is some means of keeping hold of the Person of Christ in His work, and that this is not effectively done apart from the New Testament belief in the Resurrection. There is no doubt that in speaking of the death of Christ as that through which the forgiveness of sins is mediated to us we are liable to think of it as if it were only an event in the past. We take the representation of it in the Gospel and say, 'Such and such is the impression which this event produces upon me; I feel in it how God is opposed to sin, and how I ought to be opposed to it; I feel in it how God's love appeals to me to share His mind about sin; and as I yield to this appeal I am at once set free from sin and assured of pardon; this is the only ethical forgiveness; to know this experimentally is to know the Gospel.' No one can have any interest in disputing another's obligation to Christ, but it may fairly be questioned whether this kind of obligation to Christ amounts to Christianity in the sense of the New Testament. There is no living Christ here, no coming of the living Christ to the soul, in the power of the Atonement, to bring it to God. But this is what the New Testament shows us. It is *He* who is the propitiation for our sins—He who died for them and rose again. The New Testament preaches a Christ who was dead and is alive, not a Christ who was alive and is dead. It is a mistake to suppose that the New Testament conception of the Gospel, involving as it does the spiritual presence and action of Christ, in the power of the Atonement, is a matter of indifference to us, and that in all our thinking and preaching we must remain within purely historical limits if by purely historical limits is meant that our creed must end with the words ' crucified, dead, and buried.' To preach the Atonement means not only to preach One who bore our sins in death, but One who by rising again from the dead demonstrated the final defeat of sin, and One who comes in the power of His risen life—which means, in the power of the Atonement accepted by God—to make all who commit themselves to Him in faith partakers in His victory. It is not His death, as an incident in the remote past, however significant it may be; it is the Lord Himself, appealing to us in the virtue of His death, who assures us of pardon and restores our souls.

One of the most singular phenomena in the attitude of many modern minds to the Atonement is the disposition to plead against the Atonement what the New Testament represents as its fruits. It is as though it had done its work so thoroughly that people could not believe that it ever needed to be done at all. The idea of fellowship with Christ, for example, is constantly urged against the idea that Christ died for us, and by His death made all mankind His debtors in a way in which we cannot make debtors of each other. The New Testament itself is pressed into the service. It is pointed out that our Lord called His disciples to drink of His cup and to be baptized with His baptism, where the baptism and the cup are figures of His Passion; and it is argued that there cannot be anything unique in His experience or service, anything which He does for men which it is beyond the power of His disciples to do also. Or again, reference is made to St. Paul's words to the Colossians: 'Now I rejoice in my sufferings on your behalf, and fill up on my part that which is lacking of the afflictions of Christ in my flesh for His body's sake, which is the Church'; and it is argued that St. Paul here represents himself as doing exactly what Christ did, or even as supplementing a work which Christ admittedly left imperfect. The same idea is traced where the Christian is represented as called into the fellowship of the Son of God, or more specifically as called to know the fellowship of His sufferings by becoming conformed to His death. It is seen pervading the New Testament in the conception of the Christian as a man *in Christ*. And to descend from the apostolic age to our own, it has been put by an American theologian into the epigrammatic form that Christ redeems us by making us redeemers. What, it may be asked, is the truth in all this? and how is it related to what we have already seen cause to assert about the uniqueness of Christ's work in making atonement for sin, or mediating the divine forgiveness to man?

I do not think it is impossible or even difficult to reconcile the two: it is done, indeed, whenever we see that the life to which we are summoned, in the fellowship of Christ, is a life which we owe altogether to Him, and which He does not in the least owe to us. The question really raised is this: Has Jesus Christ a place of His own in the Christian religion? Is it true that there is one Mediator between God and man, Himself man, this man, Christ Jesus?

In spite of the paradoxical assertion of Harnack to the contrary, it is not possible to deny, with any plausibility, that this was the mind of Christ Himself, and that it has been the mind of all who call Him Lord. He knew and taught, what they have learned by experience as well as by His word, that all men must owe to Him their knowledge of the Father, their place in the Kingdom of God, and their part in all its blessings. He could not have taught this of any but Himself, nor is it the experience of the Church that such blessings come through any other. Accordingly, when Christ calls on men to drink His cup and to be baptized with His baptism, while He may quite well mean, and does mean, that His life and death are to be the inspiration of theirs, and while He may quite well encourage them to believe that sacrifice on their part, as on His, will contribute to bless the world, He need not mean, and we may be sure He does not mean, that their blood is, like His, the blood of the covenant, or that their sinful lives, even when purged and quickened by His Spirit, could be, like His sinless life, described as the world's ransom. The same considerations apply to the passages quoted from St. Paul, and especially to the words in Colossians i. 24. The very purpose of the Epistle to the Colossians is to assert the exclusive and perfect mediatorship of Christ, alike in creation and redemption; all that we call being, and all that we call reconciliation, has to be defined by relation to Him, and not by relation to any other persons or powers, visible or invisible; and however gladly Paul might reflect that in his enthusiasm for suffering he was continuing Christ's work, and exhausting some of the afflictions—they were Christ's own afflictions—which had yet to be endured ere the Church could be made perfect, it is nothing short of grotesque to suppose that in this connection he conceived of himself as doing what Christ did, atoning for sin, and reconciling the world to God. All this was done already, perfectly done, done for the whole world; and it was on the basis of it, and under the inspiration of it, that the apostle sustained his enthusiasm for a life of toil and pain in the service of men. Always, where we have Christian experience to deal with, it is the Christ through whom the divine forgiveness comes to us at the Cross—the Christ of the substitutionary Atonement, who bore all our burden alone, and did a work to which we can for ever recur, but to which we did not and do not and never can contribute at all—it is this Christ who constrains us to find our representative with God in Himself, and to become ourselves His representatives to men. It is as we truly represent Him that we can expect our testimony to Him to find acceptance, but that testimony far transcends everything that our service enables men to measure. What is anything that a sinful man, saved by grace, can do for his Lord or for his kind, compared with what the sinless Lord has done for the sinful race? It is true that He calls us to drink of His cup, to learn the fellowship of His sufferings, even to be conformed to His death; but under all the intimate relationship the eternal difference remains which makes Him *Lord*—He knew no sin, and we could make no atonement. It is the goal of our life to be found in Him; but I cannot understand the man who thinks it more profound to identify himself with Christ and share in the work of redeeming the world, than to abandon himself to Christ and share in the world's experience of being redeemed. And I am very sure that in the New Testament the last is first and fundamental.

1981-82 TITLES

0102	Blaikie, W. G.	Heroes of Israel	19.50
0103	Bush, George	Genesis (2 vol.)	29.95
0202	Bush, George	Exodus	22.50
0302	Bush, George	Leviticus	10.50
0401	Bush, George	Numbers	17.75
0501	Cumming, John	The Book of Deuteronomy	16.00
0602	Bush, George	Joshua & Judges (2 vol. in 1)	17.95
2101	MacDonald, James M.	The Book of Ecclesiastes	15.50
2201	Durham, James	An Exposition on the Song of Solomon	17.25
2302	Alexander, Joseph	Isaiah (2 vol.)	29.95
3001	Cripps, Richard S.	A Commentary on the Book of Amos	13.50
3201	Burns, Samuel C.	The Prophet Jonah	11.25
4001	Morison, James	The Gospel According to Matthew	24.95
4102	Morison, James	The Gospel According to Mark	21.00
4403	Stier, Rudolf E.	Words of the Apostles	18.75
4502	Moule, H. C. G.	The Epistle to the Romans	16.25
4802	Brown, John	An Exposition of the Epistle of Paul to the Galatians	16.00
5102	Westcott, F. B.	The Epistle to the Colossians	7.50
5103	Eadie, John	Colossians	10.50
6201	Lias, John J.	The First Epistle of John	15.75
8602	Shedd, W. G. T.	Theological Essays (2 vol. in 1)	26.00
8603	McIntosh, Hugh	Is Christ Infallible and the Bible True?	27.00
9507	Denney, James	The Death of Christ	12.50
9508	Farrar, F. W.	The Life of Christ	24.95
9509	Dalman, Gustav H.	The Words of Christ	13.50
9510	Andrews & Gifford	Man and the Incarnation & The Incarnation (2 vol. in 1)	15.00
9511	Baron, David	Types, Psalms and Prophecies	14.00
9512	Stier, Rudolf E.	Words of the Risen Christ	8.25
9803	Gilpin, Richard	Biblical Demonology: A Treatise on Satan's Temptations	20.00
9804	Andrews, S. J.	Christianity and Anti-Christianity in Their Final Conflict	15.00

TITLES CURRENTLY AVAILABLE